Visual Occupations

Perverse Modernities | *A Series Edited by Jack Halberstam and Lisa Lowe*

Visual Occupations

Violence and Visibility in a Conflict Zone | Gil Z. Hochberg

DUKE UNIVERSITY PRESS *Durham and London* 2015

Typeset in Quadraat and Quadraat Sans
by Tseng Information Systems, Inc.

Library of Congress Cataloging-
in-Publication Data
Hochberg, Gil Z., 1969–
Visual occupations : violence and visibility in a conflict zone / Gil Z. Hochberg.
pages cm—(Perverse modernities)
Includes bibliographical references and index.
ISBN 978-0-8223-5901-2 (hardcover : alk. paper)
ISBN 978-0-8223-5887-9 (pbk. : alk. paper)
ISBN 978-0-8223-7551-7 (e-book)
1. Visual communication—Political aspects—Palestine. 2. Arab-Israeli
conflict—Mass media and the conflict. 3. Middle East—In mass media.
4. Palestine—In motion pictures. 5. Art and photography—Political
aspects—Palestine. 6. Military surveillance. 7. Zionism. I. Title.
II. Series: Perverse modernities.
P95.82.P19H634 2015
302.2095694—dc23
2014041992

Cover art: Khaled Jarrar, I. Soldier. 45 × 187 cm. Courtesy of the artist.

To the memory my father, Yosef Hochberg | *October 14, 1945–April 29, 2013*

Contents

Acknowledgments

Like all creations, this book is an outcome of a collegial effort. Many friends, students, family members, and colleagues have accompanied me throughout the extended period of researching and writing this book, providing me with invaluable support. I am deeply grateful to Shukri Abed, Paul Amar, Amal Amireh, Ariella Azoulay, S. A. Bachman, Ella Shohat, Rebecca Stein, Nadia Yaqub, and, last but not least, Simon Faulkner, for the many stimulating conversations I have had with each of them about vision, politics, and art and for a long-lasting intellectual dialogue.

This project would have never come to life without the inspiration I found in the work of numerous artists and political activists. I have had the fortune of forming special friendships and benefiting from the remarkably inspiring artistic and political work of Basel Abbas, Ruanne Abou-Rahme, Udi Aloni, Yael Bartana, Rula Halawani, Khaled Jarrar, Ilana Salama Ortar, Larissa Sansour, Miri Segal, and Sharif Waked. I thank all these outstanding artists for sharing their creative inner world with me.

For reading and commenting on several different sections of this book, I extend my gratitude to the wonderful members of the UCLA faculty writing group, which met regularly in 2012: Christine Chism, Elizabeth DeLoughrey, Helen Deutsch, Rachel Lee, Francoise Lionnet, Kathleen McHugh, and Shu-mei Shih. Our conversations and exchange of writings remains one of the most constructive experiences I have had.

At UCLA I continue to benefit from an enriching intellectual environment. I thank my friends at the Comparative Literature department and the Gender Studies department for their collegiality. I would like to extend my innermost appreciation to Ali Behdad, Michael Cooperson, Nouri Gana, Sondra Hale, Abeer Mohammed, Aamir Mufti, Todd Presner, and David

Schanberg for their continual support and friendship, and to express my deepest gratitude to Efrain Kristal: as the chair of my home department, Comparative Literature, he has offered me his relentless support not only as an academic mentor but also as a motivating figure at the UCLA gym.

Other close friends have followed the project from early on, offering their support and encouragement in so many ways. I am immensely thankful to PP for accompanying me through the many phases of the journey. I thank Tamar Assal, Ayelet Ben-Yishai, Mel Y. Chen, Eliane Fersan, Sarah Gualtieri, Macarena Gomez-Barris, Maria-Elena Martinez, Chana Kronfeld, Anna More, Yonit Efron, and Naomi Kanuik for meaningful friendships that nourish both mind and soul. My heartfelt appreciation goes to my dear friend Jack Halbertstam, who has read the manuscript more than once, offering me priceless remarks along with confirming reassurance at times I needed it most.

Special thanks are also extended to my students from the graduate seminar on visual culture (2011). Many of the ideas in this book crystalized as an outcome of the conversations we held in this seminar. To Hoda El Shakry, Ethan Pack, Shir Alon, and Simchi Cohen, my graduate students past and present, I owe a great debt. Their dedicated research assistance has proven vital to the completion of this manuscript.

At Duke University Press I was met with the most wonderful group of individuals. I am deeply obliged to Ken Wissoker, who has followed this project from very early on, offering me his generous support and encouragement throughout. I am also thankful to Kathleen Kageff for her careful copyediting and generosity, for Jade Brook for her assistance in every stage of production, and to the two anonymous readers, who have read more than one draft of this manuscript. Their constructive comments and insightful suggestions have played a crucial role in bringing the book to its final form.

Colleen Jankovic came on board in 2014. Her dedication to this project has been very meaningful to me. I am profoundly thankful for her careful reading of the manuscript and for her editorial help, in additional to her guidance with formatting, image capturing, image improving, and much more.

The last words of thankfulness are reserved for my family: I thank my mother, Ruth Ramot, for believing in the project and serving as my main advocate. I thank my two wonderful brothers, Daniel Tsur and Itamar Tsur, for enduring my (often) unrestrained chattering about the past, present, and future of the Israeli-Palestinian conflict. I thank my stepfather, Yaron Tsur, for asking me the kind of questions historians ask and encouraging me to frame my arguments historically.

Finally, and as always, my deepest gratitude is offered to my partner, Keri J. Kanetsky (who has read and reread all-too-many drafts over the years), and our two beautiful children, Ella and Omri Kanetsky. The love the three of you share with me is the meaning of it all.

Introduction

Visual Politics in a Conflict Zone

Vision is always a question of the power to see—and perhaps of the violence implicit in our visualizing practices. With whose blood were my eyes crafted?
—Donna Haraway, "Situated Knowledge: The Science Question in Feminism and the Privilege of Partial Knowledge"

In 2008, DAAR (Decolonizing Architecture Art Residency), a collective based in Beit Sahour, Palestine, launched one of its simplest yet most spectacular projects of decolonizing architecture.[1] The project involved the transformation of a military water tower located at the summit of the deserted Israeli army base Oush Grab into an open-air cinema screen, thus "taking a vision of control and turning it into a vision of another nature" (DAAR, "Vision").[2] Like other projects launched by DAAR, the improvised open-air cinema highlights the fact that Israel's spatial control within the Occupied Territories produces gray zones and sites of ambiguity (whether in the form of leftover ruins, demolished houses, or extraterritorial spaces left out of clear legal jurisdictions) that carry within them the potential to reveal and expose the workings of power. The old water tank transformed into an open-air cinema is a concrete example of how the militarized and colonial power of the Israeli state, which itself relies heavily on vision and surveillance as its mode of domination, can become visible (if provisionally), further challenged, and perhaps undermined (see figure I.1).

This simple act of projection not only changed the original use of the water tower by turning it into a flat screen, but it also resulted in a spectator image that literally subverted the direction of the gaze and replaced the military gaze with another kind of gaze. Staging the projector so that the screen was located at the summit—the place has served as an Israeli army

1.1 | The water tower of the deserted military base Oush Grab converted into an open-air cinema. *Oush Grab*. Photomontage, 2008, by DAAR.

base from which the Palestinian residents of Beit Sahour (the city residing just below) have been placed under surveillance and rendered visible to Israeli military eyes for several decades — the project redirected the gaze from top-down (the perspective of the soldiers) to bottom-up (the perspective of the city dwellers turned cinema spectators). Similarly, the direction of the light was altered: the projecting light, a memory of the projecting surveillance light that had for years terrorized the inhabitants of Beit Sahour, was now repositioned so that the light came from the direction of the city and onto the summit, this time keeping the residents of Beit Sahour in the dark like the invisible audience sitting in a cinema theater (see figure 1.2).

The possibility of redirecting the gaze or manipulating visions of control in order to create new ways of seeing is of course rarely so easily achieved, nor does it normally take such a literal form. Even in this example, we must remember that the direct artistic intervention was attainable mainly thanks to the fact that the military base was fully evacuated at the time. I open this book with this example precisely because I want to emphasize that undoing visions of violence, or creating new perspectives and new modes of looking, is never a simple task. As the various examples discussed throughout the book demonstrate, it is a long and bumpy process to reshape a visual

1.2 | Screening from bottom up. *Oush Grab*. Photomontage, 2008, by DAAR.

field that dominates and sustains a conflict of the magnitude we are discussing here. This process involves not just tactical, physical interventions into the landscape, but also the manipulation of visual positions, new settings for spectatorship, new modes of appearance, and at times new modes of disappearance, concealment, or refusal to appear. It also involves the ability to see one's own blindness and render visible one's failure to see.

Visual Occupations explores various artistic (cinematic, photographic, literary) attempts to expose and reframe the conditions of vision that underlie the Israeli-Palestinian conflict. These conditions of vision dictate the oppressive relationship between the Israeli occupiers and the Palestinian occupied, which is articulated through and manifested in uneven distribution of "visual rights" rooted in the historical and geopolitical conditions associated with the 1948 establishment of the state of Israel as a settler colony (Mirzoeff, "Invisible Empire" 40). The oft-quoted Zionist phrase "a land without a people for a people without a land" encapsulates a profound failure or refusal to see, and thus to recognize the political agency of, the native Palestinian inhabitants.[3] The land was never "without a people," but these people failed to appear from the perspective of Zionist settlers. Years later they still remain invisible, not only to Golda Meir, who famously announced in 1961 that "the Palestinian people do not exist," but also to subsequent generations (Giles 12).[4] However, as the following chapters demonstrate, this uneven distribution of visual rights takes different forms and shapes throughout the relatively short history of the so-called Israeli-Palestinian conflict. Most notably, following the 1967 war, the occupation of the Palestinian territories in the West Bank and Gaza, and the later annexation of East Jerusalem and the Golan Heights, Palestinians visually were unequally distributed and managed by Israel along divisions the Israeli state created among the Palestinian population, designating most specifically three main groups: Palestinian "citizens of Israel" (residents of the 1948 borders and the annexed Golan Heights); Palestinian "residents of Israel" (including the majority of the Palestinians living in the annexed parts of East Jerusalem, where few Palestinians are granted Israeli citizenship); and Palestinian "noncitizens" (Palestinians living in the West Bank and Gaza, who, since 1995, hold a Palestinian passport issued by the Palestinian authority, but whose resident status continues to be managed by Israel, which issues them IDs but not citizenship).

Visual Occupations offers an overview of these developments by tracing the visual politics sustaining the Israeli-Palestinian conflict's various contingent and contextual appearances from its initial evocation to the present. Chapters center on distinct historical moments or phases of this conflict, including (and not necessarily in progressive order) the *Nakba* and the establishment of the state of Israel (1948), the 1967 war and occupation of Palestinian territories (known in Arabic as *al-naksa*, the Setback), Israel's invasion of Lebanon in 1982, the so-called Oslo period (1993–2000), the Second Intifada (2000–2004), and the massive Israeli military attack on Gaza (Operation Cast Lead) in 2008. The book by no means purports to trace a comprehensive or detailed historical chronicle of these political changes. Instead, the book aims at identifying the main trends and forces that organize the visual field of the Israeli-Palestinian conflict *across and throughout* these different historical moments, weaving diverse spatial organizations, architectural forms, and technologies of control under the nevertheless distinguishable overarching Israeli Zionist settler colonial geopolitical imagination.

It is within this elastic historical framework, then, that the book addresses the relationship between visuality, power, domination, and control, paying attention to the conditions of visibility as created under particular moments or phases of the conflict, and with regard to the ongoing changing landscape and spatial arrangements of the Israeli Occupation. Nevertheless, the book insists that the profoundly uneven distribution of visual rights separating Israelis and Palestinians today finds its roots in the Zionist separatist ethnonational ideology and colonial settler practices *before and beyond* any such historical, geographical, or spatial specificities. The book intentionally evokes and focuses on this tension, at moments tracing the uneven distribution of visual rights in Israel/Palestine back to the fundamental conditions of the Zionist settler colonial national project, and at other times ascribing it more specifically to the particular geopolitical and spatial arrangements associated with the changing nature of the Israeli Occupation. By creating a kind of bridge between the discussion of the colonial settler nature of the Israeli state and the critique of the Israeli Occupation, *Visual Occupations* rejects the 1948/1967 divide as a prevailing analytical framework that has long dominated the study of the Israeli-Palestinian conflict and has tended to sharply distinguish between the history of Israel's 1948 establishment and the later 1967 occupation of the West Bank and Gaza. While it is certainly important to study the history of the Occupation in its relation to particular developments in spatial and population control (the excellent work of Eyal Weizman, Ariella Azoulay, Adi Ophir, Neve Gordon, Ariel Handel, and Sari Hanafi immediately comes to mind), it is equally important to highlight the ideological continuity that links the conditions of visibility created back in 1948 to those found in Israel/Palestine today; these conditions have deep roots in a colonial settler and ethnonational separatist spatial imagination out of which the Occupation's monstrosity has emerged.[5]

In the broadest sense, then, *Visual Occupations* can be said to be an inquiry into the visual configurations that make up the contours through which the Israeli-Palestinian conflict appears. What does it mean to speak about a conflict in terms of how it appears or how we come to see it? To begin with, it means that we do not take the conflict as our point of departure (asking, for example, how it is re-presented in the media), but that we rather explore the very *making* of the conflict—its contours and mappings—by focusing on the distribution of the visual and asking, for example, what or who can be seen, what or who remains invisible, who can see and whose vision is compromised? As the above questions make clear, *Visual Occupations* is preoccupied with the denaturalization of vision and the political construction of sight and visibility as practices of reading.[6] How much one can see, what one can see, and in what way one can see or be seen are all outcomes of specific visual arrangements that are created and sustained through particular configurations of space and various processes of *differentiations* along national, ethnic, racial, religious, gender, and sexual lines. If this is true in general (that is, across societies and times), it is most certainly true for extreme cases of formalized social inequality such as colonialism or military occupation, which sanction and prescribe the right to see and to be seen.

Looking at the vast majority of images that make up the international media spectacle of the Israeli-Palestinian conflict, however, one cannot fail to notice how severely limiting these images are and how violently they restrict our ability to read them. These images include the all-too-familiar photographs of Palestinian masses crowded at the checkpoints, sobbing Palestinian women, ruins of demolished houses, armed Palestinian militants, the aftermaths of suicide bombing attacks in Israeli streets, and, of course, youthful Israeli soldiers. Given the repetitive nature of these (always already) familiar images, a highly restrictive visual framework is constructed. Palestinians and Israelis appear in this predetermined visual field, time and time again, as familiar objects. Indeed, within the contours of this familiar visual frame, the Israeli Occupation can be seen only through the banality of its cruelty, while Palestinians become recognized as political agents only insofar as they are seen through a fetishized visual frame of destruction, violence, and loss.[7]

As an attempt to break through the blinding impact of such recurring images, *Visual Occupations* shifts attention away from populist media representations and their role in circumscribing the field of visuality (plenty of studies dedicated to the matter already exist).[8] Instead the book focuses on the political importance of various artistic attempts to redistribute the visible by altering, queering, and manipulating hegemonic modes of representation. More specifically, the book engages with artistic interventions that center thematically or structurally on the mechanism of the gaze and that question common distributions of the visible. In short, this book examines cultural works that place the question of visuality (the politics of the visual) at the heart of their intervention into, and interrogation of, the body politics of the conflict.

Building in part on Jacque Rancière's understanding of politics as "a question of aesthetics and a matter of appearances" (*Disagreement* 74), I propose that an effective political act necessitates an interruption and reworking of dominant visual fields, and that generating new *ways of seeing* is the precondition for overcoming oppressive geo-sociopolitical orders. My readings highlight the intricate relationship between power and vision, suggesting that there is much more at stake than a direct link between the two. If vision is often equated with power ("The gaze that sees is a gaze that dominates," Foucault has famously stated[9]), the following chapters present a more complicated picture by demonstrating the fact that while seeing (and being seen) commonly ensures political empowerment, these positions may in fact function as oppressive forces. Political transformation and empowerment, *Visual Occupations* suggests, are dependent on opacity, the ability to disappear, blindness, failed vision, and invisibility *at least as much* as they are on visibility, being visible, or having access to the gaze.

The book engages with a wide range of works (including literature, painting, photography, video, and film) primarily by Israeli and Palestinian artists. What we find in this rich archive of works, I argue, is a great deal more than critical reflections on the current Israeli-Palestinian visual regimes. Centering on the limits of dominant modes of visual distribution, these works, I suggest, challenge and denaturalize the visual regimes that currently limit our common understanding of the conflict, offering us in turn an expanded visual vocabulary that significantly alters the realm of what can be seen, who can be seen, how, and from what position.

The overarching argument of the book is that if we are to fully understand the Israeli-Palestinian conflict we cannot simply or only analyze it in terms of colonial land-grabbing, competing national narratives, the removal of peoples, or even the specific spatial arrangement of enclosement and separation. Rather, we must further recognize the conditions through which the geopolitical arrangement of space and the classification of distinct ethnonational and religious identities involved in this conflict are themselves created and solidified through particular visual practices and distributions of visibility that tend to remain *invisible* as such. These include practices engendered by the Israeli state and army as well as visual practices generated in response to Israeli visual domination from both within and outside of Palestine. To this end, *Visual Occupations* sets out to identify *three organizing principles* responsible for the configuration of visibility and the common borders of the seeable within the context of the Israeli Occupation and the ongoing Israeli-Palestinian conflict more broadly speaking. *Concealment*, I contend, is the key principle organizing the dominant Israeli (civil society) visual field, a visual field restricted by a vast mechanism of erasure, denial, and obstructions of sight since 1948 and increasingly so throughout the present. The first two chapters of the book focus on this principle and address questions of Israeli blindness and Palestinian invisibility *both* as byproducts of political denial and as conditions for articulating modes of political resistance. *Surveillance*, I suggest, is the key principle organizing the visual field that dominates the life of Palestinians living in the Occupied Territories. Chapters 3 and 4 center on this principle and address questions concerning the power of the military gaze and the ability to use artistic interventions so as to redirect and undermine this power. Here I build on the vast amount of critical work that follows Foucault's insights about panoptic vision and modernity, and I make clear the specificity of the mechanisms of surveillance in the context of the Israeli Occupation of Palestinian territories. Finally, *witnessing* is the principle that shapes what I identify as the main countervisual practice set up to undermine Israeli visual dominance. The two final chapters of the book focus on this principle and on the role of eyewitness accounts and visual evidence of Palestinian hardship in forming an alternative archive of seeing, while they further question the limits of these visual documenting practices in light of the ubiquity of the international media's gaze and the dominance of the humanitarian project in Palestine.

Before moving on to a more elaborate account of these three principles and a detailed description of the chapters included under each, a few points of clarification must be made. To begin with, it is important to distinguish throughout our conversation between *two distinct levels of inquiry*: The first relates to the "actors" themselves, Israelis and Palestinians, and to their different "ways of seeing." The second relates to the position of external viewers as what we might consider the conflict's spectators. The characteristic visual field of each of these positions and their differences must be taken into account.

"Ways of Seeing": Israelis, Palestinians, and the Partition of Vision

My lead question with regard to Israeli and Palestinian vision is: do the two collectives actually see the same reality? For example, when an Israeli Jew looks at the Separation Wall, does s/he *see* the same image that the Palestinian, located on the other side of the Wall, sees? Given that a radically different ethnic/national episteme governs and encloses most individuals on each side of the Wall, I think it is safe to say that for the majority of Israelis and Palestinians the answer to this question is an unequivocal "no."[10] Engrained in a psychic of fear, the Israeli dominant field of vision superimposes a fantasy of radical separation between Israelis and Palestinians. Within this fantasy, the Separation Wall, like all other military apparatuses such as checkpoints, sieges, and separate roads, is seen not as sign of military force or aggression but as a legitimate and protective border against terrorism and suicide bombers. Seen through this prism of fear, even the image of an armed Israeli soldier pointing a gun at a group of young Palestinian children is *seen* as an image of self-defense. From the Palestinian viewpoint, things obviously look different, with all of the examples mentioned above, seen as "visual evidence" of Israeli brutality. Another example that demonstrates the schism between common Israeli and Palestinian ways of seeing is the popular Palestinian posters displaying portraits of dead armed Palestinian freedom fighters (*shahids*). These posters, covering street walls throughout the Occupied Territories, commonly circulate within Israeli and other Western media as visual evidence of Palestinian cultural "glorification of death."[11] However, from the Palestinian perspective the same image functions as a defiant practice of anti-colonial national remembering.

The two radically different and competing visual fields (one Israeli the other Palestinian) are not, however, an outcome only of different national, ethnic, and historical epistemes that are "produced as the visible" (Judith Butler "Endangered/Endangering," 17). This process of *partitioned vision* further relies on two distinct configurations or politics of visual representation. Central in this regard is the question of the parameters placed on the legitimacy of displaying and circulating certain images in public. As shown by David Campbell, great differences appear between the standards followed by Western and Israeli media and those followed by Arab media concerning the circulation of graphic images of violence from Palestine: "While American, European and Israeli media regard the use of graphic pictures of death and injury as (in the words of a *Jerusalem Post* editorial) 'voyeuristic, nearly pornographic,' the Arab media consider these visceral images to be a sign of accurate reporting and legitimate journalism necessary for the true representation of war and its consequences" (21). It is important to realize, however, that these differences have little if anything to do with innate cultural differences, and everything to do with the different political positions Israelis and Palestinians hold vis-à-vis sovereign power. In the presence of an official army and state, Israel is capable of maintaining its *façade of normalcy* by artificially and successfully presenting an image of separation between its civil order and its militarized one, thus obscuring the impact militarism has on every single aspect of everyday Israeli life. In Israel, there is *no need* to circulate images of young warriors or dead victims publically, at least not any longer. On the contrary, there is a need to *conceal* such images or, more accurately, to keep them in a separate sphere from the civil realm in order to protect the image of Israel as a modern, democratic, and *normal* society—a society dedicated to prosperity and life that faces an enemy with a so-called passion for death: "The problem Israel faces is that we [Israelis] are facing an enemy whose culture is a 'culture of death.' For them 'death' is a good thing. You cannot confront a culture like this and tell them to lift a white flag just because you killed a hundred or even a thousand of their people. For them this is a victory" (Sharon, "Culture of Life"). Indeed, Israel's own image of normality greatly depends on the production and circulation of Palestine as an image of violence, self-destruction, victimization, and (a culture of) death. In response to widely circulated photographs of Palestinian children dressed as armed martyrs/freedom fighters, Western media posits that these images serve as proof of a social pathology. While some right-wing commentators associate this social pathology with "Islamic influences," other leftist critics ascribe it to the negative impact of decades of life under Israeli Occupation. The questions often presented in Western media in relation to these images ("What normal healthy culture raises its children to kill and die?" or "What mother sends her child to kill and die?") are rhetorical gestures through which a radical distinction is made between a dignified ("Western") ethical standard and the cultural and ethical standards of the Arab/Muslim world. Given, however, that it is mandatory for every eighteen-year-old in Israel to serve in the Israeli army, is it not accurate to conclude that, in principle, and statistically speaking, the majority of Israeli families make precisely the same choices in relation to their own children? The main difference between the two collectives is thus found in their radically different distribution of visibility with regard to militarization.

Belonging to an occupied society without a sovereign government or army, Palestinians, unlike Israelis, depend on the circulation of images of armed civilians and victims as perhaps one of *the only* symbolic means of promoting a communal sense of empowerment, resistance, and collective mourning. As a society that cannot even pretend to generate a façade of normalcy, Palestinians often highlight images of armed conflict in part to make the conditions of living under military occupation *visible* to others. By contrast, Israel invests in making the militarized formation of its society as *invisible* as possible, even though militarism is embedded into the habitus of every Israeli citizen, beginning with the fact that armed security guards check everyone's bags in the entrance to all shopping centers, museums, or theaters, and ending with the fact that young people in army uniforms are visible practically everywhere in the streets, cafés, cinemas, buses, beaches, and so on. While such markers of a highly militarized society are ubiquitous (indeed they make for a central part of the everyday landscape of today's modern, urban Israel), they are nevertheless disguised under a blinding ideological framework that emphasizes youthfulness, life, normality, and playfulness. Seen through this prism, the uniform and weapons themselves *appear* as harmless customs and toys. Visible, yet completely invisible, these armed soldiers tend to pass as joyful boy scouts and girl scouts.

Consider in this regard how Israel strategically uses female soldiers as visual icons. While, on the one hand, the circulation of images of female soldiers serves as a means of normalizing the militarization of the Israeli society as a whole (sending a message that each mother, wife, and daughter is also a soldier), it also manages to simultaneously hide militarization behind a mask of feminine tropes—a light, pretty, and sexy version of war meant to conceal the violence these soldiers take part in.[12] A catalogue of interviews and photographs of Israeli Defense Force (IDF) female soldiers released by the Israeli army for Israel's sixtieth anniversary demonstrates this well. The cover of the catalogue reads: "60 Years of Women's Service in the IDF: 1948–2008." The image on the cover is divided in half: on the top we see a female soldier's face colored in combat camouflage makeup, and to the side a small, feminine hand holds a makeup container. In the bottom part of the frame we see a less visibly identifiable body (is it a body of a man or a woman?) and an extended arm holding a gun. The arm is firm as it leans against the army pants with a wide belt. The contrast between the makeup container and the gun, the small hand and the stronger one, and the delicate features of the soldier's face and the wide pants and belt pose the masculine/feminine contrast; the fact that the makeup container looks like a peace sign (though upside down) helps solidify the softening version of militarism.

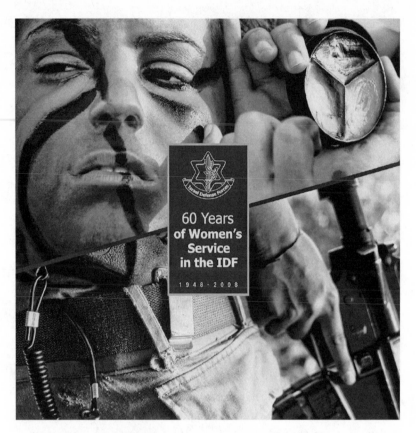

1.3 | Cover of the IDF catalogue *60 Years of Women's Service in the IDF*, 2008, from the official IDF blog.

The split image seems to suggest that IDF women soldiers can be both feminine and masculine or both *real* women and *real* warriors. At the same time, the emphasis placed on the makeup draws attention away from the violence of the gun, as if flirting with the idea that what we see in front of us is in essence not different from other popular images of women and their accessories, which are an integral part of any so-called women's interest magazine (see figure 1.3).

Popular Israeli images of male Israeli soldiers also tend to downplay the militarized nature of the soldier, emphasizing instead the soldiers' youth, playfulness, sexiness, and livelihood (a recent Google search for images of Israeli soldiers revealed that there is even an online following dedicated to images of shirtless Israeli soldiers). Among the most explicit examples

1.4 | Screen capture from YouTube video *Cellcom TV Commercial*, Uploaded July 13, 2009. https://www.youtube.com/watch?v=AH02uc1vB4k.

of this playful version of light militarism is a TV commercial for the leading Israeli cell phone company Cellcom, which aired during the summer of 2009. The commercial features a group of Israeli soldiers playing soccer with invisible Palestinian partners behind the Wall, set to the sound of cheering Israeli female soldiers. The commercial ends with the voice-over: "After all, what do we all want—just to have some fun!" (*Ki ma be-sakh ha-kol kulanu rotsim? Sh-yhiyhe ktsat kef*) (Cellcom) (see figure 1.4).

With regards, more specifically, to external (international) viewers, who come to see the conflict primarily through circulating media images, the most important factor, at least as so far as Israel's public relations efforts are concerned, is the management and distribution of violent images. In this respect we must pay attention to the fact that not all violence becomes easily visible to external viewers, and that some modes of violence systematically continue to fall out of sight. While sudden eruptions of violence associated with large-scale military assaults or terrorist attacks widely circulate, with this type of "spectacular violence" drawing attention to itself as *violence par excellence*, other more mundane and persistent types of violence ("slow violence" to use Anne McClintock's term, or "suspended violence" to use Ophir and Azoulay's term), such as the violence experienced daily by a great number of Palestinians living in the Occupied Palestinian Territories, remains almost entirely *invisible* to external viewers.[13]

Much of how external viewers come to see the conflict has to do with the different degrees of visibility ascribed to various modes of violence. Thus, the underlying and ongoing violence Israel carries out against Palestinians, independent of any eruption of sudden violent spectacles, tends to escape the radar of sight. As a result, everyday life under the Israeli Occupation fails to *appear* violent unless it is presented as a sudden (and often uncontextualized) eruption of what is quickly reframed and labeled exceptional and scandalous. Given the selective visual economy through which only a few images come to be recognized as violent (while the ongoing violence underlining the everyday existence in the Occupied Territories remains *invisible*), it is important that we take a closer look at the nature of the images that are said to capture so-called sudden eruptions or scandalous Israeli violence. These images somehow manage to break through the screen of suspended, slow, or invisible violence by doing little more than *framing* or calling attention to their status *as images*.

Take, for example, the case of the mini-scandal that erupted in 2010 when a former Israeli female soldier by the name of Eden Aberjil posted photos on her Facebook page of herself smiling and sitting by the side of two bound and blindfolded Palestinian men (see figure 1.5).

The event was but a pale reminder of the much bigger scandal that took place in 2004 when CBS exposed photos of American soldiers at Abu Ghraib prison posing alongside dead or wounded Iraqi detainees, and yet it nevertheless resembled the latter in that the Israeli military quickly framed the event as exceptional. In response to the release of the photos, Barak Raz, the spokesman for the IDF, issued a statement declaring that the photos were "disgraceful and in total opposition to the values and ethical code . . . which is the foundation of the IDF" ("Capt. Barak Raz Responds to Shameful Photos"). Reacting to these words, Aberjil told an interviewer that she did not "understand what's wrong with the photographs," which in her words, "were taken in good will and carry no political statement" ("Eden Aberjil Facebook Photos Controversy"). It was relatively easy for the Israeli army to dismiss the case as an exception (not unlike the American framing of female soldier Lynndie England and her soldier friends as a few bad apples), turning her response ("I don't understand what is wrong with the photographs") into proof of her extreme idiocy and lack of com-

1.5 | A picture originally posted on a Facebook page belonging to Eden Aberjil, 2010.

mon sense. Indeed, the case was eventually dismissed as "something very foolish and stupid [that shouldn't] be of any media interest" (Shabi, "Anger over Ex-Israeli Soldier's Facebook Photos").[14]

But what if we were to take Aberjil's confusion seriously and ask ourselves what *is* wrong with the photographs? Is it that she is smiling, clearly having a good time while the men next to her are bound and blindfolded? (Would it be different if she weren't grinning?) Is it that she posted the photos online and made further jokes about them? (Below one of her photographs, in which she is leaning toward a blindfolded young man, a comment posted by her friend stated: "You look the sexiest here." Aberjil replied: "Yeah I know . . . I wonder if he's got a Facebook account, I'll have to tag him in this picture!"). Or is it that she has captured, framed, and *made visible*—without apologies or any sense of wrongdoing—a daily (indeed mundane) reality of oppression and violence that is meant to remain *invisible* in accordance with the Israeli army's so-called high moral standards?[15] Framing Aberjil's display of photos as an exception and a scandal only conceals the fact that the display, vulgar as it is, is far from the worst crime associated with the Israeli Occupation. At best, it can be described as a mimetic aftereffect of the violence performed routinely: a slow violence that remains mostly *invisible* and fails to appear as such. Indeed, unlike the Abu Ghraib photos, which almost all capture staged and performative scenarios of torture and humiliation, resembling in their perverse logic the aesthetic of snuff movies, Aberjil's photos stage little if anything. After all, blindfolded detainees seated next to an Israeli soldier is but a typical scene at the checkpoint, part and parcel of a much larger system of oppression and humiliation that constitutes the Occupation's suspended (hence invisible) violence, which if revealed must be rendered exceptional and scandalous, and thus can hardly appear at all.

Furthermore, it is not insignificant that the images posted by Aberjil depict blinded captives. Indeed, the camera captures and renders sensational the disparity in the position of the Israeli soldier and her captives: while her captives cannot see, she sees them and documents their nonseeing. The camera captures her looking, but the detainees cannot look back. Do they even know they are being photographed? The image of the blindfolded men seated next to the grinning soldier thus frames and freezes a reality of occupation in a theatrical image of power, domination, and pleasure (the very pleasure that sustains domination). It presents an image of power that centers on the drama of the eye: who can see whom, what, and how. If these photographs reveal any grand atrocity (much worse things happen to Palestinians than being blindfolded and photographed), it is that they successfully capture the underlying gratification involved in the *visualization* and *display* of power—a visualization and display without which power itself fails to appear.

Finally, in this case, as in the case of Lynndie England, the American female soldier who appeared in the most famous Abu Ghraib photographs, gender plays a significant role in the scandalous framing of the images. Indeed, the fact that the tormenting soldiers in both cases are women, and that they find pleasure in posing as torturers (of *men* nonetheless), clearly upsets the more familiar and banal visual iconography of war violence in which images of tortured women at the hands of torturing men can hardly circulate as scandalous.

In the following pages, I refer back to these distinct and partitioned fields of vision as I delve into a more detailed presentation of each of the three principles around which the visuality of the Israeli-Palestinian conflict is organized, namely, *concealment, surveillance, and witnessing*. While these principles are introduced separately as governing a sociopolitical reality that functions for the most part independent of the others, the book as a whole situates these principles in relation to each other, suggesting that it is only by taking into consideration their accumulated impact that we may gain access into what is in effect the *complex* (rather than single or unified) visual regime through which we come to see the Israeli-Palestinian conflict.

Concealment: Israeli Blindness, Palestinian Invisibility

"The whole history of the Palestinian struggle," Edward Said famously remarked, "has to do with the desire to be visible" (Preface, *Dreams of a Nation*, 2). This ongoing Palestinian struggle for visibility is staged against the historical, theological, and political potency of the Zionist national narrative that involves in the imaginary (and overtly Christian) redemptive framework of bringing together "a land without a people" and "a people without a land," thus redeeming both the (promised) land and the (Jewish) people. If Palestinians have historically struggled to bring their grievance into the Israeli and international field of vision, the Israeli state has, from very early on, responded to such "intrusions" by developing a vast array of vision-blocking mechanisms, including naming the Palestinians who left their homes temporarily during the 1948 war as "present absentees"; replacing the original Arabic names of towns and villages with new Hebrew names; planting forests over Palestinian ruins; and following 1967, closing the Palestinian Occupied Territories to international media and, perhaps most visibly recognizable, erecting a *hypervisible* eight-meter-high wall that literally blocks off Palestinians from sight.

Palestinians residing within the 1948 borders are commonly referred to in Hebrew as "Israeli Arabs" (*Aravim israelim*) or as the "Arab minority" (*ha-meeut ha-aravi*), names that intentionally ignore their national affiliation as Palestinians and their native status as pre-1948 inhabitants of the land. Their invisibility, in other words, is based on the erasure of their Palestinian-ness in favor of a vague Arab-ness that *as such* (that is, in being vague and *not* Palestinian, that is to say, not national) can be incorporated into Israel and Israeli-ness as a docile "minority." I elaborate more on this mode of invisibility in chapter 2, which is dedicated to the cinematic work of the acclaimed Palestinian Israeli director Elia Suleiman. The invisibility of Palestinians living in the 1967 Occupied Territories (the West Bank and Gaza) is managed quite differently, primarily because Israel continues to hold these territories in an ambiguous position: *not* part of Israel per se, yet also not quite *not* part of Israel per se. The Palestinian residents of the Occupied Territories are not granted Israeli citizenship; indeed, unlike their "Israeli

Arab" cousins, they are not considered Israeli. Their Palestinian-ness is overtly accepted, but as such it must remain clearly and securely *out* of Israel and out of Israeli sight. Tucked away behind walls, fences, and roadblocks, and set apart by separate road systems, Palestinians in the West Bank and Gaza have become gradually more invisible to Israelis over the years. Accounting for this invisibility, Israeli journalist Amira Hass writes, "A person could travel the length and breadth of the West Bank without ever knowing—not only the names of the villages and cities whose lands were confiscated in order to build the Jewish settlements and neighborhoods, but even the fact that they exist" (Hass, "You Can Drive Along"). Creating two parallel spatial and geopolitical realities within one geographical territorial space, Israel has managed to keep Palestinians almost completely invisible to Israeli eyes even as Israelis travel through the West bank. While Israelis drive on highways above, Palestinians for the most part drive in tunnels below, unseen from above. Driving on Highway 443, for example, a major road connecting the city of Modiin to Jerusalem through the West Bank, one has to strain the eye in order to see the Palestinian villages residing just below in the valley[16] (see figures 1.6 and 1.7).

The aim of erasure in this case is not simply to render Palestinians invisible to Israeli eyes but to further render the *very process of erasure* invisible as well. The same can be said about the Separation Wall, referred to in Hebrew as a "security fence" (*gader ha-bitachon*) and in Arabic as the "racist segregation wall" (*jidar al-fasl al-'ansuri*). Built very close to Palestinian houses, schools, and other populated centers, the Wall is seen from nearly everywhere on the Palestinian side. It is "assertive, dominant and spectacular" (Rotbard, "Wall and Tower" 47). It is however significantly less visible and certainly less monstrous on the Israeli side, given that it is built at a significant distance from any Israeli Jewish settlement. Thus, while the Wall can be seen from the vantage point of all Palestinian urban centers and residential areas, seen from the Israeli side the wall always appears in a distance and behind a vast empty section of (annexed) land.[17] In some sections on the Israeli side, the Wall appears partially covered and concealed. For Israeli drivers who pass through Highway 6, for example, the enclosed Palestinian cities of Tulkarm and Qalqilya are hardly visible, and the Wall itself is hidden behind trees and other plants that cover a great portion of the concrete, which make it seem small and harmless, if even noticeable. In other sections on the Israeli side, the wall is decorated (as in figure 1.6,

1.6 | Highway 443 on the outskirts of Jerusalem. Photograph by Amir Terkel, 2009.
1.7 | The reality "underneath" 443, the road connecting the Palestinian village Jeeb to the West Bank. Photograph by the author, January 2013.

1.8 | A portion of the wall around the Gilo Jewish settlement in East Jerusalem. Photograph by Colleen Jankovic, 2010.

a photo of the wall along Highway 443). An extreme example of an attempt to disguise the ugliness of the Wall with images of open landscape creating a kind of trompe l'oeil effect of an open vast space was found in the section of the Wall that was built in 2002 around the Jewish settlement of Gilo (this part of the Wall has since been removed following Israel's High Court order in 2010). The cement blocks separating Gilo from the nearby Palestinian village Beit Jala were covered with landscape paintings capturing biblical scenes and offering an optical illusion of both historical and topographic continuation. The paintings presented a direct link from biblical times to the present in the image of a peaceful vast terrain, devoid of Palestinians and free of security fences, gates, and walls (see figure 1.8).

A somewhat less imaginative example of concealment can be found at the site of Rachel's Tomb, located at the outskirts of Bethlehem. The area has been confiscated by the Israeli army and surrounded by walls and watchtowers, making what is for many a holy place look like a top security prison[18] (see figure 1.9).

To make the site appear somewhat more welcoming and holy to the Jews (mainly women) who come to pray here, a colorful painting of the old tomb was recently attached to a section of the wall located next to the parking lot. This painting blocks the view of the Palestinian residential build-

I.9 | Entrance to Rachel's Tomb. Photograph by the author, 2012.

ings of Bethlehem that are located just on the other side of the Wall. The painted canvas often crumbles and reveals the ugly truth of the cement (see figure I.10).

Thus, since 1948, and particularly in relation to the Palestinian presence in the 1967 Occupied Territories, concealment functions as the dominating principle shaping the Israeli field of vision. This principle seeks not only to hide Palestinians or render their existence invisible in the eyes of Israelis, but also to further conceal the act of erasure itself. Subjected to what Dalit Baum and Ruchama Marton call "state propelled active non-seeing mechanisms," the great majority of Israelis remain blind not only to the existence of Palestinians, but perhaps more significantly, to the blinding mechanism that renders them invisible to begin with (214). Consider in this regard the provocative commercial filmed in the summer of 2004 by the Israeli elite women's clothing design brand Comme Il Faut.

The two-minute video commercial was shot near a section of the Separation Wall just outside of Jerusalem and approximately two years following its construction. The clip, an addition to the company's photocatalogue for its summer collection, featured six international models with differ-

1.10 | An image of the old tomb painted on fabric attached to the Separation Wall. Photograph by the author, 2012.

ent skin colors and appearances parading along the Wall to the sound of Neneh Cherry's "Woman" ("This is a woman's world, this is my world") (Davidovitz). The video opens with an image of two (what else but) veiled Palestinian women walking with their heads lowered as the camera swiftly moves to capture the more rebellious (Western, modern, liberated, fashionable) models, who, unlike the Palestinian women in the clip, stare defiantly at the Israeli soldiers as they pass by them, marching along the Wall. The confrontational exchange of gazes with the soldiers is staged in explicitly *gendered terms*: the camera shifts between the two camps — on the one side we see Israeli soldiers with guns, and on the other, defiant women in fashionable clothes. Palestinians, for their part, play only a small role in this drama. Palestinian men are altogether absent from the scene, while the women seen momentarily in the opening have no role other than serving as the Oriental background and passive prelude against which the fashion show unfolds (see figure 1.11).

The theme of the collection, "Women Cross Borders" (*Nashim chotsot gvulot*), suggested that Comme Il Faut is part of a promising cross-cultural

I.11 | Image from *Summer Collection*, catalogue for Comme Il Faut, 2004.

and border-free feminist political commerce movement/market. The goal of the fashion show, as the company's CEO Sybil Goldfiner remarked, was to encourage Israeli and Palestinian women to work together for peace: "We offer a suggestion, or the hope, that women from both sides who bring life into the world will unify to stop this killing that has gone on for too long" (quoted in "Fashion on Israel's Frontline"). The fact that no Palestinians took part in the exchange did not seem to pose a problem for Comme Il Faut and its message of a feminist coexistence.[19] I mention this example because I believe it makes visible beyond all doubt just how profoundly ingrained Palestinian invisibility is for Israeli eyes—so much so that even within a visual framework that alleges to challenge separations and borders and to create a message of coexistence, Palestinians remain *out of the frame*. Worse, their visible absence—particularly disturbing in this context—appears to go unnoticed.

I elaborate on this problem of blindness and radical invisibility in the first two chapters of the book. Chapter 1, "Visible Invisibility: On Ruins, Erasure, and Haunting," explores the impact of haunting as a sociopolitical force and an alternative mode of visibility that operates within the Israeli mainstream visual field *despite* the blinding mechanisms that dominate it. The chapter centers on the figure/image of ruins (of Palestinian villages) as a central motif in Israeli culture, from as early as 1948, suggesting that their haunting expands the realm of visibility by introducing the *visibility of the invisible*. Informed by the work of Avery Gordon, Abraham and Torok, and Derrida, the chapter offers a new reading of several key Israeli literary works and paintings and suggests that the unresolved and ongoing historical violence associated with the forced deportation of Palestinians in 1948 (the Nakba), while seemingly invisible within canonical Israeli texts, nevertheless finds its way into the Israeli public sphere under the sign of a growing phantasmatic and ghostly *visible invisibility*. Chapter 2, "From Invisible Spectators to the Spectacle of Terror," examines the radical invisibility of Palestinians within the Israeli visual field by looking closer at the absurdist terrain of being rendered invisible in one's own home(land). The chapter probes the twofold position of the circulating image of the Palestinian, marked by both invisibility (absence, un-image-ability) and hypervisibility (a visual archetype conflated with the spectacle of terror), as I analyze two films by the acclaimed Palestinian director Elia Suleiman. My reading of the films further highlights the different mechanisms involved in rendering invisible Palestinian citizens of Israel on the one hand, and in concealing Palestinians living in the Occupied Territories on the other.

While the book's first two chapters focus on the dominant Israeli visual field marked by blindness, the failure or refusal to see, haunting and the visible invisibility of the Palestinian, the following two chapters shift attention to the visual field created within the 1967 Palestinian Occupied Territories—a visual field that is governed by the principle of surveillance and characterized by violence, the power of the gaze, and the spectacle of power. These chapters show how the tensions between the omnipresence of the Israeli militarized gaze on the one hand, and the blindness characteristic of the greater Israeli public on the other hand, dictate most forms of Palestinian resistance. Indeed, while Palestinians struggle to become visible in the eyes of their Israeli occupiers and the world at large (against the erasure imposed by Israel), they must also escape the dominating gaze of surveillance that renders them visible at all times by finding ways to temporarily disappear or become invisible altogether.

Surveillance: The Power of the Gaze and the Spectacle of Power

If the main principle governing the Israeli (civil society) visual field is that of concealment, the main principle governing the visual field created within the Occupied Palestinian Territories, securing the hierarchal and oppressive relationship between Israelis as occupiers and Palestinians

I.12 | Hebron—the Old City. (The sign beneath reads: "This land was stolen by Arabs following the massacre of Hebron Jews in 1929.") Photograph by the author, 2012.

as occupied, is the principle of surveillance—a principle that guarantees maximum subjection of Palestinians to the Israeli military gaze as well as maximum visibility of this monitoring gaze to Palestinian eyes. This uneven visual field is characterized by its "one-way hierarchy of vision," in which only Israelis are allowed to do the looking, while Palestinians are constantly *looked at* (Weizman, *Hollow Land* 133) (see figure I.12).

Building on Foucault's analysis of the Panopticon in *Discipline and Punish*, Umut Ozguc has argued that Palestinians in the Occupied Territories are placed under uninterrupted Israeli surveillance.[20] Among the means used to render Palestinians visible at all times, Ozguc mentions the checkpoints, the settlements, the Wall, the satellite images, and numerous other practices of classification, categorization, and mapping of populations. Together these modes of inspection create "a monstrous reality" in which "the panoptic gaze of Israeli authorities is always already found everywhere" (Ozguc 4). Eyal Weizman has similarly suggested that Israel's elaborate surveillance mechanism has successfully mapped the entire Palestinian Occupied Territory into a "purely visual plane," in which Palestinian living space has become nothing more than little objects and dots mapped onto a screen ("The Politics of Verticality"). And finally, Derek

Gregory has argued that the intricate system of Israeli monitoring in the Occupied Territories, including "passive sensors, observation towers, satellite images and photographs from reconnaissance planes," has managed to render Palestinians visible to the Israeli guarding eyes at all times: "every floor in every house, every car, every telephone call or radio transmission can be monitored" (*The Colonial Present* 117). Mobilizing Giorgio Agamben's notion of "bare life," Gregory concludes that Israel's advanced surveillance apparatus has turned the Palestinian people "not only into enemies," who must therefore be closely watched, "but [also] into aliens" who reside, live, and die in the space "of abandonment within which the sovereign power had suspended its own law" ("Palestine and the 'War on Terror,'" 186).[21]

While these are astute observations, critics emphasizing the omnipresent, advanced technology of Israeli surveillance and its detrimental impact on Palestinian life in the Occupied Territories tend to overlook the fact that, in order for this elaborate apparatus of control to be effective, Israel's surveillance power must itself be rendered visible at all times. This need to ensure the visibility of Israeli dominance often means that Israel relies on the visual presence of the most primitive and unsophisticated modes of surveillance and control (namely, watchtowers, aiming guns, and checkpoints) at least as much as it does on elaborate, hypermodern, and technologically advanced ones. Indeed, without these old guards—the visible sight of the gun, the checkpoint, or the tower—Israel risks its entire complex surveillance system's efficacy. To put it differently: Palestinians who are subjected to the militarized Israeli gaze of surveillance must simultaneously be exposed to the sight of this gaze as a spectacle of power, without which, as Neve Gordon phrases it, "power itself becomes powerless" ("On Visibility and Power" 137).

In this sense there is a significant difference between Foucault's account of the work of surveillance in modern times and the militarized version of this phenomenon in the Israeli Occupation context. For Foucault, one must remember, the main trap associated with visibility has to do with the internalized gaze of the guard/the state. Modern subjects, he argues, have already internalized the normativizing gaze of the state, and it is for this reason that there is no more need for "arms, physical violence, or material constrains. Just a gaze. An inspecting gaze, a gaze which each individual under its weight will end by interiorizing to the point that he is his own observer, each individual under its weight thus exercises this surveillance over, and against, himself" (*Discipline and Punish* 155). One could hardly, however, make a similar argument about the majority of the Palestinians living under Israeli Occupation. As noncitizens, Palestinians do not recognize themselves in the law of the (Israeli) state. In this case, the gaze alone cannot secure domination. Control works not by means of *internalized* surveillance, but simply and most explicitly by the continual threat of a very real punishment imposed from without. In other words, the *visible presence* of power and signs of control (the gun, the watchtower, the surveillance camera, the tank) are needed in order to ensure obedience, which in this case can hardly be described as "identification with the normativizing gaze." Unlike Foucault's modern subject, who has internalized the normativizing gaze of the state, Palestinians living under occupation are placed under surveillance, which loses all its power and credibility without the support of visible armed forces—the guns and the threatening tanks. If there is any attempt to conceal the process of surveillance, then, it surely does not take place vis-à-vis the Palestinians who are subjected to this gaze. It is rather directed at the Israeli citizens who are subjected to state-controlled blinding mechanisms meant to conceal the *fact of occupation* from disturbing the projected fantasy of the Israeli state's normality.

Israel's militarized architectural organization of the landscape is thus based on a carefully crafted logic of visibility and invisibility that renders Palestinians visible to military eyes while further rendering the power of surveillance itself visible to Palestinians and, whenever possible, invisible to Israelis. This involves, for example, building hilltop settlements from which the settlers have full visual domination over the Palestinian population residing below but, no less significantly, from which the settlements themselves are hypervisible as a site of domination. "I want the Arabs to see Jewish lights every night 500 meters from them," Ariel Sharon, the lead engineer of the settlements back in the late 1970s famously declared (Sivan, "The Lights of Netzarim"). And indeed, the settlements—with their iconic red roofs and excessive lights—are seen from virtually everywhere throughout the West Bank. These sights function as a visible *display* of power: a reminder of Israel's domination and a means of carrying on a psychological war (see figure I.13).

Israel uses various other means to effectively militarize the local terrain through the gaze. These include walls, checkpoints, watchtowers,

1.13 | The village of Nahalin (below) and the settlement Bitar Ailit (above). Photograph by the author, 2013.

closed-circuit cameras, and elaborate road systems that subject the Palestinian population to uninterrupted surveillance while simultaneously drawing attention to Israeli's dominance and control. This is particularly true for urban spaces where Jewish settlements are located at the heart of Palestinian residential areas. In such cases — for instance in Hebron or the old city of Jerusalem — monitors, cameras, and manned towers, as well as Israeli flags, are visible literally everywhere (see figure 1.14).

Chapters 3 and 4 focus on the relationship created in such settings between the gaze, power, and domination. Both chapters center on artistic projects that I argue aim at undoing or overcoming the "one-way hierarchy of vision" that restricts Palestinians' right to look, while at the same time rendering them visible to the Israeli controlling gaze. Chapter 3, "The (Soldier's) Gaze and the (Palestinian) Body," visits the visual field created at the checkpoint, one of the only sites left today for a direct interaction between Israelis and Palestinians. Through a close reading of *Chic Point: Fashion for Israeli Checkpoints* (2003), a film (video/stills) by the Palestinian artist Sharif Waked, the chapter explores the violence involved in the meeting between

I.14 | Hebron. Entrance to the old city. Photograph by author, 2012.

the eyes of the soldiers and the bodies of Palestinians placed under examination. My readings further render visible the commonly *invisible* erotic and libidinal implications of the Israeli militarized gaze, suggesting that if homoeroticism in this context surely belongs to the realm of colonial fantasies about the "sexy terrorist," it nevertheless also serves as a means of challenging the otherwise fixed power relationship between the Israeli gaze and the Palestinian who is subjected to it. Chapter 4, "Visual Rights and the Prospect of Exchange: The Photographic Event Placed under Duress," returns to the question of the gaze as an apparatus of control, asking under what conditions of spectatorship, production, and distribution might photography become a means of intervention into, or manipulation of, the visual field that currently binds Israelis and Palestinians together under an extremely uneven distribution of visual rights. Centered on a comparative look at two photographic projects: *Intimacy* (2004), a photographic series by the Jerusalem-based Palestinian photographer Rula Halawani, and *At the Checkpoint* (2007), a photo exhibit/performance by the Ramallah-based Palestinian artist Khaled Jarrar, the chapter further engages in a critical dialogue with Ariella Azoulay's conceptualization of photography's capacity to function as a "civil contract" (*The Civil Contract of Photography*).

The third and final section of this book shifts attention to what I call the crisis of witnessing. Witnessing, I suggest, is the main governing principle of the *counter* visual fields generated by both Palestinians and Israelis in direct response to the Israeli state's visual dominance. The two final chapters of the book center accordingly on the politics and ethics of bearing witness in light of the growing impact of the humanitarian project on the politics of visibility and the standards of representation associated with the Israeli-Palestinian conflict.

Witnessing: Bearing Witness and the Ethics of Spectatorship

It has become almost a cliché to suggest that we live a so-called era of the witness.[22] Within the context of the growth of humanitarian organizations and the centrality of the discourse of international human rights formed after World War II, witnessing has indeed become "the idiom in which individuals speak back to power" (Givoni 149). Associated with the ability and mission of *exposure* of otherwise unreported, invisible, or undermined atrocities, witnessing/testimony has come to be considered as "the primary ethical configuration of the age of globalism" (Givoni 162).

In the context of the Israeli-Palestinian conflict and the fight against the Israeli Occupation, the global humanitarian project has accordingly increased its impact over the years, placing emphasis on the collection of eyewitness accounts and visual documentation of Palestinian suffering and Israeli atrocities. During the period following the outbreak of the Second Intifada in particular, human rights nongovernment organizations (NGOs) located in the West Bank and elsewhere have become key players in producing and circulating such visual documentation by assigning Palestinians the "right-bearing suffering subject position" (Allen, "Martyr Bodies" 161–62). Within this practice of documentation, *visual evidence* of Palestinian suffering is often understood to be the most effective means for gaining support for the Palestinian cause given that such images serve as proof that Palestinians *too* have a part in the "humanity shared in common with the international community" (Allen, "Martyr Bodies" 162).

On the Israeli side, the incentive to bear witness has also grown significantly, but mainly in relation to what is known as "perpetrator's trauma" — feelings of guilt, remorse, and shame, particularly of Israeli soldiers who have been involved in violent acts or have witnessed atrocities committed by their fellow warriors. Given that so-called confessions from the battlefield are received with less suspicion and hostility by most Israelis than the testimonial reports produced by various Israeli human rights organizations (B'tselem, Machsom Watch), these modes of firsthand combat confessions often result in a greater public outcry. Most significant in this context is the work of the Israeli organization Shovrim Shtika (Breaking the Silence), whose members are IDF veterans. The goal of the movement, as indicated on its webpage, is to "open the eyes" of Israelis to the reality in the "state's backyard"—a reality that the great majority of Israelis do not see nor wish to see. In this case, bearing witness functions as a means of personal healing, but also as an attempt to educate and heal the Israeli collective from its wishful blindness.[23]

But practices of bearing witness, documenting, and testifying as a means of exposing otherwise invisible atrocities also have clear limits. Thus, while the growing circulation of images of Palestinian suffering produced by various Palestinian, Israeli, and international human rights organizations have surely contributed to the growing visibility of the Palestinian cause in the West, the actual political merit of such widespread circulation of testimonial images remains questionable. According to Ronit Avni, founder and director of Just Vision, "the situation with regard to the protection and promotion of human rights within the context of the Israeli-Palestinian conflict has in fact deteriorated over the years . . . despite widespread graphic and unflattering media coverage" (Avni 206). Furthermore, this reliance on eyewitnessing produces particular and rather confined political subjects. On the Palestinian side we find "the sympathy-deserving suffering human" whose damaged body attests to the fact that s/he "naturally deserves the human rights others enjoy" (Campbell 22). Meanwhile, on the Israeli side we find the remorseful soldier, the warrior who shoots and cries and whose remorse can be easily incorporated into the Israeli national narrative of the most moral army in the world.

Chapter 5, "'Nothing to Look At,'" tackles the "crisis of witnessing" associated with the demand imposed on Palestinians from both human rights NGOs and the global media to provide visual proof and eyewitness accounts of their suffering and hardship. The chapter engages with two essay films that I argue deliberately refuse to provide such visual evidence, *Nervus Rerum* (2008) by the London-based artistic collaborative the Otolith Group (members: Kondwo Eshun and Anjalika Sagar) and *We Began by Measuring Distance* (2009) by the Beirut-based Palestinian director Basma Al

Sharif. I show how the films' investigations of the limits of documentation (as an ethical act and as a cinematic genre) generate in turn an alternative visual syntax elaborated via a poetics of opacity and a politics of disappearance.

Chapter 6, "Shooting War," pivots on the question of witnessing as well, but this time by focusing on the perpetrators of violence. Dedicated to two recent Israeli films, *Waltz with Bashir* (Ari Folman, 2008) and *Lebanon* (Samuel Maoz, 2009), this chapter examines the ability articulated within these films to generate an effective ethical and political stance based on a logic of documentation that involves an act of witnessing one's past failure to see on time. If the crisis of witnessing addressed in chapter 5 has do with the demand imposed on Palestinians to serve as witnesses of their own suffering, the crisis of witnessing examined in chapter 6 has to do with role of the witness assigned to the Israeli soldier as a perpetrator of violence who carries the ethical responsibility of awakening others.

....

Visual Occupations is the outcome of several years of research and numerous field research trips to Israel and Palestine. During 2012–13, I had the opportunity to spend the whole year in Israel and Palestine, or rather on the *seam line* that radically separates the two communities: the Israeli Jewish and the Palestinian. I worked and studied in East Jerusalem and Abu Dis (a neighborhood in the West Bank that borders Jerusalem, but is separated by the Separation Wall), but I lived in Tel Aviv. The almost daily trips back and forth between these two locations — so close yet so far away — proved to be significantly harder than I expected. While the drive took less than one hour each way, my need to readjust to the radically different configuration of space and reality in each of these two locations took much longer. These daily trips made me realize that the partition separating Israeli Jews and Palestinians splits the visual field in such a drastic manner that the two communities can hardly be said to see the same reality. Rarely, if ever, do these communities have the opportunity to see each other.

This description of my travel itinerary provides an opportunity for me to say a little more about my own privileged position as an inside-outsider who could navigate between visibility and invisibility in order to ease my mobility through and across this fragmented land, itself crisscrossed by mechanisms of seeing and concealing. Armed with an American academic affiliation and passport as well as the knowledge of both Hebrew and Arabic, I moved around with relative ease, unlike many Israelis and certainly almost all Palestinians. But my position as an inside-outsider also greatly contributed to my ability to see. Indeed, it was not until I left Israel (in my mid twenties, almost twenty years ago) that I came to finally see what I had previously failed to see or even realize was there for me to observe—my own blindness. Growing up in a small suburb near Tel Aviv University in a leftist Israeli household, I was well versed in the history of the so-called Israeli-Palestinian conflict. What I had discovered only years after living outside of Israel was that my knowledge of the conflict did not translate into a practice of seeing. Indeed, reflecting back on the years of living in Israel I came to realize that what I knew about Israel, Palestine, and the Occupation and what I saw in my everyday life had little relation to each other. I knew there was a so-called Palestinian problem. I knew there were refugees. I knew Israel had forcefully evacuated Palestinians out of their villages in 1948. I knew there were a growing number of Palestinians living under direct military occupation since 1967. I knew Palestinian houses were demolished and that Jewish houses were built in their place throughout Israel and the Occupied Territories. But I saw only the green hills around Tel Aviv University. I saw people hanging out in spacious cafes. I saw the calmness of the beach. I saw a beautiful landscape. This schism between what I knew and what I saw never became visible in itself. Looking back, already partially as an outsider, I began to realize that the greatest power of the Israeli state (perhaps of all states) lies in its ability to conceal its violence and manipulate its citizens' frame of vision even and despite what may be their well-informed understanding and capacity to analyze their political reality.

I began to see my own blindness, not because I learned anything I didn't already know about Israel, Palestine, or the Occupation, but simply because being elsewhere enabled me to alter my frame of vision. Rewarding as this experience has been, it has also been at times quite difficult. I am reminded of the moving words Israeli painter Larry Abramson uses to depict his own awakening from his blind love for the rocky hills around Jerusalem, the landscape of his childhood: "It was 1993. The Oslo peace negotiations just began and I felt I was finally ready to see everything that my blind love prevented me from seeing: the mountains covered with terraces were still beautiful, but now they looked less as the ancient landscape of my biblical fathers and more like the deserted fields of Palestinian farmers who since 1948 were forced to live in remote refugee camps. The ruins that were left among the fruit trees also no longer looked like romantic European sights, but more like the empty remains of depopulated Palestinian home" ("Ma ha-nof rotse" 5). Waking up from a blind love can be painful, especially when one is convinced (as one usually is) that her/his love is not blind. *Visual Occupations* is, to certain degree, a book about this painful experience of coming to terms with my own blindness. But as such, it is also a book about the need to mobilize such awakenings in order to move beyond the melancholia involved in letting go of an old blind love toward the creation of a new and more lasting love modeled on new ways of seeing.

Read as a whole, *Visual Occupation* advances its arguments by offering a series of readings that demonstrate just how thoroughly the visual architecture of control, concealment, and separation has been disseminated throughout Israel and Palestine. These readings aim at expanding our understanding of the visual politics of the conflict to include *not just* the current distribution of the visual and its policed order, but also, and more importantly, the political potential found in the prospect of *redirecting* such visions of control and classified conditions of invisibility so as to generate new modes of seeing and new distributions of the seeable.

The examples I discuss present modes of visibility and practices of seeing that reside in the margins and on the far fringes of the hegemonic fields of vision that currently dominate the ways we have come to see the Israeli-Palestinian conflict. Unlike the majority of the popular circulating images of the conflict and the Israeli Occupation that seek immediate readability (for example, the ubiquity of the Separation Wall as a visual icon), the realm of visuality explored in these artworks relies not on immediacy but rather on *slowing down* and becoming aware of our process of reading the images.[24] My own readings, presented in the following chapters, are accordingly offered as an invitation to slow down and to replace our reliance on familiar images, which *blind us* by showing us nothing we have not already seen, with re-visions based on alternative visual configurations, which render our political reality less immediately decipherable. For if it is true that "the world is *what we see*," it is also true that we nonetheless "must learn to see it" (Merleau-Ponty 4).

PART I *Concealment*

Chapter One

Visible Invisibility

On Ruins, Erasure, and Haunting

The [Palestinian] villages that no longer exist were pushed out of the [Israeli] public sphere. They carry new names of Hebrew settlements (*yeshuvim ivriyim*). But these villages left some traces in these new settlements . . . a stone fence, bricks of ruined houses.
—Azmi Bishara, "Between Place and Space"

To be sure, the Nakba exists in the landscape. There are hundreds of ruined Palestinian villages throughout Israel, many of which are still surrounded by the sabra cactus . . . but for some reason the ruins of villages across the countryside [fail to] register among the Jewish Israeli population.
—Neve Gordon, "Erasing the Nakba"

There is an ambivalence [that] lays deep at the heart of Israeli thinking and culture . . . a denial of the persistent, ghostly presence of the Palestinian absentees amid the ruins of their homes and their neglected fields.
—Yehudit Kirstein Keshet, *Checkpoint Watch: Testimonies from Occupied Palestine*

This book deals with questions of vision and visibility, particularly the ability to see and be seen. But the parameters by which we determine what is or isn't included within the realm of the visual is itself a matter open to dispute. Following the image of the ruins of depopulated Palestinian villages within the Israeli public sphere and culture, this chapter investigates how a certain *failure to see* or *to appear* generates an alternative mode of visuality associated with the sociopolitical power of ghostly haunting.

Informed by the work of Avery Gordon, Jacque Derrida, and Nicholas Abraham and Maria Torok, I suggest that haunting expands the realm of the visible to include the visibility of the invisible. The chapter engages several key Israeli literary and artworks to examine how the unresolved and ongoing historical violence associated with the Palestinian forced exile of 1948, referred to in Arabic as the Nakba (the catastrophe), is seemingly erased or hidden from Israeli eyes, and yet nevertheless finds its way into the Israeli visual field as a haunting presence of a *visible invisibility*.

To be sure, the dominant Israeli visual field—not unlike that of other settler colonial societies—is created, guarded, and sustained through various state-governed blinding mechanisms that conceal and erase the history of past inhabitants' relationship to the land. In the case of Israel, these erasures include rhetorical acts such as the replacement of the Arabic names of villages with new Hebrew names, the use of the term "present absentees" to denote Palestinians who fled their homes in 1948, and the replacement of the term "Palestinians" with the term "Israeli Arabs" in reference to Palestinian citizens of Israel. The erasure also takes the form of particular spatial arrangements, such as the planting of numerous national forests over the remains of Palestinian villages; and the separation of Jewish Israelis and Palestinian Israelis so that the visibility of the other remains as minimal as possible, including the construction of the Separation Wall, which keeps the Palestinians of the West Bank out of the Israeli visual field, and the construction of distinct road systems for Israeli Jews and Palestinians, which again minimizes the visibility of the other through the imposition of two radically separate geopolitical realities on the same territorial landscape (see Weizman, "Politics of Verticality").

And yet, unlike what we might consider other, more successful settler colonial projects, the Zionist Israeli Jewish enterprise failed both in removing the original inhabitants of the land and in concealing their traces.[1] This means, among other things, that compared to Australia, New Zealand, or the United States, Israel has not succeeded in generating a myth of a unified democratic collective origin, or in hiding the ongoing violence involved in the state's establishment. It also means that despite Israel's ongoing and persistent attempts to cover up, remove, hide, and eliminate anything Palestinian, the "stubbornly persistent Palestinian presence" nevertheless manages to invade almost every aspect of everyday Israeli life (Makdisi, "The Architecture of Erasure" 527). Indeed, the common Hebrew phrase is *kfarim netushim*, which literally translates to "deserted villages." Focusing on the image of the ruins of depopulated Palestinian villages within Israeli culture, this chapter traces the growing *visible invisibility* of the Palestinian Nakba as a ghostly haunting that continues to taunt the Israeli visual field despite the state's elaborate attempts to do away with it once and for all.

The Landscape of Ruins

For anyone familiar with the Israeli landscape, the sight of ruins of destroyed Palestinian villages is not unusual. Usually one finds but a few remaining structures: an arch, a gate, a half-standing house, a broken water tank. It is true that a great number of the more than the four hundred Palestinian villages depopulated following the 1948 war were completely demolished by Israel, leaving no trace behind. But there have also been instances in which ruins have been left visible, and in some cases they have even been carefully preserved and exposed as parts of touristic sites open to the general public.[2] If the majority of the ruins were thus destroyed in a process of historical erasure, others were erased in a more complex manner: while the ruins were left visible, they were incorporated into the hegemonic Zionist narrative through a process of *resignification*.[3] At times this process of resignification involved the transformation of the Palestinian ruins into symbols of biblical times, whereby the ruins are imagined as ancient remains that offer an insight into the life of the Israelites. At other times, the ruins were preserved and presented as an organic part of the landscape: "a-historical natural entities, like rivers or water pools" (Kadman 70–71).

The image of Palestinian ruins has found its way into numerous Israeli landscape paintings, films, and literary texts, becoming an integral part of the projected new Israeli landscape and a significant element of so-called authentic Israeli culture (Ofrat 19).[4] Examining the status of Palestinian ruins in these cultural texts, one finds a similar tendency to resignify, de-historicize, and naturalize. Thus, in many of the Israeli abstract landscape paintings from the 1950s and 1960s, Palestinian ruins are included in the frame but only through the selective gaze of the new colonial settlers who overlook the immediate historical context of violence and destruction and instead incorporate the ruins as elements of a lyrical and abstract composition (see figure 1.1).[5]

A similar tendency characterizes many Israeli literary texts. Consider, for example, a scene from Amos Oz's novel *A Perfect Peace* (*Menucha nekhona*, 1982) in which the narrator (Yonatan Lifshitz), who often visits the ruins

1.1 | *Ruins*, by Jakob Eisenscher. Watercolor, date unknown. Courtesy of Arie Albert Eisenscher and Tamar Eisenscher Lavner.

of the Palestinian village Sheikh Dahr, bordering his kibbutz, appears to be taken by the force of a sudden melancholy: "On the hilltop, against the sky, backed by blue clouds, stood the ruins of Sheikh Dahr, light slashing through the gaping windows like an eviscerating sword, the out-of-doors just as bright on the side of the smashed, charred, homeless walls as on the other. Rubble from fallen roofs lay in the heaps. Here and there an un-submitting grape vine had run wild, clung with bared claws to a remnant of a standing stonewall. Above the ravaged village rose its shattered mina-ret" (127).Yonatan is taken by the image of the ruins and is reminded of his childhood sense of uncanny feelings each time he sees them. But Oz's language depicts this experience with such a romantic flair that it reads more like an encounter with nature's sublime forces than with a concrete and recent history of violence and destruction.

The figure of speech "the deserted Arab Village" (*ha-kfar ha-aravi ha-natush*) is also prevalent in 1950s Hebrew poetry. The expression func-tions as a paradoxical means of memorialization and erasure. On the one hand, the ruins are repeatedly mentioned, but on the other hand they are described as "deserted," a term that hides the fact that Palestinians were forced out of their villages and suggests instead that the villages were deserted by their past inhabitants for some unknown and mysterious reasons — as if "the ruins rather than the villagers are the actual victims of this process of ruination" (Hever, Al Tagidu 14).[6]

These repeated attempts to erase, resignify, and evacuate the historical meaning of the Palestinian ruins, characteristic of these dominant Israeli modes of representations, nevertheless fail (they are *bound to fail*) to successfully repress the haunting impact that these ruins continue to have over Israelis and Israeli culture. Thus, despite the fact that Palestinian ruins have been manipulatively incorporated into the master Zionist narrative of Jewish return (to the land and to history) as either symbols of an authentic Israelite biblical time, or as a symbol of a pastoral, simple way of living associated with the Orient, a closer look reveals the fact that in effect these ruins continue to *animate resistance*. As a poetic device, ruins highlight an unobservable tension that disturbs, haunts, and taunts the Zionist national narrative from within. I shall demonstrate this by tracing the figure of the Palestinian ruin in three key Israeli literary texts: S. Yizhar's novella *Khirbet Khizeh*, first published in 1949, A. B. Yehoshua's novella *Mul ha-ye'arot* (*Facing the Forests*), first published in 1963, and Yeshayahu Koren's novel *Levaya ba-tsohora'im* (*Funeral at Noon*) from 1974. My readings highlight the allegorical function of the figure of the ruins within the texts as a poetic device that unearths the ghostly presence of the Palestinian Nakba within the Israeli visual field *despite* its ongoing erasure and concealment.[7] Specifically, I will show how a certain failure to appear (the failure of the Nakba to become fully visible and accountable within Israeli texts) translates into a *growing visible invisibility*: an invisibility that calls attention to itself as such. The second part of the chapter moves from literature to painting to propose a correlated political utilization of failed vision.

Haunting and (In)visibility

"Haunting," Avery Gordon tells us, "describes that which appears to be not there," but it is a "not there" that nevertheless acts on and meddles with "taken-for-granted realities" (8). Haunting takes place when we encounter a ghost, itself a presence unlike any other presence: a presence "seemingly not there to our supposedly well-trained eyes" (8). Freud also famously mobilizes the language of haunting in order to account for the sudden emergence of the repressed from its long hibernation in the un-consciousness and into a sudden return of a view ("The Uncanny" sec. 3: 222). What seems to me to be most significant about these accounts is that they capture not only the fact that being haunted has to do with coming to terms with something that has been previously repressed, but also the fact that through the psychic experience of haunting something *happens to visi-bility*. Something happens that puts into question the borders between the visible and the invisible, the known and the unknown, that which is clearly present and that which continues to escape our eyes.[8] Another way to say this is to suggest that the psychic experience of being haunted involves not only the sudden resurfacing of the repressed, but also the appearance of a *visible absence* or a *visible invisibility* that draws attention to itself, "however symptomatically" (A. Gordon 15).

Taking this understanding as my point of departure, I describe the ghost that runs through many key Israeli cultural texts not simply in terms of a concrete figure or image (the ruins) but more significantly in terms of a cer-tain *crisis of visibility*. I ask: What kind of seeing could possibly render this ghost visible? What kind of seeing could identify that which by definition escapes our normal field of visibility? Wrestling with the question of the specter's visibility, Derrida has suggested, "the specter, as its name indi-cates, is the *frequency* of a certain visibility" (100). If we are able to see the specter and render it visible, it is only insofar as what we see as the *marked absence* left by the ghost's appearance: "at the time and place where [the specter] appears, there something disappeared, departed in the appari-tion itself as reapportion of the departed" (Derrida 6). In other words, the kind of seeing enabled by the psychic experience of being haunted is dif-ferent from the seeing we normally experience. Haunting renders visible the *invisibility* that marks the limits of our common practices of seeing and makes us see, as in recognize, that there is a presence before us, which we nevertheless fail to see with our naked eyes.

Closely engaging with several Israeli texts (literature and painting) in the next section, I seek to unearth the haunting presence of the *visible in-visibility* of the Palestinian Nakba, which I show to be a central feature of Israeli cultural and political imagination. My readings follow a two-stage process. First, I look at three principal Israeli literary texts (published in 1949, 1963, and 1974) and trace in them a progressive narrative of haunt-ing associated with a culture of denial, blindness, and failed vision. In the second part, I turn to a painting exhibit by the acclaimed Israeli artist Larry Abramson. The exhibit, Tsŏob'ä (1994), situates the question of failed vision and the symptomatic blindness of Zionism at the heart of the artist's investigation of the relationship between national ideology and landscape paintings and, more specifically, between the displacement and concealment of Palestinian ruins and the greater tradition of modernist Israeli landscape paintings. What is therefore symptomatically present in the literary texts that I analyze — the haunting of the visible invisibility associated with the repressed history of these ruins — reemerges in Abramson's work as a meta-artistic commentary that is as much about the *image* of these ruins as it is about the *ruin* of the image. I will return to this point following my discussion of the literary texts.

From Yizhar's Khirbeh to Yehoshua's Ruins and Koren's Crypts: A Growing Visible Invisibility

The figure of the "deserted Arab village" (ha-kfar ha-aravi ha-natush) appears, reappears, and disappears in Yizhar's, Yehoshua's, and Koren's texts, making visible the unresolved history of violence and repression located (and hidden) at the heart of the Israeli Jewish Zionist narrative advanced and undermined by these authors. In Yizhar's groundbreaking text, written less than a year after the 1948 war, we are confronted with the *hirbeh*, Arabic for "ruined structure" (the Arabic word literally translates to something which is destroyed, broken, or spoiled). Within the story, the term is used by the Israeli soldiers in reference to a Palestinian village they are *about to destroy* and turn into ruins. Close to twenty years later, Yehoshua's text momentarily reveals to the reader, only to quickly reconceal, the hidden ruins of an Arab village located in the midst of a recently planted Israeli national forest. A little less than a decade later we find the same figure of speech ("the ruins of the deserted Arab village") in Koren's novel, only this time the ruins seem to have already become "a crypt" in the sense advanced by Abraham and Torok: "a burial site" where a past trauma and the failure to face it are sealed and "kept out of sight."[9] The emptied ("deserted") Arab villages to which Yizhar's early novella introduces us, and which reappear in Yehoshua's text as hidden ruins and in Koren's novel as crypts, unfold a semantics of ambiguity located between presence and absence, the present and the past, the visible and the invisible, and the living and the dead. Located in the liminal spaces (hidden in the forest or marking the exterior of a thriving settlement), these ruins come to us not only as images of a violent past, but also, I suggest, as a reminder of "a space that is still in becoming" (Eshel 147). They are, in other words, figures (and figures of speech) animated in their haunting.

....

Khirbet Khizeh was published in 1949 under the name S. Yizhar (pen name of Yizhar Smilansky), a writer who was born in Palestine in 1916 and became one of Israel's most renowned writers before passing away in 2006.[10] The title of the novella uses the Arabic word Hirbeh (the Hebrew word is churva) in reference to an evacuated Arab village attacked by Jewish soldiers during the 1948 war. The story, which accounts for the expulsion of Palestinian villagers from their homes and the destruction of their village, was published just a few months following the end of the 1948 war and the establishment of the state of Israel. It therefore situates the Palestinian narrative of forced exile and loss at the very heart of what has become a foundational (perhaps the founding) text of modern Hebrew statehood literature.[11]

The centrality of this narrative of violence and loss within a text that early on became a canonical Hebrew literary work has invited numerous explanations and interpretations over the years.[12] The novella has long been read as a testimonial text dealing primarily with the moral dilemmas and internal conflicts of a soldier with a conscience (the protagonist) rather than with the historical and political question of Palestinian forced exile and loss. It is within this limited framework that critics have continued to debate over the exact ethical and political implications of the text.[13] In their rush to determine the political message of the text and assess its ethical implications, however, critics seemed to have overlooked, if not totally ignored, one of the most fascinating stylistic features of Yizhar's text: namely, the fact that its "time is out of joint."[14] Paying close attention to this time lag, my own reading moves away from the testimonial model and suggests we should instead read the text for its prophetic quality.

The story opens with the narrator recalling: "true, all this happened a long time ago, but it has haunted me ever since. I tried to bury the memory away in the rush of everyday life, to underplay it and make it less sharp by passing time. Sometimes I was even successful" (Khirbet 33). Yizhar, who published the story just weeks after the end of the war, situates his narrator in a long-distant future ("it all happened a long time ago"). Thus, the act of narration itself unfolds through an anticipated haunting yet to come: the return of the past as an anticipated future, to paraphrase Derrida.[15] Furthermore, the Arab village ordered for destruction is itself caught in limbo. At times referred to as a "village" (in Hebrew: kfar) and at times a "waste-land"/"ruin site" (in Arabic: hirbeh), the village appears to be precisely that: an emptied village *on the way to becoming ruins*. As such, its appearance in the text is always already ghostly: it is a site already destroyed and yet ordered for future destruction. In short, I suggest that Khirbet Khizeh is not simply a testimonial text that recounts a young Jewish soldier's experiences expelling Palestinians from their homes. Rather, and perhaps more importantly, it is a prophetic text predicting the inescapable haunting impact this expulsion is bound to have on future Israeli generations.

Arriving at a hill overlooking an almost empty village, the narrator and his fellow soldiers await an order to attack. It is within this transformative moment when the village is about to become ruins, envisioned by a soldier who is about to take part in the destruction, that Yizhar implants his warning of a haunting yet to come:

> These empty villages. A day arrives and they begin to scream. You walk through them and suddenly in front of you, without you knowing where it comes from, you are met with hidden eyes of walls, yards, and alleys that accompany you silently. . . . And there are cases where suddenly in the middle of the day or the early evening, when the village, that was until then simply a bunch of empty houses engraved in their silence, bursts with the sound of the objects that have lost their soul: the song of human deeds that returns to their core in distortion; the song of an announced sudden catastrophe that froze and remains like a curse . . . and fear, and horror, and a flitting sign of revenge cries out from there . . . from these empty villages. . . . Big shadows of things whose death is still unconceivable circle around, harassing. (41)

The sign of the ghost inscribes Yizhar's language. He names the ghost the "unburied dead" and warns us of its *unavoidable* return, since, truthfully speaking, the dead have never left: "the air is still filled with their sounds, voices and gazes" (47, 77).

Yizhar's narrator predicts what has indeed become a state-led strategy to erase and forcibly forget the past: "New Jewish immigrants would be settled in this 'whatever its name is' village. Who would even imagine that there was once some kind of an Arab hirbeh here?" (Yizhar, *Khirbet* 76). Yet he accompanies this prediction of a state-governed politics of memory and forgetting with a warning about its inevitable failure: "But those who would end up living here, in this village, would the walls not scream in their ears? And all these images and cries, those which were voiced and those that were not . . . would the air not be filled with all these sounds, voices, and gazes?" (77). Time will pass, the houses will be resettled, and no visible mark of the past will be left, Yizhar tells us, already predicting the success of the Zionist resettling enterprise. No matter how many efforts are put into covering, erasing, concealing, and hiding, the haunting visible invisibility of the ghost will continue to taunt.

Fourteen years separate *Khirbet Khizeh* from A. B. Yehoshua's renowned novella *Mul Ha-ye'arot (Facing the Forests)*.[16] During those years, the JNF (Jewish National Fund), the global Zionist organization in charge of purchasing land and encouraging Jewish settlement in Palestine, embarked on a massive project of forestation, particularly around Jerusalem and throughout Galilee.[17] Planting trees and creating national forests have long functioned as part of the Zionist mechanism of altering and reshaping the landscape. The official narrative promoted by the JNF is that the forests helped dry the swamps and make the desert bloom and provided work for the numerous new Jewish immigrants, reenforcing the ties between Jews and (their promised) land. But these massive plantings have also served as a means of literally covering up the Palestinian past. Planted over and around numerous sites of destroyed Palestinian villages, such forestation violently obscures the visible marks of a recent past: forced expulsion, atrocities, and violence.[18]

Yehoshua's text addresses this historical erasure explicitly. The protagonist is an older graduate student struggling to complete his dissertation. In his desperate attempt to find peace, he decides to leave the city and take up a job as a forest fire watcher in one of the national parks. Bored with his studies and overwhelmed by the loneliness, the protagonist spends hours dazed, falling in and out of sleep, or simply staring out of the window at the forest through his binoculars, waiting for "action" in the form of a fire's eruption, which would justify his position. Several months pass before the fire watcher finds out (from curious tourists visiting the forest) that the forest covers the ruins of a destroyed Arab village. Obsessed with the desire to find and expose these ruins, the fire watcher indirectly (yet suggestively) entices an old mute Arab groundskeeper (his sole companion) to burn down the forest, no doubt providing himself with some long-awaited excitement. Following the fire and the exposure of the ruins, the police interrogate the fire watcher, who frames the old Arab and then heads back to the city to resume his life as a failed student.

This seemingly aimless circularity with which the novella closes and the enigmatic nature of the plot as a whole has long earned the text the descriptions "uncanny," "haunting," and "bizarre."[19] While some critics have focused on the role of the ruins in the novella, pointing at their enigmatic status, none seem to have noticed or paid attention to the close relationship formed within the text between the ruins and the protagonist's *visual deficiency*. Indeed, the protagonist's ability to see straight is cast into doubt very early on. We are told that the student's "compromised vision makes many things appear doubtful" (Mul 99). The supervisor who hires him to guard the forest also questions his capability to take on the job based on his bad vision: "perhaps he doesn't see clearly after all? Maybe he needs stronger glasses? Should he take another pair with him?" (Mul 102). Hired to watch for fires, the student spends all day just looking out of his window. Armed with his binoculars, he gazes at the forest, "which approaches him, seeming all blurry" (Mul 103). When he learns that ruins of a Palestinian village are hidden somewhere in the forest, he becomes obsessed with the desire to *see* them and make them visible. At the same time the text frames his entire mission of exposure within a narrative about his impaired vision and partial blindness. At times he wakes up "blinded with a red burning color in his glasses," and at other times he cannot see well because of his "foggy shades" (Mul 104). Struggling to see clearly, and relying on the glasses and binoculars, the student either sees things that aren't there ("at noon he is distracted by the sight of a flame burning in the trees. He follows it for hours only to discover at evening that it is only the red dress of the little Arab girl who is running among the trees"), or he fails to see things that are there ("an Arab village? He looks at them with his tired eyes, no. There is no Arab village here, the map must be wrong") (Mul 106–7, 113).

Moving back and forth between seeing clearly and barely seeing, the protagonist struggles to distinguish between optical illusions and obscured realities: "the trees look like a group of soldiers awaiting their commander. . . . Flickering light and shadows" bring life into the quiet forest, which otherwise resembles "a graveyard" (Mul 109). Growing more and more obsessed with what are no longer simply illusionary visions of fire, but rather a deep yearning to finally see the forest on fire, the protagonist sees the forest covered by smoke. Realizing there is no fire, he concludes, "the spectacles are to blame" (Mul 116). Even after the forest is finally burned, the "green forests continue to grow in front of his angry eyes" (Mul 127). With this focus on vision and visual deficiency, Yehoshua prepares the grounds for asking what I believe is the main question raised within the novella: what kind of seeing (or compromised seeing) is required in order to see that which remains invisible, or that which remains visible in its invisibility?

The protagonist of the novella is clearly haunted by a past he does not understand and eventually fails to see. The ruins, hidden in the forest, seem to work on him, while their exposure does little if anything to change his clueless position. Instead, he turns his back on the old Arab and returns to his meaningless life in the city, far away from the burned forest and the exposed ruins. In a manner similar to that of Yizhar's text, Yehoshua's novella includes *within it* not only a story about haunting but also a story about the failure or inability to face the ghosts of the past: a failure that alone ensures that haunting will continue. Indeed, like *Khirbet Khizeh*, *Facing the Forests* delivers an *unresolved haunting* as a narrative about the failure to see the visible invisibility of the ghost.

Social haunting takes place, Abraham and Torok argue, as long as an individual or a collective continues to fail to come to terms with "the lacunas imprinted on it by the secrets of others," which are the secrets of previous generations (427). The ruins in Yehoshua's story, I suggest, stand for the secrets of the founding generations that are hidden and abruptly exposed, only to be hidden yet again. "What happened here?" the protagonist wonders when he first encounters the ruins; "probably the women were killed too, when the houses were destroyed; without doubt, a shady thing" (Mul 121–22). Within the framework of the novella, this haunting finds no resolution. On the contrary, with the student returning to his old routine and everything going back to normal, as it were, we get a clear sense that shady things *continue* to take place. But what *within the story* remains an unresolved pathological and ongoing shady thing that *as such* carries a productive poetic force? The ruins remain disruptions that are unable to be consumed by or integrated into the narrative as a whole even when they finally appear. They function as a reminder of the open secret situated at the heart of the Israeli national narrative.

A little over a decade after the publication of *Facing the Forests*, Yisha'ayahu Koren published his remarkable, if lesser-known novel *Funeral at Noon* (1974). The novel, published right after the Yom Kippur War (the 1973 war), can be read as a poetic rendition of the confusion, shock, and speechlessness that characterized the Israeli state of mind at the end of a war that took Israel by surprise and almost resulted in catastrophic defeat only seven years after Israel marked its swift victory in the 1967 war (the Six Day War or *Milchemet sheshet ha-yamim*). Indeed, Koren's novel is full of gaps, silences, dysfunctional characters, and death. It is also, I believe, the Israeli literary text that best captures and animates the haunting impact of the Palestinian Nakba on Israeli society.[20]

The entire plot of *Funeral at Noon* takes place in the *vicinity of* and *in relation to* the ruins of a destroyed, nameless Arab village. The protagonist of the novel is a woman by the name of Hagar. We know very little about her aside from the fact that she is married to Tuvia Erlikh, about whom we know even less. The other character we meet is the neighbor's ten-year-old son, Yiftach, whom Hagar befriends and with whom she spends most of her time roaming through the nearby ruins of a destroyed Arab village. During one of their visits to the ruins, Hagar finds a military canteen and decides to find the original owner. One event leads to another, and Hagar eventually meets a young Israeli soldier who denies owning the canteen. The two have sex hiding among the ruins, after which Yiftach disappears and is later found dead. The novel reads like a mystery but follows an unresolved plot: we never learn why Hagar repeatedly visits the ruins, why she becomes obsessed with finding the owner of the canteen, how she meets the soldier, or how Yiftach, who follows her to her secret love meeting in the ruins, eventually dies. The endless details Koren provides never conjure up a coherent narrative. We learn little about the relationship between the various disjointed and fragmented stories told in the novel and even less so about the untold story of the Arab ruins, which serve as the stage for this enigmatic plot.

The phrase "the deserted Arab village" (*ha-kfar ha-azuv*) is mentioned throughout the novel, haunting page after page. These words do not denote a place as much as a secret. The phrase functions as a set of "phantom words," to borrow Abraham's term ("Notes on the Phantom" in Abraham and Torok, 174), and stands for an attempt to capture *in language* (as a visible mark) a secret otherwise unattainable. Moreover, the phrase represents an attempt to "force the ghosts of violent history into the open" by generating a haunted language that literally functions as a burial site for what is simultaneously "hidden as it is revealed" (174). In other words, the figure of the Arab ruins, mentioned throughout the novel but never becoming an integral part of the plot, function as a *crypt* or "psychic tomb" that harbors the undead ghosts and hides them "in language" (Abraham and Torok 6, 22, 130). More literally, *within the novel* the ruins are where the body of young Yiftach is eventually found after his mysterious death. The novel thus seems to grants the ruins the status of *real crypt*: the site where the unspeakable traumatic past continues to haunt and act on the present, mashing together the living and the dead.[21]

The silences, displaced transitions, gaps, and missing information that make the novel so enigmatic draw attention to the haunting presence of these phantom words: "the deserted Arab village." The traumatic past encrypted into the words "the deserted Arab village" (ha-kfar ha-azuv) or the "ruined village" (*ha-kfar ha-charev*) hover over the novel as a haunting phantom: disrupting and unsettling. As Palestinian Israeli writer and literary critic Ayman Siksek notes:"Empty, nameless, destroyed, the remains of the village stand there in an unbearable proximity to the town where Tuvia and Hagar live. It is an astonishingly passive body: the past inhabitants of its destroyed houses are none other than ghosts about whom we know nothing: did they escape, did they fight back, and were they killed?" ("Ta'atu'ai ke'elu"). What should we make of this silencing? Koren's enigmatic style may be accused of failing to articulate a clear moral condemnation or an effective political response to the historical violence it indirectly (yet repeatedly) alludes to. Indeed, the figure of the nameless, empty, and destroyed Arab village in the text could even be said constitute a fetish. As fetish, these words stand in for an unresolved anxiety and repression that the characters, and perhaps even Koren himself, may be accused of failing to come to terms with. And yet it is also significant that this enigmatic, nameless, destroyed village (whose "past is expelled out of the text," to borrow Siksek's words) frames—from the first line of the novel to its end—the entire narrative. It is without doubt the ghostly presence that mobilizes Hagar, leading her time and again to leave her house and roam the destroyed, empty village. It is there that she finds the water container and then a lover, and it is there that she loses her only friend. Hagar is compelled to return to the destroyed houses and the village ruins. We never learn what motivates her, nor does it seem like Hagar has insight into her own actions. As in the case of Yehoshua's fire watcher, the destroyed village appears to *act on her*.

Narratologically speaking, the force of the ruins lies in their negativity. Their appearance marks a void that calls attention to itself as such.[22] The "deserted Arab village"—a place that has become bereft of the people who make it a place in the first place—is the phrase that punctuates the narrative not by infusing it with details of past memories or accounts of violence and loss, but rather by drawing attention to the absence of any such account. This ghostly presence, made visible through the negativity of the ruins, haunts Koren's novel and its characters, leaving readers hoping to find closure or resolution. Instead we are left with a crushing and unresolved sense of discomfort. The novel's enigmatic and uncanny narrative tells us only that something remains undisclosed: *visible in its invisibility*.

Indeed, Koren's novel joins Yizhar's and Yehoshua's earlier efforts to underscore the afterlives of ruins. The three novels remind us, "something unidentified remains hidden behind the 'visible' parts of the story, something that seeks to be exposed, but which as such remains beyond our reach" (Siksek). While the protagonists in each of these texts remain blind and clueless—failing to grasp and come to terms with the haunting historical force of the ruins—the texts draw attention to such failures as a means of capturing *in language* an alternative mode of visuality directed not so much at the visibility of the ruins but at the *visible invisibility* of the historical violence these ruins encrypt. The sudden and momentary haunting *reappearance* of this historical violence often marks its immediate *disappearance* into the Israeli landscape. In other words I suggest that the *spectral quality* of these texts draws attention to the status of these ruins within the dominate Israeli visual field by reminding us that more important than seeing the ruins is seeing their disappearance: seeing, that is, their *visible invisibility*. A similar position is advanced, I suggest (and this time explicitly and critically rather than symptomatically), in Larry Abramson's memorable painting series Tsŏob'ä (1993–94).

The Image of the Ruin and the Ruin of the Image:
Larry Abramson's Tsŏob´ä

From 1993 to 1994 the prominent Israeli artist Larry Abramson repeatedly painted a single image: the remains of the Palestinian village Suba adjacent to kibbutz Tsuba.[23] The final exhibited project (named Tsŏob´ä) included thirty-eight landscape oil paintings of the Tsuba mountain in which the top layer of paint ("the greasy layer," to use curator Tali Tamir's words) was removed by old newspapers that were stuck to the paint and then detached; the thirty-eight old newspaper prints with the mirror images and traces of colors of the paintings; and thirteen small paintings of branches taken from the vicinity of the destroyed village (see figures 1.2.1–1.2.4).[24]

Abramson's choice of the ruins of Suba was not accidental. Rather, it marked his choice to enter an explicit dialogue with the identifiable tradition of Israeli abstract landscape paintings. Abramson's project offers a critical reexamination of one of Israel's most acclaimed founding painters, Yossef Zritsky, who, from his studio in Kibbutz Tsuba, throughout the 1970s and 1980s painted numerous landscape pictures known as his "Tsuba paintings." Commenting on these paintings, Abramson writes, "the ruins of the village are invisible. They have become an integral part of the landscape: part of a beautiful, romantic and pastoral unity [blended into] the soft harmony of his beautifully mastered abstract style" ("What Does the Landscape Want?" 5).[25] Returning to Zritsky's work to reevaluate the long tradition of Israeli abstract landscape painting, Abramson concludes, "the art of abstraction has long functioned as Israel's ultimate visual regime . . . its most effective art of disguise" (5).

The main question Abramson's own work sets out to investigate is: what modes of seeing and representations could possibly rescue these Palestinian ruins from vanishing into the Israeli landscape and into the arms of universalizing and abstracting modernism? The question seems to be directed first of all in relation to the general history of landscape painting, which as W. J. T. Mitchell remind us "is often a place of amnesia and erasure, a strategic site for burying the past and veiling history with 'natural beauty'" ("Holy Landscape" 195). More urgently, Abramson's series calls attention to the specific blinding mechanisms that inform the Israeli Zionist visual field, in which the land (of Israel) is imagined as an empty (abstract) space: a tabula rasa on which Jewish history can be created anew.

1.2.1, 1.2.2, 1.2.3, and 1.2.4 | Larry Abramson, from his series Tsŏob′ä, 1993–94, consisting of thirty-eight landscape paintings, oil on canvas, 25 × 25 cm each; thirty-eight impressions on newspaper, 40 × 28 cm each; thirteen still-life paintings after flora samples, oil on canvas, various sizes. Private collection, Tel Aviv. Courtesy of the artist.

Within such visual imagination, the ruins of a Palestinian village inevitably *disappear* at the very moment they *appear*, for their appearance is immediately incorporated into the broader frame of the Zionist geopolitical imagination of Jewish historical revival.

Working with visual materials rather than words, Abramson's quest is to find a visual arrangement to capture this process of disappearance: this *visible invisibility* of the ruins. Simply painting the ruins as they appear in the telescopic photographs Abramson himself captured (and on which he based all thirty-eight ruin paintings) would do little to confront the larger framing view of the Israeli visual field in which these ruins are always already *seen in their disappearance*. Abramson's series approaches this problem by turning this drama of erasure and disappearance into an investigation of *the image of the ruins* (the history of Israeli landscape paintings), which is, at the same time, a process that involves the *ruination of the image*.

In a manner similar to that found in Koren's phantom words, Yehoshua's fragmented narrative, and Yizhar's time lag, Abramson's paintings include *within them* the visual failure (the failure to appear/the failure to see) that paradoxically functions as the key component of the ability to capture and render visible the *visible invisibility* of the Palestinian ruins. Painting the ruins and then partially erasing them while further destroying the image (removing the top layer of the paint), Abramson's series makes the ruins less visible and, by the same token, draws attention to their *visible invisibility* within the general Israeli visual field and in the Israeli landscape painting tradition.

Abramson successfully concretizes Eduardo Cadava's suggestion that "the image of the ruin is also the ruin of the image" by making the process of *looking at* the ruins and capturing them as an image the subject of his series. Indeed, Abramson's destroyed paintings of the ruins of Suba are, in their final form, also ruined paintings. Conceptualizing the image of ruins from this point of view means thinking about the limits of representation—the limits of the image's capacity "to show, to represent, to address, to evoke the persons, events, truths, histories, lives and deaths to which it would refer" ("Lapsus Imaginis" 35–36). It also means thinking about how this limit may itself be represented. Abramson's ruined paintings introduce us to traces, gaps, and failures insofar as the scrapped paint calls attention to the fact that something else might have been there, has escaped the final frame, has been violently erased, but is nevertheless signified as a reminder of absence and erasure—a *visible invisibility* located somewhere between the image and its erasure, appearance, and disappearance, the past and the present, the paint that remains and that which was scraped away.

In other words, while Abramson's paintings visualize the process of seeing, they also render visible the limits and structured blindness involved in the process of an Israeli artist looking at Palestinian ruins and attempting to capture them as image. Hence the final images (the paintings) are *ruined images.* These ruined images, I suggest, join Yizhar's, Yehoshua's, and Koren's disjointed narratives in rendering visible the phantasmatic nature of the Israeli visual field, haunted as it is by the visible invisibility of the Palestinian Nakba. Scattered all over Israel, these ruins remain barely visible even when they are overtly visible. And yet, as these texts remind us, it is from their marginal, erased, and concealed position within the dominant Israeli cultural imagination and geopolitical landscape that these ruins continue to haunt. Absent in their presence, invisible in their visibility, and visible in their invisibility, these ruins continue to animate resistance, functioning as the specter that accompanies and disputes the hegemonic Zionist narrative about "a people without a land" retuning to "a land without a people."[26]

Chapter Two

From Invisible Spectators to the Spectacle of Terror

Chronicles of a Contested Citizenship

Chronicle is the silence before the storm. *Divine Intervention* is the very early stages of a
volcanic eruption.
—Elia Suleiman, in "The Occupation (and life) through an Absurdist Lens"

The previous chapter explored the phantasmatic nature of the Israeli visual
field, haunted by the visible invisibility of the Palestinian Nakba. Turning
in this chapter to the cinematic work of the acclaimed Palestinian Israeli
director Elia Suleiman, one must first note Suleiman's own conspicuous
status within the Israeli cinematic scene as a visible invisible ghost. Suleiman was born and raised in Nazareth, Israel. His films, particularly his
cinematic trilogy comprising *Chronicle of a Disappearance* (*Segell ikhtifa*, 1996),
Divine Intervention (*Yadon ilaheyya*, 2002), and *The Time That Remains* (*Al-zaman
al-baqi*, 2009)—the first of which was funded by Israeli Fund for Quality
Films—remain visibly invisible in Israel. Upon their international release,
these films (each shot primarily in Israel) had limited screenings, often
showing for a brief period at a small number of art-house cinemas and/or
as part of a special film festival before vanishing from the screens. In short,
they appeared only to quickly disappear.

Suleiman's films explicitly deal with the invisibility of Palestinians living
within the Jewish state of Israel and annexed Jerusalem, where Palestinians citizens of Israel make for over 20 percent of the state's population and
the approximately 375,000 Palestinians living in East Jerusalem with the
status of "permanent residents" make for another 4.4 percent. His cinematic oeuvre's invisibility in Israel is particularly alarming as it signifies
a failure, refusal, or inability on the part of most Israelis to see the invisibility that continues to escape the dominant Israeli visual field, and which

2.1 | Screen capture from *The Time That Remains* (dir. Elia Suleiman, 2009).

as such functions (not unlike the ruins discussed in the previous chapter), as the ghostly specter that haunts from within.[1]

Suleiman's cinematic persona and protagonist in all three films, the introvert spectator E.S., appears to be modeled on the figure of the ghost: he is the silent spectator, often located on the very edge of the frame. He remains largely invisible to the Jewish characters in the films, but from his position of invisibility he continues to watch. As spectators of the films, we see not only his invisibility in the eyes of the Israelis around him, but also his eyes: watching, following, haunting (see figure 2.1).

Most critics writing about Palestinian cinema identify the conundrum, located at the core of this body of work, invoked in Palestinian cinema's task to "stand against invisibility" and "represent the unrepresentable" (Said, Preface 3; Dabashi, Introduction 148). Under the conditions of Palestine's geographical absence and the overbearing power of the Zionist narrative, the cinematic virtual image of Palestine is often said to present an alternative location from which to render visible the Palestinian plight that otherwise remains invisible. My following engagement with Suleiman's films is similarly tuned to the tensions between visibility and invisibility, representation and unrepresentability. However, I argue that insufficient attention has so far been given to the unique political and poetic use Suleiman makes of this tension as a means not for representing the unrepresentable, but rather as a deliberate refusal to do so.

This chapter engages closely with the first two films of Suleiman's trilogy and explores the absurdist terrain of being rendered invisible in one's own home(land).[2] I suggest that Suleiman mobilizes the tension between visibility and invisibility in order to achieve two things at once: to visualize the invisible status of Palestinians, and to deny his cinematic subjects a so-called proper or restorative representation. Furthermore, Suleiman's cinema manages to bring the question of Palestine into the visible realm as a narrative, a historical position, and a political reality by focusing on the least visible Palestinian or on the most invisible figure of this conflict, namely the Palestinian citizen of Israel. This is a figure whose ghostly existence, unlike that of the more familiar icon of the Palestinian living under direct military Israeli Occupation, continues to escape most of the dominant visual frameworks through which the Israeli-Palestinian conflict appears. Indeed, if the image of the (either suffering or heroic) Occupied Palestinian body has long gained an iconic status within the international visual representations of the conflict, Palestinian citizens of Israel (and, to a lesser degree, the East Jerusalem Palestinians who have been partially incorporated into the fabric of the Israeli society under the conspicuous status of permanent residents) remain almost entirely invisible to external viewers.[3]

While Suleiman's cinema renders visible the conspicuous invisibility of Palestinians residing within Israel (and East Jerusalem), his cinematic practice nevertheless avoids representation insofar as it refuses to render Palestinians (Israeli or otherwise) more visible. In other words, Suleiman avoids the kind of visibility associated with filling the void (representing the unrepresentable) by instead advancing either a "poetics of invisibility" (Chronicle of a Disappearance) or a "poetics of hypervisibility" (Divine Intervention), which are cinematic languages that highlight two sides of the same coin.

Situating Suleiman's films in the immediate historical and sociopolitical context out of which they emerge — the so-called Oslo period in Chronicle of a Disappearance and the beginning of the Second Palestinian Intifada in Divine Intervention — provides a partial explanation for the noticeable stylistic differences between the two films, particularly in relation to the transition from Suleiman's early poetics of invisibility to his later investment in hypervisibility. On the most simplistic level, the change in Suleiman's cinematic language reflects the changes in the distribution of Palestinian visibility during this period: from a tamed partner during peace negotiations to a violent objector after the Intifada's outbreak. Indeed, this may be what Suleiman means when he says "*Chronicle* is the silence before the storm [and] *Divine Intervention* is the very early stages of a volcanic eruption" ("The Occupation" 64–65).

Aiming for a deeper historical reading, I suggest that we pay closer attention to the particular status of the Palestinian citizen of Israel who is Suleiman's films' protagonist as well as the central figure of his cinematic interrogation of, and intervention into, the dominant Israeli, Palestinian, and international visual renditions of the conflict. Tracing the drastic changes in this particular figure's visibility between the Oslo period and the beginning of the Second Intifada may give us some insight into the stylistic changes in Suleiman's cinema. This said, one must proceed with great caution when seeking to historically contextualize Suleiman's films, which are after all inherently fragmented and resistant to the narrative closures commonly advanced by strictly historical or political interpretive frameworks. The following readings of *Chronicle* and *Divine Intervention* seek to maintain the films' ambivalent relationship to history and historical context by recognizing the impact of the specific historical and political conditions out of which Suleiman's films emerge (and with which they undoubtedly engage), while nevertheless emphasizing the inadequacy of such readings to fully account for the films' internal stylistic grammar, which positions cinematic images in a purposefully antagonistic relationship with any overarching or fully decipherable meaning.

Chronicle of a Disappearance: *The Poetics of Invisibility*

Faint background music accompanies the sound of deep breaths. A blurry close-up of a black-and-white image appears on the screen; it is unidentifiable. Slowly, more light enters the frame, and the blurry image begins to reveal itself: first a hand, then a nose, and then eyes. The camera zooms out, and we can finally identify the image: an old man's face, his head leaning on his hand, moving steadily to the rhythm of his breath, his eyes shut. With this opening scene, *Chronicle of a Disappearance* launches its exploration of a "poetics of invisibility," itself an oxymoronic task of visualizing absence and disappearance.

Introducing a rich visual grammar of concealment and invisibility, *Chronicle* locates its characters partially outside of the camera frame, uses primarily long shots that do not allow spectators to see facial expressions, and blurs some of the images to a degree that makes them unidentifiable. From beginning to end, the film is preoccupied with questions concerning the relationship between in/visibility and power: who is seen, and who remains invisible? Who or what can be seen from the location of invisibility? My reading of the film suggests that it troubles and queers the conventional association of visibility and power, exposing instead the political potential found in the position of the invisible spectator: the ghost who, from his position of invisibility, continues to watch and haunt.[4]

Chronicle of a Disappearance was shot and produced mainly in Israel during the height of the so-called Oslo period, a period roughly associated with the early to mid-1990s and marked by overt (mainly Israeli) optimism about the prospect of peace. This fantasy of coexistence was modeled on the two-state solution, which proposed an independent Palestinian state, located somewhere within the terrain of the Occupied Territories, side by side with a Jewish Israeli state. Chronicle's poetics of invisibility traces its Palestinian protagonists' gradual disappearance back to their paradoxical existence as citizens of the Israeli Jewish democratic state. Defending Israel's status as both Jewish and democratic, Palestinian Israeli Knesset member Ahmad Tibi's biting statement aptly captures Palestinians' paradoxical presence: "The truth is, Israel is a Jewish democracy: democratic towards Jews and Jewish towards Arabs." However, given the historical moment out of which the film emerged, we must also read the film's focus on the invisibility of the Palestinian residing in Israel as an explicit critical commentary and sober meditation on the premature jubilation over the Oslo peace negotiations' promise.[5] More specifically, with the ghostly main protagonist, E.S., and his family unnoticeably roaming Israeli streets or dozing off to televised broadcasts of the Jewish Israeli anthem, I argue that the film's focus on 1948 Palestinians' invisibility directly references the settler colonial nature of the Zionist project in Palestine and the ethno-religious-national character of the Jewish Israeli state, but is further mobilized as a critique of the specific (and particularly alarming) invisibility of this population throughout the entire process of the Oslo peace negotiations. The film's female protagonist, whose radical invisibility as a Palestinian resident of Jerusalem allows her to manipulate the entire Israeli police force and ultimately order their full evacuation from East Jerusalem, provocatively announces that "Jerusalem is no longer unified," highlighting the conspicuous absence of the question of Jerusalem from the framework of the Oslo negotiation.

Indeed, the Oslo negotiations' focus on the two-state solution left the question of 1948 Palestinians unaddressed, if not altogether forgotten. In other words, promising as it may have been, insofar as Palestinian citizens of Israel were concerned (and to a lesser degree Palestinian residents of East Jerusalem, an area of conflict that was deliberately bypassed and deferred throughout the negotiations), the Oslo period was marked by a profound invisibility. As suggested by Jonathan Cook, during this "hopeful period" the Palestinian citizen of Israel become more startling and paradoxically invisible than ever before: "The Palestinian leadership [overlooked the fact] that the division of the land would [cut off] the Palestinian [population in Israel] from its ties to the rest of its people forever; and Israel [continued] to treat its Palestinian community as little more than temporary residents of a Jewish state, a demographic nuisance [or perhaps even] a bargaining chip to be exchanged for land" ("What Future" 19).[6] In short, I propose that *Chronicle of a Disappearance* explores the visual poetics of invisibility in order to investigate the general conditions of invisibility associated with Palestinians residing within Israel (as a Jewish Democratic state), and as a means for further exposing the optimistic Oslo period as itself politically blind.

Without a doubt, the film focuses on the political predicament of the invisible Palestinian citizens and residents of Israel and alludes to their alarming disappearance or absence from the Oslo negotiations. And yet, containing Suleiman's film within this or any other fully defined historical and political context, or even securing the subject of his film, remains challenging. The film's fragmented structure and evasive visual vocabulary strongly resist any decisive or complete closure between image and reference. Consequently, an attentive reading of Suleiman's film must keep in mind the centrifugal force of its images and their defiance of familiar and pregiven political or historical frameworks as the setting for their interpretation. Accounting for this rejection of so-called politically oriented narrative cinema, Suleiman notes: "I am trying to create an image that transcends the ideological definitions of what it means to be a Palestinian. . . . My challenge is to avoid a centralized, unified image. . . . I don't want to tell the story of Palestine; I want to open the way to multiple spaces that lend themselves to different readings" ("Cinema of Nowhere" 97–98). Mobiliz-

2.2 | Screen capture from *Chronicle of a Disappearance* (dir. Elia Suleiman, 1996).

ing the format of a personal diary, *Chronicle* introduces a series of disparate vignettes that capture a variety of mundane events taking place in Nazareth and Jerusalem during the short visit of E.S. (played by Elia Suleiman), a Palestinian film director who returns from abroad to visit his hometown and make a film about peace. The parts shot in Nazareth follow the title "A Personal Diary" and are mainly composed of seemingly unremarkable images of everyday family life: people eating, smoking, sitting, and falling asleep in front of the TV screen.

Nazareth, the largest urban center of Palestinians in Israel, appears in *Chronicle* as a ghostly city: an empty, dull, and quiet place on the verge of disappearance. Appropriately, many of the scenes take place in front of an empty tourist shop, where souvenirs are piled in anticipation of visitors who never arrive, or in front of the local coffee shop, where only a few men gather to pass long hours in silence.[7] Without the presence of tanks, soldiers, checkpoints, Israeli police forces, or Jewish Israelis, the only visible sign of the Israeli occupation in Suleiman's Nazareth are the kitschy Zionist souvenirs at the tourist store: a postcard featuring a falafel sandwich topped with a miniature Israeli flag, and a wooden camel dressed in blue and white—the colors of the Israeli flag (see figure 2.2).

If this first part of the film focuses on the invisibility of the Israeli occupation and the absence of any visible marks of occupation in Nazareth, the second part of the film, "Jerusalem: A Political Diary," shifts attention

2.3 | Screen capture from *Chronicle of a Disappearance* (dir. Elia Suleiman, 1996).

to the invisibility of Palestinians in the state's capital. The silent, empty streets of Nazareth are accordingly replaced with images of frantic Israeli militarized activity in Jerusalem: honking police cars, sirens, and troops of Israeli security men who are constantly looking for, or chasing after, invisible Palestinian suspects. This futile chase after an invisible suspect is captured in one of the films' finest and most humorous scenes. A group of armed Israeli security force agents bursts into E.S.'s apartment to the sound of an action-movie soundtrack, reporting their "suspicious findings" on their walkie-talkies: "one chair, a pack of cigarettes, a window, two doors, a picture." The men continuously pass by their suspect, E.S., failing to notice him despite the fact that he is standing directly in front of them. It is only after they have searched the entire apartment and are ready to leave that they notice E.S. standing by the door. Even then, the security agents simply categorize and report him as another object found in the missing suspect's house: "one man in pajamas." In a parallel scene, a group of Israeli policeman arrest A'dan, the Palestinian female protagonist of the film, after realizing she has been interfering with the police radio airwaves. Soon after, she manages to escape, unnoticed, and instead the police arrest a life-sized mannequin dressed in a traditional Palestinian gown, again not noticing the difference (see figure 2.3).

Alternating between its focus on an invisible occupation (Nazareth) and on invisible Palestinians (Jerusalem), *Chronicle* makes no attempt to unveil or expose anything, and no effort to bring into visibility the otherwise invisible reality of Palestinians residing within Israel, whether as citizens or as permanent residents. One finds here no corrective, no positive or otherwise informative representations of a ghostly population that remains invisible to its Jewish surroundings. Instead, the film traces what can be called the invisible force of invisibility: the political and poetic potential found in being unseen. Indeed, it is important to note that invisibility itself does not amount in the film to simple erasure: it is never simply an outcome of a systematic write-off of Palestinians who thus lose their political agency. On the contrary, remaining invisible in *Chronicle* represents both the mark of a systematic oppression and an empowering subversive opportunity, which involves becoming an invisible spectator whose productive act of looking escapes state surveillance.

It is from the point of view of the invisible spectator, or ghost (a position shared by Palestinian protagonists E.S. and A'dan), that we get to see the ridiculously crazed and paranoid state of militarized Israeli society. Furthermore, it is from their positions as invisible spectators that E.S. and A'dan are capable of intervening and changing the course of events while at the same time remaining unnoticeable. Thus, E.S. is looking out of his apartment window when he notices a police van making a sudden brisk stop, letting out a group of ten armed Israeli policeman who jump out and immediately line up by a wall to urinate in perfect synchrony. Hurrying back into the van, they leave behind a walkie-talkie, which E.S. picks up without being noticed. It is this same walkie-talkie that is soon found by A'dan, who uses it to orchestrate her own theatrical show. Armed with the walkie-talkie, A'dan orders all the Israeli police units to vacate East Jerusalem immediately, announcing, "Jerusalem is no longer united." Remaining invisible to the Israeli police, E.S. and A'dan are able not only to steer chaos, but also to further enjoy watching the crazed Israeli security forces in action. From the invisible, safe positions of their balcony windows, they watch as if they were spectators for an action movie they are also directing.

The figure of the invisible spectator in Suleiman's film stands for the figure of an invisible minority that paradoxically finds empowerment in its marginalized position of invisibility: "Many Israelis don't realize that the Arabs in Israel live their own identity . . . that there is a society there, enclosed on itself, practicing a sense of their own identity. . . . They think we are affiliated with the state . . . that we are 'their' Arabs [they fail to see] the foreigner who lives among them" (Aufderheide 75, 77). Reinforcing this point, the film closes with the image of E.S.'s elderly parents drifting off asleep in front of the televisual image of Israeli flag and the sound of the Israeli national anthem that closes the broadcast day. They are like foreigners living amidst the Israeli society. Dozing to the sight of the flag and the sound of the national anthem, the parents mark their indifference and detachment from the symbols of the Israeli state. The flag and anthem have invaded their living room but have not invaded their hearts. Their sleeping must be understood as a looking away: a disengagement that corresponds to the exclusionary practices of the Jewish state with regards to its non-Jewish Palestinian citizens.[8] This mode of disengagement and looking away presents us with yet another mode of invisibility addressed by Suleiman's film: the invisibility of this subtle and quiet mode of resistance, which, unlike the spectacular armed resistance of Palestinians in the Occupied Territories, fails to appear. Since it escapes the visual threshold of the common spectacle of resistance, this invisible resistance may not look like resistance at all, particularly when compared to the stereotypical paralysis ("the masked Arab, the kufiyya, the stone-throwing Palestinian," to borrow Edward Said's words [Preface 3]) that frames the familiar context of the Palestinian struggle and restricts the Palestinian people's visibility so that Palestine emerges only as a "tragic-heroic fetish object" (Stein and Swedenburg, "Popular Culture" 14). Yet this highly invisible form of resistance is practiced daily by a great number of invisible people who live under an invisible occupation. Like many other settler-colonial societies, this invisible occupation is predominantly maintained by forces that tend to escape the threshold of visibility (systematic discrepancies in the allocation of public funds, systematic cultural discrimination, and various acts of so-called soft racism). One could say that it is easier to visualize a military occupation such as the one practiced in the Occupied Palestinian Territories since the images are familiar and accessible: soldiers, checkpoints, roadblocks, walls, tanks, security towers, and so on. In accounting for the lives of Palestinians living within the 1948 borders of Israel, Chronicle seeks to capture an occupation much more difficult to visualize as such. If there remains an incentive for increased Palestinian visibility, particularly within Israel, I maintain that Chronicle of a Disappearance indeed brings this matter to the forefront, but rather than answering the call, the film instead offers an elaborate visual commentary on the limits of the political terrain framing the quest for visibility.

Produced six years later, *Divine Intervention* shares much with *Chronicle*. The films share the protagonist E.S. (Elia Suleiman), who returns for a short visit to his hometown of Nazareth, and in both cases this lead character is accompanied by a female protagonist who primarily functions as his alternate ego.[9] Both films reject the traditional narrative structure in favor of a series of loosely connected sequences located in two primary centers, Nazareth and Jerusalem, and both films advance a unique cinematic style that fuses lyrical melancholy and theatrical parody.

As in his earlier film, *Divine*'s protagonist is a silent, invisible spectator. While he remains hardly noticeable to his Israeli surroundings, he continuously watches reality unfold before him—gazing out of his apartment's window, peeking through cracks in the wall, staring through open doors, or looking out of his car. The recurring image of E.S. and his female lover (in this film, Manal Khader) sitting silently in their parked car (as they hold hands and stare at the figures of the Israeli soldiers at the nearby checkpoint) looks like a dark rendition of more familiar populist cinematic depictions of lovers sitting in an outdoor cinema. Like ordinary moviegoers, the two lovers sit silently in the dark. Invisible to the soldiers, they watch the checkpoint as if they were watching a movie. Still, the grim setting of the checkpoint's parking lot is hard to miss (see figure 2.4).

The years separating *Chronicle* and *Divine Intervention* mark an important historical and political transition from the calmer "Oslo period" to the outbreak of the Second Palestinian Intifada. Among other things, this shift was reflected in a drastic change in the visibility of the Palestinian citizen of Israel, at least within the mainstream Israeli media.[10] Perhaps for the first time since 1948, the latter has gained the kind of visibility previously accredited only to the Palestinian "enemy" in the Occupied Territories. Indeed, with the collapse of the Oslo negotiations and the subsequent events of October 2000, in which thirteen Palestinian Israelis rallying in support of the Palestinian uprising in the Occupied Territories were shot and killed by the Israeli police, Palestinian citizens of Israel were no longer (only) invisible, second-rate citizens—they had become an overtly discriminated-against minority.[11] From a supposedly absent, and seemingly un-imageable citizen (known as an "Arab Israeli citizen"), the Palestinian citizen

2.4 | Screen capture from *Divine Intervention* (dir. Elia Suleiman, 2002).

of Israel almost overnight achieves a dangerous fifth-column status. Accordingly, their invisibility was replaced with the hypervisibility reserved for the figure of the Palestinian terrorist.[12] Like other Palestinian Israeli film directors (Nizar Hassan, Juliano Mer-Khamis, Mohammad Bakhri, Michel Khleifi), Suleiman's post-Oslo, early Intifada cinema responds to these changes by emphasizing the shared destiny of Palestinians living in the Occupied Territories and those living within the 1948 Israeli borders. In *Divine Intervention*, this bond crystallizes in the figure of the lovers. E.S., the Palestinian Israeli from Nazareth, and his female lover from the West Bank meet regularly in the parking lot just outside the checkpoint separating Jerusalem and Ramallah.[13] The checkpoint, seen as the violent artificial cut separating the lovers (and the 1948 Palestinians from the Palestinians of the Occupied Territories), becomes in *Divine Intervention* the main location of their defiant union as well as the site for the film's most spectacular images.

Divine Intervention: *From Invisibility to Hypervisibility*

Shot between 2000 and 2002, *Divine Intervention* turns its attention to what appears as an inescapable condition of hypervisibility during the Second Intifada, including the widely circulating images of Palestinians as suicide bombers/martyrs and terrorists/freedom fighters. In short, Palestinians

2.5 | Screen capture from *Divine Intervention* (dir. Elia Suleiman, 2002).

were represented via the kind of hypervisibility that comes with the terrain of armed resistance and the enchanting spectacle of terror. While the protagonist E.S. remains in the position of the invisible spectator/the ghost, this later film elaborates the role of his female counterpart to the level of a full-fledged cinematic spoof. She plays multiple roles as a ninja martial arts warrior, a seductive femme fatal, and a determined Palestinian freedom fighter. Through this character Suleiman expands the role given to the spectacle of violence, drawing heavily on familiar and iconic popular media representations of the figure known to some as terrorist, and to others as freedom fighter. Grounding these visual explorations and cinematic citations in the immediate political context of the Second Palestinian Intifada, *Divine Intervention* offers a harsh (if indirect) critique of the dominant visual representations of the Israeli-Palestinian conflict, as well as a model for how to exceed these dominant representational modes with parodic repetition and fantastic identifications (see figure 2.5).[14]

Opening with the image of a bleeding Santa Claus, a huge knife stabbed in his chest, running through the hills of Nazareth to escape a gang of young boys, *Divine Intervention* unfolds a sequence of violent scenes that take place in E.S.'s hometown—another group of kids and young men stand in a circle and beat a snake to death; a grenade is thrown from a passing car into a house; neighbors dump their trash in each other's backyard; and so on. The film provides little explanation for its excessive use of violence, but

2.6 | Screen capture from *Divine Intervention* (dir. Elia Suleiman, 2002).

it makes clear from the outset that its preoccupation with violence is first and foremost a preoccupation with images and therefore with the spectacle of violence.

Later images from Jerusalem and the Al-Ram Checkpoint are more politically recognizable. Here we find the familiar images of the Israeli occupation: soldiers, guns, watchtowers, and so on. But these images also appear excessively theatrical and spectacular. For instance, an Israeli soldier (Menashe Noi) orders all Palestinians in line to switch cars as he begins to dance wildly and scream into a megaphone, "long live the people of Israel!" Alternatively, we follow a Palestinian femme fatal (Manal Khader) who refuses the soldiers' order to stop, and instead marches through the checkpoint, leaving the soldiers astonished and causing the watchtower to collapse behind her. Other no less fantastic and spectacular images soon follow. The protagonist tosses an apricot pit out of his car window, hitting a tank and causing it to promptly explode into small pieces of steel and flames, and a Palestinian freedom fighter/ninja warrior single-handedly wipes out an entire Israeli commando team with her crescent moon–shaped darts, a few rocks, and a golden shield carved in the shape of the map of Palestine (see figure 2.6).

While there is nothing particularly violent about exploding a tank (with a pit), collapsing a military watchtower, or fighting an armed commando unit, the spectacle of these acts, which includes explosions, shootings, killing (what John Menick calls the film's "flare-ups of political halluci-

2.7 | Screen capture from *Divine Intervention* (dir. Elia Suleiman, 2002).

natory longing" or "Technicolor daydreams"), is reminiscent of other explosions and shootings directly associated with the tactics of armed resistance practiced by Palestinians during the Second Palestinian intifada
("The Occupied Imagination") (see figure 2.7).

The significance of these spectacles of violence is not found in their
direct parodist and surreal reference, however, but rather in their image.
While violence is surely an integral part of everyday life in Israel/Pales-
tine, *Divine Intervention*'s visual rendition of violence, far from rendering this
reality of violence visible, instead replaces the imperative to document with
a fantastic visual imagery of violence more akin to Quentin Tarantino's styl-
ized spoof B movies. Indeed, the actual violence that takes place daily at
checkpoints and elsewhere is almost completely absent from Suleiman's
film: "there are no crazed shots of chanting adolescent protestors [here]
and no excruciating depictions of numbing gore and victimhood" (Menick). Instead of realistic documentation of the actual violence Palestinians
endure or inflict, what we see on the screen is a visibly staged and overtly
performative form of spectacular violence that draws attention to its own
status as a mode of cinematic entertainment (see figure 2.8).

The film's title, *Divine Intervention*, suggests the possibility of a sudden
flare-up of potential radical transformation (call it "violence") that makes
for a fantastic victory and a victory of the fantastic. But what is the status of
fantasy within the framework of this spectacular cinematic bravado? Several critics have suggested that the fantastic scenes of Palestinian triumph

2.8 | Screen capture from *Divine Intervention* (dir. Elia Suleiman, 2002).

stand for a Palestinian collective fantasy of victory or revenge. Rasha Salti, for example, suggests that they "enact Palestinians' wildest and simplest fantasies and dreams—dreams that are, conversely, Israeli nightmares" (52). Menick similarly suggests that these scenes reenact "secret dreams [that are] likely running through the minds of millions" ("The Occupied Imagination").[15] Other less sympathetic critics have accused Suleiman of cultivating revenge fantasies and endorsing, if not promoting, actual violence.[16] Still, supportive and antagonistic critics equally underestimate the role of parody in shaping these sequences and rendering them inherently ambiguous with regard to their origin (whose fantasy is it?) and to their signification. Take, for example, the infamous closing ninja scene in which the female protagonist overpowers and kills an entire troop of Israeli warriors. While one could certainly claim that it expresses a Palestinian collective fantasy of revenge, one could just as convincingly argue that it represents an Israeli, or broader Western, projected fantasy of Palestinian violence. Indeed, the parody works precisely because it is directed both at common Palestinian triumphant fantasies and at common Israeli and Western media representations of Palestinians as always already revenge-driven terrorists. Finally, one must not forget that as spectators of the film (a Palestinian film, more specifically; about the conflict, even more specifically; a film shot and screened during the Second Intifada, to be even more precise), we are just as much the target of this parodic rendition. Does this spectacular rendition of violence not derive from our own set of expectations, if not from our own hunger for the spectacle of violence that we associate in advance with Palestine?

Keeping the source of the fantasy and the target of the parody ambiguous, *Divine Intervention* is just as much a film about reel violence as it is a film about real violence. In this regard, it is particularly interesting to think about *Divine Intervention* in relation to Hany Abu-Assad's *Paradise Now*, released in 2005. Where the latter avoids the spectacle of violence expected from a film about suicide bombers and thus, as Nouri Gana writes, denies the spectators the "consumption of reel violence," *Divine Intervention* relishes in the spectacle of violence by emphasizing the status of this spectacle as a cinematic image, a simulacrum, a "visual event," and an artifact (36).

Both films confront viewers with their own set of expectations and their desire for the spectacle of (Palestinian) violence, but each achieves this in a radically different way. *Paradise Now* unfolds a psychological narrative about the reasons and events that lead up to a suicide bombing, building up the expectation for the spectacle of terror and then withholding it. *Divine Intervention*, far from withholding the spectacle, inflates it but empties it from any narrative. In other words, if *Paradise Now* seeks to narrate the antinarrative of the terrorist by avoiding the spectacle of terror, offering instead an elaborate (psychological) narrative of the inner life of suicide bombers, *Divine Intervention* operates in an almost opposite manner, offering an abundance of spectacle devoid of narrative—psychological or otherwise. What we get, then, is the spectacle of violence in and of itself, drawing attention to the spectacle's own status as a gimmick of reel violence.

Commenting on the goal of Palestinian cinema, Michel Khleifi suggested that the most important thing is to avoid making films that generate "an automatic response" based on "ready to serve images" (Sabouraud and Toubiana 111). If Suleiman's film achieves this goal it is not because it avoids "ready to serve images," but rather because it mobilizes an excessive arsenal of such images (including Arafat's portrait, the Al Aqsa mosque, the map of Palestine, and a Kuffiya), which thus gain the status of citational parodic statements.[17]

Take, for example, the celebrated scene of the red balloon E.S. flies out of the car as he and his lover sit watching the Israeli soldiers at the checkpoint. Carrying the portrait of Yasser Arafat, the balloon flies high up in the sky, over the checkpoint and into Jerusalem, eventually landing on the

2.9 | Screen capture from *Divine Intervention* (dir. Elia Suleiman, 2002).

dome of the Al Aqsa mosque, where the Second Intifada first erupted. Most critics have read the scene as indicative of the impossibility to arrest the Palestinian "dream of a nation" (see Gertz and Khleifi, "Between Exile and Homeland," as well as Dabashi, *Dreams of a Nation*). Instead, I suggest that we focus on the bewilderment exhibited by the Israeli soldiers as they gaze at the flying balloon, and take their astonishment as a key for our own open-ended reading of the scene. Is the blown-up portrait of Arafat a reassertion of his image as a key national icon, or a sheer caricature? Is the arrival of the balloon at the top of the mosque an indication of future national victory, or a mockery of the visual grammar of such aspirations? Answering these questions with a less-than-ambiguous answer stands in sharp contradiction with the film's overall poetics of visual excess and spectacular indeterminacy (see figure 2.9).

Commenting on the political significance of the poetic indecisiveness of his cinematic images, Suleiman notes: "if you can create images that call into question this [or that] 'truth' and open new horizons, you can constantly rewrite the story or at least create the possibility of rewriting the story. That's what my films try to do" ("Cinema of Nowhere" 97). Exploring the generative poetic and political force of the image insofar as it does not work in the service of any predetermined narrative, Suleiman's films transform the task of politically committed cinema from that of visualizing or rendering visible the plight of the oppressed to that of loosening "the bonds that enclose spectacles within pre-determined forms of visibility" (Rancière, Carnevale, and Kelsey, "Art of the Possible"). If *Chronicle of a Disappearance* achieves this loosening through a critical embracement of invisibility (invisible people, invisible occupation, invisible resistance), *Divine Intervention* brings about this loosening by embracing the spectacle associated with the hypervisibility of the always already cinematic figure of the terrorist/freedom fighter. Shared by both poetic practices is the deliberate visualization of the conditions of Palestinian invisibility (for which hypervisibility marks but the other end) that nevertheless refuses the visual vocabulary of representation. Another way to say this is that both Suleiman's films maintain the tension between visibility/invisibility not only as a tension between the image and the referent (asking, for example, how can one visualize the invisible or the hypervisible?), but also as a tension within the image itself insofar as its meaning remains at once historically contextualized and forever un-decodable, unstable, and only partially visible. It is in short a cinematic, but also political, attempt to free the image from the tyranny of signification without, however, losing its power (as image) to expand the borders of the seeable and challenge hegemonic distributions of visibility, which are always already subjected to a particular geopolitical and historical configuration.

PART II *Surveillance*

Chapter Three

The (Soldier's) Gaze and the (Palestinian) Body

Power, Fantasy, and Desire in the Militarized Contact Zone

It was approximately 11:00 pm on 13 May 2006. The soldiers ordered us in Arabic through loud speakers to take off our clothes. [They] ordered us to lift up our shirts and pull down our trousers . . . [we] pulled down the trousers a little but the soldiers asked [us] to remove the trousers and take them off.
—Testimony quoted in Grazia Careccia and John J. Reynolds, "Al-Nu'man Village: A Case Study of Indirect Forcible Transfer"

The perverse relationship between Israelis and Palestinians is a depressing B movie that the entire world daily watches [but] despite the attraction to action, not many realize that the Israeli occupation is all about the body: sweat, heavy breathing, desire . . . inspecting, identifying, examining, searching, and stripping the body.
—Yael Berda, "The Erotics of the Occupation"

Chapters 1 and 2 explored the dominant Israeli visual field, marked by blindness, haunting, and the underlying visible invisibility of the Palestinian. This chapter attends to the visual field created within the Palestinian Occupied Territories, which is governed by the principle of surveillance and characterized by the domination of the Israeli militarized gaze. Focusing in particular on the visual field created at the checkpoint, one of the only sites left for direct interaction between Israelis and Palestinians, this chapter centers on the extremely uneven power relationship between the Israeli (soldier), the owner of the gaze, and the gazed-on Palestinian, and it further explores the possibilities of queering and partially transgressing this structure of power and domination.

Dividing territories and people, as well as severely restricting Palestinians (people, cars, and goods included), Israeli checkpoints are currently spread across and throughout the Palestinian Occupied Territories. According to the statistics published by the Israeli human rights watch group B'tselem, in September 2013 there were ninety-nine permanent checkpoints in the West Bank, plus hundreds of surprise so-called flying checkpoints in the West Bank and East Jerusalem. These checkpoints function as contact zones between the Israeli state and the Palestinians; as such, they are also the main sites through which Palestinians are *produced* as occupied subjects (Amir and Kotef, "Between Imaginary Lines" 64). It should be remembered, however, that the checkpoint system in the Occupied Palestinian Territories is a fairly recent phenomenon. From 1967 to the late 1980s there was very little direct Israeli control over Palestinian mobility and entrance into Israel, facilitating the Palestinian economy's dependence on the Israeli economy (see Shira Havkin). Checkpoints began to spread across the Occupied Palestinian Territories in the early 1990s, growing in number after 1995, when Israel (responding to a growing number of Palestinian suicide bombings in Israel) effectively separated the Israeli and Palestinian populations by building a vast web of checkpoints along the so-called buffer zone separating the Occupied Territories and Israel. Since the 1990s, the monstrosity of the checkpoints as an elaborate system of population control has evolved considerably. Indeed, since the period leading up to Second Palestinian Intifada, Israeli checkpoints have functioned as a visible display of military force, becoming *the visual icon* of Israeli dominance and brutality. Often the last and only site of direct interaction between the occupied Palestinian population and the governing Israeli forces, checkpoints serve as a stage on which daily performances of power and discrimination take place, sharply dividing the occupiers from the occupied between "those who give permission and those who need to ask for it," to borrow Azmi Bishara's words (*Al-Hajiz* 11). Passing through the checkpoint, the Palestinian is stopped and her/his body placed on display before the scrutinizing gaze of Israeli soldiers, other security personal, or, more recently, electronically stripping sensors. This violent and invasive, direct or mediated gaze examines the partly or fully stripped and undressed body standing in front of it as if "able to know the hidden truth this body [conceals]" (Azoulay, "Determined at Will" 146).

Chic Point: Fashion for Israeli Checkpoints (2003), a seven-minute film (combining video and still images) by the Palestinian Israeli artist Sharif Waked, draws attention to this intrusive gaze by focusing on one of the checkpoints' most theatrical practices of control, namely, the use of body searches and forced stripping.[1] The film revisits the visual field created through these "body searches," drawing attention to the violence involved in the meeting of the eyes of the soldiers and the bodies of Palestinians. Such actual meetings have gradually been done away with since 2006, when Israel replaced the direct process of surveillance (manned by Israeli soldiers and other guards) in most of the central checkpoints with an elaborate monitoring apparatus made of various security cameras and biometric identification devices. Under such new and supposedly modernized conditions, the direct and visible body searches of the kind Waked's film accounts for are hardly in need. Indeed, they have been replaced with procedures of stripping electronically, procedures that conceal the monitoring gaze of the Israeli soldier and his gun, and thus create an illusion of normality, to paraphrase Daniela Mansbach (263).

However, managed through the meeting point between the Israeli militarized gaze and the Palestinian exposed body, the power dynamic between Israelis and Palestinians in essence remains the same, even despite the great difference in the appearance of the checkpoints. The main difference between the old-fashioned checkpoints and the newly constructed terminals is that the latter make it significantly more difficult to see the violence involved in the subjection of Palestinians to Israeli surveillance. For instance, the new technologically advanced indirect body searches take place in enclosed terminals that effectively conceal the violence and the scrutiny of the military gaze from *both* the Palestinian passenger (s/he now faces an electronic/ biometric device rather than an a soldier with an aiming gun, although no doubt, s/he knows very well that the gun is there even as it is now invisible), *and* from outside viewers (including human rights activists and reporters) who cannot see/witness the procedures that take place behind the sealed walls (and one-way mirrors) inside the terminals.[2]

My own engagement with *Chic Point* and its preoccupation with the direct body searches typical of the premodern checkpoints is presented here not to return to and examine a particular earlier moment in the history of Israeli surveillance, but rather, and more accurately, to force (once again) back into the open *the visibility of the violence* involved in this ongoing process of surveillance (then and now). I aim specifically to work against the

3.1, 3.2, and 3.3 | (*above and opposite*) Stills from Sharif Waked's *Chic Point: Fashion for Israeli Checkpoints* (2003). Courtesy of the artist.

....

ongoing attempts of the Israeli government to conceal this violence be-hind a flurry of neoliberal consumerism and normalization rhetoric, which is represented in the new vocabulary used to refer to Palestinian passen-gers as "customers" who pass through "terminals" and "border crossings" (*ma'avarai gvul*), which themselves are said to have become "modernized" and "civil" (*izruach*).[3]

....

Divided into two main parts, *Chic Point* brings together the imaginary and the real as it subtly blurs the distinctions between the two. The first part, a colorful fashion show, introduces the latest in checkpoint fashion. One by one, young men walk down the catwalk to the sound of electronic club music and playfully model clothes equipped with zippers, openings, and holes designed to ensure efficient body exposure and quick undressing (see figures 3.1, 3.2, and 3.3).

In sharp contrast, the second part introduces a series of black-and-white photographs taken at several Israeli checkpoints and published in

various newspapers during the early years of the Second Intifada (2000–2003). These images capture the reality of harassment experienced by Palestinian men (and, to a lesser extent, women) at Israeli checkpoints, where the practice of body searches and stripping have long existed as a daily routine. But, as my reading suggests, the film further highlights the often concealed erotic implications of this meeting both in light of the colonial fantasy of the sexy terrorist *and* with regards to the ability to politically mobilize homoeroticism as a means of undermining the authority of the military gaze (see figures 3.4 and 3.5).

The justification provided by Israeli officials for its army's use of forced stripping and full body searches is commonly described as a matter of exceptional national security that requires exceptional military measurements.[4] According to this logic, Palestinians — or rather, Palestinian *bodies* — present an imminent threat (a perception greatly reinforced by the Second Intifada and the numerous suicide attacks within Israel), and must therefore be placed under strict surveillance and close regulation. Yet, if the body searches and stripping practices are presented by Israel as a necessary measurement for protecting Israeli citizens against the threat of Palestinian terrorists, these practices undoubtedly also function as a means of *producing* the Palestinian body as a symbol of imminent danger on the verge of explosion, and thus as a body which must be placed under surveillance and carefully regulated at all times.

Returning to familiar images of naked or partly naked Palestinian men facing the scrutinizing gaze of Israeli armed soldiers, *Chic Point*'s critical impact comprises two distinct, yet related effects. The first and most obvious effect is the film's ability to recapture and bring to light the cruelty and excessiveness of checkpoint stripping practices, unearthing their performative nature as a theatrical display of power. Ironic and indeed chic, *Chic Point* delivers a sophisticated and critical condemnation of these practices by visually capturing the extreme dissymmetry between the alleged endangering half-naked and unarmed suspect/terrorist and the soldier who is fully geared and backed up with guns and massive tanks. Furthermore, the film mobilizes the analogy created between our position as viewers of the fashion show and the position of the Israeli soldiers as seen in the photographs displayed in the film's second part. As the sole spectators of the fashion show, we are placed in a position parallel to that of the gazing soldiers: we are doing the looking as the stripping men march toward us,

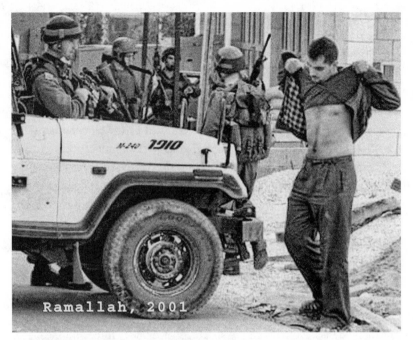

3.4 and 3.5 | Archival still images from Sharif Waked's *Chic Point: Fashion for Israeli Checkpoints* (2003). Courtesy of the artist.

exposing their bodies. But from this very position, and by means of the analogy created in the film between the setting of the fashion show and that of the checkpoint, we are also called on to look at and critically examine the intrusive nature of our own gaze, and by extension, that of the soldiers. When the film shifts from the first part (the fashion show) to the second (the archival photographs), we at first feel embarrassed for enjoying the fashion show—for being entertained by the chic models. This embarrassment is achieved primarily thanks to the symmetry created between our own position as spectators and that of the soldiers seen in the photographs. We realize that, like them, we have been taking pleasure in watching these partly naked bodies parading before us. But it is precisely this sudden embarrassment and momentary shame that also encourages us to look closer at the soldiers' gaze. We realize the radical distinction between *our* gaze at the film and fashion show and *their* military gaze, which is backed by guns and tanks.

The second, less immediately evident effect has to do with the film's ability to challenge the prevailing myths of masculinity (as either heroic or damaged) associated with the spectacle of military force and theatrical public humiliations of these ceremonial checkpoint bodily searches. Key to this critique is *Chic Point's* embracement of queer aesthetics. The film opens with what is normally viewed through an exclusively heterosexual frame of analysis to include an explicit and critical engagement with homosexuality as both a driving force of state violence and a potential means of transgression. I will return to this point shortly. First, a few words must be said about the hegemonic heterosexual frame of analysis with which *Chic Point* wrestles. This frame of analysis presumes a natural bond between national potency and healthy (that is, always already heterosexual) masculinity and thus accounts for national defeat in terms of "a loss of male virility" (Amireh 751).[5]

In the context of the war between Israeli and Palestinian masculinities, the figure of the Israeli soldier, as Joseph Massad notes, comes to embody regenerated and triumphant masculinity and is seen by both Israelis and Palestinians as a symbol of redeemed virility. Palestinian masculinity (not unlike the pre-state exilic Jewish masculinity),[6] on the other hand, is associated with femininity and weakness (the ever looming threat of homosexuality)—it is, in short, "a masculinity in crisis" and thus in need of repair.[7]

It is this same (heterosexist, misogynist, homophobic, and nationalist) framework that shapes the popular discourse describing the interactions between Israeli soldiers and Palestinian men at the checkpoints. The latter is overburdened with descriptions that affirm robust Israeli masculinity in contrast to wounded, overcompensating Palestinian masculinity. The familiar narrative goes somewhat as follows: "as [Palestinian] men have traditionally been responsible for defending the community, their inability to do so and their apparent powerlessness in the face of a militarily superior enemy has caused a crisis of masculinity" (Holt 119).

Offering what is otherwise a carefully tuned queer reading of Chic Point, Karim Tartoussieh also falls into the trap of the "masculinity in crisis" trope when describing that the Israeli checkpoint "posits a feminizing moment, where [the] powerlessness and nationlessness of the Palestinian automatically feminize him" ("Chic Point and the Spectacle of the Body"). A similar view is expressed by Dorit Naaman, who argues, "the experience [of the checkpoint] robs [Palestinian] men not only of their dignity, agency, and freedom but also of their masculinity" (175).

Viewed against the prevailing cultural trope that directly or indirectly associates national defeat with femininity, demasculinization, and homosexuality, Chic Point appears to map out an alternative arrangement of Israeli and Palestinian masculinities while at the same time continually emphasizing their codependency. Thus, even if the film presents checkpoints as instrumental sites through which Israeli and Palestinian masculinities are reaffirmed in relation to one other, it nevertheless casts doubt (in the form of irony) on the common rendition of this process through heteronormative accounts of threatened masculinity. Chic Point does not replace such heteronormative accounts with the prospect of a queer utopia (there is no redemptive love/lust/desire operating in the film). Rather, the video highlights the queerness of the exchange between the Israeli soldiers and the Palestinian men at the checkpoint as a means of bringing into the open and making visible the hidden "perversion" that "is always already installed in the project of naming the terrorist" (Puar xxiv). The following section, dedicated to a close reading of the film's campy style and its dual structure (the fashion show and the archival photographs), demonstrates the manner by which Chic Point touches the sore spot, even if it softens the strike with chic humor.

Shiny pink letters announce the opening of Waked's video-piece *Chic Point.* The credits follow, introducing the models of the upcoming fashion show. Their names—Yigal, Danny, Oded, and Nir (Hebrew), alongside Ashraf, Walid, Samir, and Saleh (Arabic)—clearly reveal the mixed ethnonational makeup of the show. Then, to the sound of electronic club music, the models emerge one by one. They are young, handsome, fit, and dressed for the occasion: preparing to cross through the Israeli checkpoints. The designs of the clothes vary significantly, but the logic remains the same. The idea is to dress up in clothes that are not only chic, but that are also easy to remove, or that expose significant parts of the body. In short, these are clothes that reveal at least as much as they conceal. Beyond the apparent irony of the performance, the rationale behind the outfits can be explained in rather serious terms. In expediting and perfecting the undressing process, the design effectively minimizes the violence involved in obeying the order to undress, and perhaps even stands for an attempt to bypass the need to obey altogether by rendering the stripping down at the command of the soldiers unnecessary, as if saying: "We know the trick . . . we have come prepared, we are 'already naked.'" The common denominator for each outfit is the ease and rapidity with which it can be removed. Indeed, the show is as much about the *removal* of clothing as it is about the clothes themselves. This makes this peculiar fashion show appear more akin to a *strip show* than a conventional runway performance. The models' conduct reinforces this impression as some of them wink or stare audaciously at the camera as they unzip their clothing, and as others intimately toy with themselves before sashaying offstage.

With fluorescent hot-pink lights, dark irony, androgynous clothing and gestures, exaggerated theatricality, and dance club music, Waked's fashion/strip show is unmistakably camp. Indeed, the show adopts all the recognizable features of what Susan Sontag has famously described as "Camp taste" and which she (and many followers since) attributes to queer sensibility.[8] But *Chic Point's* campiness is not simply a replica of dominant Western-gay-cosmopolitan iconography. On the contrary, the film fuses the grammar of familiar Western cosmopolitan camp with foreign influences, such as traditional Arab garments (*jallabiya,* hijab) and the lingering close-ups of dark, hairy male abdomens. These elements draw our attention

3.6 | Still from Sharif Waked's *Chic Point: Fashion for Israeli Checkpoints* (2003). Courtesy of the artist.

to the specific ("Semitic") locality of the fashion show and take us far away from the iconic image of the hairless, oily Armani model and the skinny, pale, and hairless Calvin Klein look.

The first model, a tall, slim man, walks in wearing a cropped black evening suit that exposes his abdomen and lower back. The camera zooms in on his exposed flesh, capturing the movement of his skin and then lingering for a few seconds on his buttocks as he swaggers off stage. The next model appears wearing an updated version of the jallabiya, his hand caressing his exposed chest through the large opening in the fabric as he stares provocatively at the camera. The third model lifts up his shirt by pulling on a hidden accordion string. As the shirt lifts up, his arm slides down to touch his abdomen and glide over his groin. Other models introduce an array of see-through outfits: a blue evening shirt with Velcro replacing buttons for speedy exposure; an elegant white shirt with wide zippers for a swift opening; and a tight black mesh shirt attached to a black headscarf for a truly androgynous look (see figure 3.6).

The last model, slim and feminine, takes the stage. He is wearing a short blue net-dress over a pair of tight, white boxer shorts. As he melancholically gazes at the camera, the music fades out and the colorful images are replaced with a black screen. After a brief intermission, the piece's second part begins. A series of black-and-white photographs appear in succession, including images of ordinary Palestinian men—old, young, tall, short, slim, and heavy—stripping at various Israeli checkpoints. They expose their upper bodies with lifted shirts and open jackets. Some have their pants pulled down, some are kneeling, and several of them are blindfolded. The upbeat music accompanying the film's first part (the fashion/strip show) slowly fades away as we are confronted with these grim images. The abrupt transition from the film's first part to the second surely calls attention to the sharp contrast between them: the mobility, vibrant colors, and upbeat sounds of the filmed fashion show contrast with the motionless, black and white, and silent presentation of the still photographs. These distinctions in medium and form highlight the obvious differences between the two settings: glamour, youth, and beauty clash with the quotidian; the direct, even provocative gaze of the models clashes with the blindfolded eyes of the photographed men; the eroticized bodies of the models clash with the image of forced nudity; and the explicitly theatrical setting of the fashion show contrasts with the archival status of the photos, highlighting the obvious chasm between the superfluous world of fashion and the harsh reality of living under military occupation. And yet, the very *being together* of these two parts within the frame of one work compels us to read them comparatively.

Bringing together these two seemingly clashing parts, Chic Point advances its scandalous revisitation of the visual field born at the checkpoint. Prefacing the archival photographs of stripped Palestinian men facing the scrutinizing gaze of the armed Israeli soldiers with the campy fashion/strip show, Chic Point does not simply contrast the scenarios. More accurately, it forces us to see the photographs in relation to, and through the prism of, the fashion/strip show and the parameters it has set forth. Indeed, after watching the fashion/strip show, one cannot but look perversely at the proceeding checkpoint photographs. Seen from this perspective, the issue of security (the official justification provided by the Israeli for the stripping rituals) appears as a mere pretext for an altogether different purpose. Stripping is restaged as a source of entertainment and a setting for Israeli soldiers (like spectators of a fashion show, or better yet, a strip show) to watch as Palestinian men undress for the occasion. In other words, with the fashion/strip show's colorful images setting the tone for the work as a whole, the images of forced exposure at the checkpoints come to resemble a staged performance or show in which each side fulfills its predetermined role: one as spectator, the other as model/stripper. The images of Palestinian men lifting up their shirts, pulling down their pants, or opening their jackets as they face armed soldiers thus come to convey more than a documentary and prosaic message of submission and humiliation. They emerge as images of men flashing, teasing, toying with, and seducing the Israeli soldiers.

The provocative impact of the film as a whole, then, relies on the double and contradictory effect created by the bringing together of its two main parts. This double move of contrasting and comparing the fashion show with the archival photographs is translated into the film's unresolved tension: between the perception of the body as an object of desire, and the perception of the body as an object of military surveillance; between the free body and the occupied body; between the notion of the body as empowered by self-fashioning and performativity, and the notion of the body as fully subject to oppressive external regulations. At the heart of this visual experience stands the interplay between the body and the gaze, including the gaze of fashion consumers and the models' bodies, the gaze of the soldiers and the Palestinian bodies, and our own gaze as viewers and spectators of both the fashion show and the archival photographs. Chic Point offers a critical visual commentary on the relationship between violence, desire, and spectatorship as it calls attention to the fact that the exploitive relationship between the gaze and the body in the context of checkpoints is not just about military power (the need to control, consume, and put under surveillance), but also about fantasy and desire. Better yet, the film enables us to see the inseparability of the two. "To become a target," Chic Point reminds us, "the enemy must be sexualized" (Kaplan 193–94). Accordingly, the suspected body of the enemy (the potential terrorist) emerges here not only as a symbol of captivity, oppression, humiliation, and torture, but also as a site of desire and seduction. And while the scrutinizing gaze of the soldier appears violent and pornographic, it too is vulnerable to forbidden lusting, fantasy, and attraction.

The Gaze of Surveillance and the Shadow of Homosexuality

Checkpoints are an arrest, a stop, and a meeting point of sorts between the scrutinizing gaze of the state/soldiers and the bodies put under surveillance (the suspect, terrorist, the Other). As such, they represent an apparatus of power that seeks to perform, produce, and reproduce the power relationship between occupiers and occupied. It is this clear-cut power inequality that Waked confronts and attempts to (partially) subvert in *Chic Point*. Waked rejects the monopolized authority of the strictly documentary representation of Israeli checkpoints in favor of an overtly staged representation that mobilizes the ironic, the fantastic, and the theatrical. In *Chic Point*, the concealed fantasy of the sexy terrorist is unveiled as a fantasy that underlies many of the interactions that take place at the checkpoint and that bring together Palestinian bodies and Israeli eyes (and guns).[9] Clearly this fantasy, insofar as it belongs (knowingly or not) to the Israeli soldiers, is enabled by the structure of the occupation and the colonial violence it imposes on Palestinian bodies. After all, as the film makes clear, it is the Israeli soldiers alone who are empowered by the position of the gaze. They do the looking and have the power to desire, while the Palestinians are confined to the position of displaying their goods, as it were.

If the fashion/strip show focuses on the models' bodies, with the camera positioned from the vantage point of the spectators/viewers, the archival photos capture *both spectators and spectacles*, with the camera often situated behind the Palestinian men and focused on the gaze of the inspecting Israeli soldiers. This focal transition from the (seductive, teasing, fashioned, active) body to the scrutinizing gaze of the soldiers highlights the pornographic nature of this armed gaze, revealing the manner in which the act of military surveillance and checking that identifies (finds, names, creates, and invents) the terrorist entails his simultaneous perverse sexualization. But *Chic Point* further shows this *as a fantasy*, insofar as the trope of the sexy terrorist is not, and cannot, be fully subjected to the cannibalistic viewpoint of the soldiers. Waked openly engages with the fantasy (in the first part of *Chic Point*) not simply in order to scrutinize the colonial fantasy of the sexy terrorist but also, and more significantly, to redirect and reemploy the fantasy in a manner that produces an empowered representation of the occupied Palestinian body.

Armed with his desirability, Waked's Palestinian is not merely the victim of colonial violence or cannibalistic fantasies. The film's overt engagement with sexual fantasies and desirability ascribes political agency to the occupied Palestinian body, thus undermining the power of the militarized gaze of surveillance. Viewed through the frame of film's first part (the fashion show), the images of the stripped, naked, exposed, and humiliated bodies are no longer simply images of passively displayed bodies. Empowered with the ability to tease, seduce, and taunt, these bodies confront the viewer to say, "you know and I know that you want me; you know and I know what this 'security business' is all about, so let's get down to business." In other words, the stripped body seen through the prism of the fashion show is a body that speaks back to the dominating gaze of the soldiers, exposing and performing the sexual fantasy that the rhetoric of national security is meant to conceal. Indeed, in staging the fashion/strip show as a prologue to the archival photographs of checkpoint inspections, Chic Point forces us to see the ghostly, commonly invisible presence of sexual fantasies and (homosexual) desire that underlie the daily scenes of public stripping at the checkpoints, reminding us that "the shadow of homosexuality is never far" (Puar 86).

Chic Point speaks the unspeakable by rendering visible the idea of a homosexual fantasy involving Israeli soldiers and Palestinian men and in further highlighting the role of this fantasy in creating and solidifying the homoerotic bond among Israeli soldiers as they subject Palestinian men to their gaze. Indeed, the archival photographs expose the soldiers' faces, capturing their gazes and smiles and revealing the fact that many of the soldiers are busy looking at other soldiers doing the looking at least as much as they are busy looking at the Palestinians they check out. It is this *web of gazes* that renders the event so violent, and through this event the stripping of the Palestinian body for security reasons becomes a founding ritual and a right of passage in the making of Israeli masculinity. Furthermore, if the film emphasizes the sexualization of the suspected terrorist, or better yet, the manner by which he is sexualized *as* he is identified and named as such, it also defuses the common homophobic projection of queerness onto the terrorist by emphasizing instead the sexually charged quality of the soldiers' gaze. The visible homosexual overtones mark, in this case, *not* the crisis of masculinity or the dreaded effeminacy or queerness of the terrorist, but rather his *desirability*, which functions in the film as a source of empowerment. Desirability allows for self-fashioning, exhibited most explicitly by the models' behavior and further mobilized by Waked's over-

Jerusalem Checkpoint, 2002

3.7 | Archival still image from Sharif Waked's *Chic Point: Fashion for Israeli Checkpoints* (2003). Courtesy of the artist.

all chic political commentary. The fashion show stands for an explicit and deliberate stylization of the body, one that speaks directly to the threat introduced (and framed as a matter of national security) by the Palestinian body. Accordingly, this representation challenges the most prevailing depictions of the (male) Palestinian body as a marker of submission, terror, death, masculinity in crisis, and "bare life."[10]

Making visible this transgressive message, *Chic Point* closes with a photograph of a Palestinian man whose arms are pulling his jacket wide open as he exposes his upper body to a small group of armed Israeli soldiers. The camera is situated behind the man, capturing his back and the eyes (and guns) of the soldiers. Alone, this man appears to command the attention of all the soldiers around him. His gesture of opening the jacket and exposing his chest no longer conveys the predictable message of submission or humiliation, for he now appears to be proudly exhibiting his body. His body language seems confrontational and teasing, if not explicitly seductive (see figure 3.7).

All this of course is not to say that *Chic Point* undermines the oppressive impact that the military gaze and the stripping practices have on Palestinians. Rather, what I propose is that the film redirects and reframes our understanding of these practices by liberating the archival journalistic photographs, if partially, of their overdetermined meaning. In turn, the film calls our attention to the "ever present shadow of homosexuality," redirecting the power of the military gaze by making it visibly known to us as something else.

Chapter Four

Visual Rights and the Prospect of Exchange

The Photographic Event Placed under Duress

Under normal circumstances only soldiers are allowed to see Palestinians.
—Ariel Handel, "Notes on the Senses"

Returning to the question of the gaze as an apparatus of control, this chapter asks under what conditions of spectatorship, production, and distribution might photography become a means of intervention into, or manipulation of, the visual field that currently binds Israelis and Palestinians together under an extremely uneven distribution of visual rights. The chapter centers on two photographic projects: *Intimacy* (2004), a photographic series by the Jerusalem-based Palestinian photographer Rula Halawani, and *At the Checkpoint* (2007), a photo exhibit/performance by the Ramallah-based Palestinian artist Khaled Jarrar, while further engaging in a critical dialogue with Ariella Azoulay's conceptualization of photography's capacity to function as a "civil contract" based on "an exchange of gazes" between all those involved in the photographic event: the photographed, the photographer, and the spectator.[1]

Visual Rights

For Hannah Arendt, the political world is "the place of appearances": "the place where I appear to others as others appear to me" (*The Human Condition* 198–99). In a political zone marked by inequality, armed conflict, and militarized occupation, such a "place of appearances" is inevitably strained by radical discrepancies of visibility. The occupied Palestinian noncitizen de facto suffers from public invisibility insofar as s/he cannot appear before the Law. In Arendt's terms, this condition parallels that of the stateless refugee, who has a limited "natural visibility" (s/he is reduced to the condition of "the abstract nakedness of being human") yet remains publically invisible (*Origins of Totalitarianism* 299). Such limitations imposed on Palestinians' ability to appear are further enhanced by various degrees of Israeli blindness and systematic (willful or symptomatic) failures to see, as we have seen in the first two chapters of the book.

This condition of radical invisibility couples with an extreme inequality with regard to Palestinians' right to look. As noted by Ariel Handel, within the occupied territories one finds a clear and systematic policing of the gaze: "under normal circumstances only soldiers are allowed to see Palestinians," while the latter are not allowed to look back. Any other arrangement of the visual field "would certainly shake the system at its core"("Notes on the Senses" 160). In short, the visual rights of Palestinians—what Nicholas Mirzoeff has described as "the right to look" and "the right to be seen"— are severely undermined under the conditions of visuality generated within the occupied territories ("Invisible Empire" 40).

The previous chapter focused on the role of irony and queer aesthetics in Sharif Waked's *Chic Point* as well as Waked's attempt to shake the system by intervening in and altering the visual field created at the checkpoint. The current chapter considers photography's potential to examine relationship between power and the gaze *in* and *through* the photographic apparatus, which produces a web of gazes woven across the various intersections between the photographed person, the photographer, and the spectator, while further marking their different positions vis-à-vis both power and visibility.

Returning to the site of the checkpoint—the main stage where through the apparatus of the gaze the extreme and uneven power relationship between Israelis and Palestinians, occupiers and occupied, and citizens and noncitizens crystallizes—both Halawani's series *Intimacy* (2004) and Jarrar's exhibit/performance *At the Checkpoint* (2007) use the photographic image as means of expanding the field of what can be seen, how, and by whom. I propose that both artists' photographs rupture the existing social and political orders undergirding the extreme uneven distribution of visual rights among Israelis and Palestinians, *either* by removing the gaze from the photographic frame altogether (Halawani), *or* by multiplying the gaze into a series of mirroring gazes, which consequently resist the binary principle of those who do the looking versus those who are looked at (Jarrar).

4.1 | Rula Halawani, photograph from the series *Intimacy*, 2004. Courtesy of the artist and Selma Feriani Gallery, London.

Intimacy

Rula Halawani's series *Intimacy* (2004) comprises photographs taken at the Qalandia checkpoint, which is located between Ramallah and Jerusalem.[2] The series focuses on exchanges between Palestinian passengers and Israeli soldiers, uniquely avoiding photojournalism's customary wide-angle perspective. Instead of familiar images of masses waiting in long lines, armed soldiers, iron bars, traffic jams, and surveillance cameras (in short: the spectacle of the checkpoint), the series introduces close ups of hands: women's hands, men's hands, old hands, young hands, bare hands, and gloved hands (see figure 4.1).

The few faces that appear in the photographic frame are faded out and situated off center. The front stage is reserved for the hands: hands presenting identity cards, hands touching plastic bags, hands opening backpacks, or hands slightly touching each other. The photographs center on an exchange, yet through a limited frame that excludes the gazes exchanged *within* the photographic image and between the spectators and the photographed subjects. The series animates the contact zone between Israelis and Palestinians *as a contact zone*. Doing away with faces and the centrality

4.2 | Rula Halawani, photograph from the series *Intimacy*, 2004. Courtesy of the artist and Selma Feriani Gallery, London.

of eyes in the process of surveillance, inspection, and control, Halawani transforms the encounter between the two anonymous parties into an at once familiar and new image (see figure 4.2).

We are invited to look at the hands resting briefly on the cement block separating the two bodies. Two bodies appear so close, and are yet so far apart: a solder and a passenger, occupier and occupied, Israeli and Palestinian. What story do these hands tell us? In a photoessay cowritten with Rema Hammami, Halawani writes, "The only intimate exchange left between Palestinians and Israelis takes place across the smooth surface of a concrete block. One set of hands is assertive and expansive; it demands and takes. The other set is reticent and self-controlled; it waits and offers up what is demanded. . . . [I]t's a script that you repeat everyday; wait-demand-present-take-wait-demand-present-take" ("Lifta" 101). In Qalandia, as at several other central crossing areas, this limited site of intimacy no longer exists. So-called new terminals replace the old checkpoints, where sophisticated technologies of surveillance and indirect control mediate all direct contact between Israeli soldiers and Palestinian passengers. Halawani's series thus exposes the last mode of intimate, direct exchange between

Israeli soldiers and Palestinian noncitizens, which is gradually being lost to a process of "modernization."[3]

Looking at the images, without knowing in advance the reality they represent, one might not recognize the extent of the violence underlying the photographed exchange of the hands. Centered on hands, this microimage offers us a rare, often unseen, side of the checking process. "The occupation machine," Halawani notes, "is blind to our humanity," and her faceless images convey this blinding violence ("Art and Politics"). Even more significantly, they unfold a theater of gestures that reflect the larger story of power, domination, and resistance inscribed each time a Palestinian presents her/his identity card to an Israeli soldier. This theater of gestures discloses a perverse intimacy, but intimacy nevertheless.

Produced within the belly of the beast, so to speak, the photos remain disturbingly ambiguous not so much because they reinforce the faceless state of the Palestinians passing through the checkpoints, but more so because they refuse to replicate and render visible a reality that is always already seen through the dominant gaze: masses passing through, long lines of waiting people, and so on. Indeed, *Intimacy* hides at least as much as it reveals. The images suggest a brief exchange, perhaps of goods or coins. Persuading us to find something poetic in the photographed exchange, the cropped frame conceals the terrible brutality of the checkpoint. This narrow frame functions, perhaps, as a mode of dissociation, to use the psychoanalytic term, and thus reflects a *zoom in* that allows us to *zone out* and thus to block the unpleasant omnipresence of the Israeli gaze.

Halawani's decision to focus on hands ironically helped her secure permission to photograph at the checkpoint: "Israeli photographers take pictures of us all the time without ever needing our permission, but for me as a Palestinian photographer to take photographs of Israeli soldiers, that is a whole different story. . . . I had to apply and get permission to photograph. I applied several times and was denied time and time again. They didn't want me to take photos from such a close distance or to stand in such a proximity to the soldiers." Ultimately, Halawani's assurance to the Israeli military authorities that she would not take photos of any of the soldiers' faces helped her secure the permit: "when I was photographing I had to promise again and again that I am only taking picture of hands and that the solders will remain invisible."[4]

By excluding faces, Halawani's photographs may indeed secure the soldiers' anonymity, but they also further enable us to see how central the soldier's gaze is in securing the power dynamic between Israelis and Palestinians. Without the scrutinizing gaze's visible presence it would be difficult, indeed impossible, to decipher the exchange's violent, humiliating nature. Removing the gaze from the photographic frame, then, Halawani alludes to the militarized gaze's prominence in securing the power dynamic between Israelis and Palestinians (a gaze that, once removed from the scene, makes it unrecognizable) and simultaneously reveals another story (of perverse intimacy). This intimate exchange commonly remains invisible because the military gaze tends to be the key organizing principle of space and visibility at the checkpoint, and thus the focus of many photographic re-presentations of this spatial configuration. "The gaze that sees is a gaze that dominates," Foucault famously writes, yet his gaze is marked as missing in Intimacy, and as spectators we are well aware of its absence (38). Viewing the hand exchanges, we are invited to at once imagine a scene of intimacy between the two parties and to reimagine the violent visual field that dominates this impossible intimate exchange.

Halawani's deliberate avoidance of the gaze in Intimacy productively interacts with Ariella Azoulay's photographic civil contract theory, which is in effect based on the idea of a fertile exchange of gazes between the various parties involved in the photographic event, namely, the photographed, the photographer, and the spectator. Drawing on a vast critical discourse about modern citizenship (including Hannah Arendt, Etienne Balibar, and Giorgio Agamben), Azoulay suggests that photography offers us the rare opportunity to form alternative civil unions that surpass the nation-state's sovereign power and grant citizenship to all. This alternative civic community (a community yet to come), confined as it were to the "nation of photography," supposedly comes into being through a productive exchange between the photographed person, the photographer, and, most important, the spectator who by extension is the photographic message's true addressee: "when the photographed persons address me, claiming their citizenship in photography, they cease to appear as stateless or as enemies. . . . [T]hey call on me to recognize and restore their citizenship through my viewing" (Civil Contract 17). Photography, Azoulay concludes, functions as "an énoncé within the pragmatics of obligation," that is to say it operates as a speech act and a mode of direct communication through which a civil contract is created (despite, or even directly against, the sovereign order) between the spectator and the photographed subject (*Civil Contract* 25). Speaking more specifically about photography in the context of the Israeli Occupation, Azoulay notes that in many of the photographs taken by Israeli photographers one finds Palestinians either directly looking at the photographer or exposing before the photographer and by extension potential (Israeli) spectators their wounds. Azoulay suggests that we read these acts as explicit messages, presented by the noncitizen Palestinian photographed subject before the Israeli citizen spectator, in demand that the latter restore the Palestinian's civilian right to have rights.[5] In short, Azoulay assigns these photographs the role of "court of appeal," wherein the photographed subject makes a claim and addresses a spectator who in turn takes on the responsibility to answer: "photographed subjects call on me to recognize and restore their citizenship through my viewing" (*Civil Contract* 17).

Azoulay's perception of photography's political potential offers an alluringly optimistic account. In the context of so many suspicious accounts of photography (particularly photojournalism) as a desensitizing medium, this optimism is particularly appealing.[6] And yet the political promise Azoulay ascribes to photography primarily relies on the act of spectatorship and, in the context of the Israeli Occupation, on the ability (and willingness) of the (Israeli) spectator to ethically and politically respond to the appeal made to her/him by the photographed (noncitizen) Palestinian person. According to Azoulay, spectators must meet two conditions in order to be able to restore universal civil rights via photography: first, looking at or seeing photographed images must be replaced with watching. The spectator must spend time watching the photographic image as if it were a cinematic moving image unfolding over time (*Civil Contract* 14). Secondly, the spectator must understand photography's referential status not simply in terms of capturing or documenting past events (Barthes's "was there"), but also as pointing to a reality that is "still there" (*Civil Contract* 16). The transition from looking to watching and from the past to the present, Azoulay suggests, eventually brings the photographic event back to life, reviving the entire photographic situation and the "social relations that made it possible" (*Civil Contract* 127). In other words, a careful and prolonged act of watching exposes an otherwise invisible reality and turns "a still photograph into a theater stage on which what has been frozen in the photograph comes to life" (*Civil Cotract* 169).

This keen focus on the spectator's ability to replace the mere act of passively decoding images with that of actively generating information in a sense downplays the photographic scene's power to greatly limit any such interventions. Those limits are captured in important questions such as: Who has access to controlling the camera's lenses? Who controls the setting that frames any particular *énoncé* made within the photograph? Who has the right or means to watch photographs? Who is denied the position of a spectator? Halawani's series and discussion tell us a more skeptical story about the ability and limitations of photography to function as a political act or intervention modeled on a fruitful exchange.

Azoulay's conceptualization of photography's political promise is articulated in terms of an exchange of gazes. The photographed person, in this case the Palestinian, presents a demand before the spectator, in this case an Israeli, whose viewing (of the photo) in turn animates the image, thereby liberating it from "its frozen position and turning it into a theater of relationship between people" (Azoulay, *Act of State*). By contrast, Halawani's series dramatizes the noticeable limitations or impossibility of any such prospect of exchange given the extreme conditions of visual inequality that underline the relationship between the two parties. Indeed, under the circumstances generated by the Israeli occupation exchanges are limited to forms and identification cards. *Intimacy*, then, *deliberately* shifts attention away from the gaze and from the potential for a restorative exchange or a process of recognition or communication (which depends greatly on the [Israeli] spectator's ability and will), instead highlighting the *impossibility* of such a redemptive political imagination to productively operate in the context of the Israeli occupation and its particular modes of (visual) control.

The rejection of the gaze may also suggest that Halawani, like many other Palestinians, worries about mobilizing a redemptive political imagination in which the new or alternative social coalitions that are created, despite all good intentions, ultimately only replicate the Israeli colonial occupying gaze's historical violence. This violence translates into an explicit visual inequality whereby the Israelis do the looking and grant the rights (or fail to do so), whereas the Palestinian's involvement in the exchange is

4.3 | Rula Halawani, photograph from the series *Intimacy*, 2004. Courtesy of the artist and Selma Feriani Gallery, London.

limited (yet again) to her/his (already framed) position as a human rights victim who presents his/her wounds before others.[7]

"They photograph us all the time. But when we want to photograph them we need to ask for permission."[8] What happens when a Palestinian photographer takes hold of the camera, and takes pictures of Israelis soldiers moreover? What kind of exchange of gazes might we be able to trace here? And what kind of a spectatorship setting can we form with images that intentionally deny the possibility of an exchange of gazes either within the photographic frame or between the spectators and the photographed subjects? These are some of the important questions and challenges Halawani's project advances with regard to photography's role in overcoming the extreme inequality between Israelis' and Palestinians' visual rights (see figure 4.3).

Halawani's own gaze as a photographer may be said to imitate the gaze of the Palestinian passenger who, while crossing the checkpoint often, lowers their eyes in order to avoid meeting the Israeli soldiers' and guards' eyes. As such, however, these photographs also remind us that looking down or avoiding the eyes of the other is not only or necessarily an act of subordination, but also a refusal to exchange gazes, whereby looking back under conditions of extreme (visual) inequality constitutes collaboration. If Halawani responds to this inequality and violence by removing the gaze from the photographic frame altogether, Khaled Jarrar's exhibition *At the Checkpoint*, to which I now turn, uses photography to multiply the number and positions of gazes at the checkpoint so as to challenge the Israeli militarized gaze's exclusivity in the scheme of domination.

At the Checkpoint

Khaled Jarrar, a Palestinian artist born in Jenin and currently living and working in Ramallah, presented his first photography exhibit in the summer of 2007.[9] The event's title, *At the Checkpoint*, refers to the photographs' content as well as to the setting Jarrar chose for the exhibition. *At the Checkpoint* included forty-one medium-sized photographs that Jarrar took at various checkpoints. The photographs were hung on the fence at the checkpoint, first at the Hawara checkpoint (February 3, 2007), and a month later at the Qalandia checkpoint (March 2007). With the help of about fifty Israeli, Palestinian, and international activists, the photographs were quickly placed along the checkpoint fence where they remained for approximately three hours before the soldiers ordered their removal.

Jarrar's photography offers a direct artistic intervention into social space by generating an alternative public formed through a temporary community of spectators. Located at the checkpoint rather than a gallery, the audience of *At the Checkpoint* was created on the spot. Aside from the activists who installed the photographs, other spectators (primarily Israeli soldiers and Palestinian passengers) were taken by surprise. In other words, they became spectators without necessarily choosing this position. Further, Jarrar and several others photographed the event, hailing passersby as photographic spectators as well as subjects and creating a chain of images: photographic images of Palestinians and Israeli soldiers looking at photographs of Palestinians and Israeli soldiers (see figure 4.4).

At the Checkpoint could be described as an anti-exhibit exhibition or even a performance, which it resembled more than an exhibit in the traditional sense. For instance, Jarrar and several activist-volunteers assembled the show collectively, whereby hanging the photographs functioned as an indispensable part of the show. Passengers and security forces noticing the commotion quickly gathered around the improvised gallery-in-the-

4.4 | Khaled Jarrar, *At the Checkpoint*, 2007. Photograph by Rula Halawani.
Courtesy of the artists.

making.[10] During the few hours in which the photographs were displayed, Jarrar and the other activists had the opportunity to capture the event on camera. They documented some of the reactions and comments made by the audience that spontaneously formed around the photographs. This resulted in a mirroring effect that effectively blurred the divisions between viewers and viewed, spectators and photographed subjects, and the time of photographing and the time of spectatorship, thereby turning the exhibit into something more akin to a Brechtian theatrical stage.

Some of the soldiers busily searched for their own pictures. Khaled noted that at least one soldier expressed his disappointment when failing to find his image, saying, "How could you miss me, I am here every day!" Another soldier who spotted himself in the picture appeared quite happy to take part in the exhibition, whereas a female soldier told Khaled, "these pictures make us look bad" (see figure 4.5).

At the same time, several of the Palestinians crossing by questioned the logic behind the display. "Am I supposed to look at these photographs or are the images here to witness my suffering?" one woman asked. "Is this what they call an exhibition?" a man asked. After Jarrar informed him that indeed "this is an exhibition," he responded joyfully, "well then this is the first exhibition I have ever attended!" (see figure 4.6).[11]

4.5 and 4.6 | Khaled Jarrar, *At the Checkpoint*, 2007. Photographs by Rula Halawani. Courtesy of the artist.

In an interview following the event, Jarrar noted that he was originally hoping to "create a direct dialogue with the soldiers" and perhaps even to "affect their consciousness" ("Artist Profile"). Jarrar's initial intention has proven to be quite naïve. Most of the soldiers did not even bother to look at the images of the Palestinians, as they were too busy trying to find their own pictures. And yet the presence of the photographs at this contested site nevertheless opened up the space for the formation of new outlets of seeing and communicating. As an international observer at the event reported, one Palestinian man went up to an Israeli soldier, pointed at one of the photos, looked at him, and said: "Look at what you are doing to us!" The mediation of the photograph in this case enabled a speech act otherwise inconceivable in the context of the strict power relationship maintained at the checkpoint between the soldiers and the passengers.

It is under such unique conditions of display that Azoulay's idea to mobilize photography as a civil contract—a means for generating new civil alliances that trespass the current state-governed policies and overcome the radical separation between Israelis and Palestinians, citizens and noncitizens—may be best realized. And yet, as it made clear, the success of Jarrar's attempt to create such an alternative community depends little on the ability/willingness of the (Israeli) spectator to ethically respond or produce a careful, slow, and responsible reading. Indeed, the Israeli soldiers certainly did not respond to the photographs according to the ethical standards initially set forth by Jarrar, nor did they bother to spend the necessary time watching the photos and reflecting on the reality they unfold. Quite on the contrary, not only did they fail to see the suffering presented to them in the images of humiliated, threatened, and violated Palestinians, they further failed to see themselves as guilty occupiers, even when looking at their own images. Still, and despite the failure on the part of the soldiers to become good spectators, they did—and this is no minor achievement—respond.[12]

The presence of the photographs of the checkpoint at the checkpoint altered the normal visual field so that a new "theater of relationships," to borrow Azoulay's term, indeed emerged, if only for a short while. Furthermore, this theater of relationship was not, strictly speaking, limited to the photographic framework's borders (as animated by an external spectator). More accurately, and most significantly, the relationships were created through the interaction among various people who oscillated their positions between spectators and photographed persons and thereby played their part in the newly created show.

Under normal circumstances "the soldiers don't really see the Palestinians. They don't talk to them. They don't look them in the eyes. . . . [T]hey look with one eye on the target but they ignore the eye that sees a human being."[13] Therefore, the fact that some of the soldiers defensively explained themselves to Jarrar, and even accused him of defaming them, is a remarkable achievement. Jarrar notes, "when I was taking the photographs down, three soldiers came over and told me that the images 'misrepresented them' and that they portrayed a very negative image of Israeli soldiers, who for the most part are 'good guys doing what they have to do.'"[14] Prompted by the photographs and the position of power they granted to Jarrar, who was no longer just a target or passenger but suddenly an artist with his own small international crowd, the soldiers entered into an otherwise unlikely conversation under so-called normal circumstances.

The soldiers' *failure* to abide by ethical spectatorship standards, then, serves as the starting point for an exchange, limited and antagonistic as it may have been, that took place between Jarrar and the soldiers, and between the soldiers and the passengers. Displaying images *of* the checkpoints *at* the checkpoint, Jarrar's exhibition called attention to the immediate relationship between the image and the reference—does the photographed checkpoint look like the actual checkpoint or vice versa? ("Am I supposed to look at these photographs or are the images here to witness my suffering?"). With the image and the spectator "witnessing" each other, the stage set up for spectatorship radically challenged any clear division between image and reality, spectator and spectacle, and photographic frame and its background. A few months later, Jarrar was invited to exhibit the photographs at the International Academy of Art Palestine in Ramallah. He agreed, primarily because "local people will have the opportunity to see them." Yet when I asked him how he saw the difference between these two events, he replied, "at the gallery, people see the tragedy inside the pictures. At the checkpoint, they see it while it also takes place right there in front of them, outside the frame." It is this double vision created by displaying the photographs *of* the checkpoints *at* the checkpoint that invites the critical engagement with photography and the act of spectatorship. The exhibition placed the *practice of looking* under duress. It invited Palestinians to look at themselves and at the photographed images of Israeli soldiers. It also invited them to look back at the soldiers, both inside and outside of the photographs. Ultimately, the event formed a space of spectatorship where Palestinians and Israelis, citizens and noncitizens, played both roles—spectators and photographed subjects, if not necessarily by will. As noted by Jarrar, "noticing the photographs, the soldiers themselves unwittingly became a core part of the exhibition. . . . [T]hey begin looking at us [in the photos] and were visible for all of us to look at. Usually we [Palestinians] don't do the looking."[15]

The web of gazes created at the Hawara checkpoint between Israeli activists, Palestinian activists, Palestinian passengers, International NGOs, and Israeli soldiers gathering around the photographs forms a mixed, even antagonistic community of spectators, dramatically violating the state-governed visual field at its most strictly guarded. Admittedly, this altered order of things did not last for long. And yet, brief as it was, At the Checkpoint was a photographic event that successfully altered not only the visual field (as in "what can be seen") but also the scene of spectatorship (who "does the seeing," where, and how).

Comparing Halawani's and Jarrar's photographic projects (and events), different as they may be, enables us to see that if photography has the power to politically intervene and challenge the dominate gaze, this likely has little to do with an intrinsic quality of photography (its ontology) or, for that matter, with the ethical endeavors of its spectators. Rather, it has everything to do with the circumstances involved in photographic image production and display. Photography's political potential begins with the question, "who takes the photographs?" and ends with the question, "who watches them, where, and under what conditions?"

Azoulay's understanding of photography as an exchange of gazes relies on a presumed contract between photographer and photographed person, as well as between photographed person and spectator, the political promise of which greatly depends on the spectator's ability to perform a correct or ethically responsible looking ("watching"). In the context of the Israeli occupation, this model offers a great deal of political agency to Israeli spectators, but it severely limits the role assigned to Palestinians as photographed subjects, photographs, or for that matter spectators. In Halawani's series and in Jarrar's exhibit/performance we find two different attempts to expand this role and to articulate Palestinian political agency through photography, which would be free, at least partially, from the grip of the Israeli gaze. Halawani's *Intimacy* shifts attention away from the question "what can become visible?" (through the right kind of looking) to the question, "what can be done away with, or temporarily removed from the frame, with the help of the camera?" In this case, photography introduces an opportunity for *editorial intervention* into the dominant field of vision. The promise of an exchange of gazes (and its dependence on the Israeli spectator) is replaced with a *refusal* to meet the oppressor's eyes. Finally, Jarrar's *At the Checkpoint* draws attention to the importance of creating new modes of *public display* and new outlets for *public viewing* in which unaccepted spectator communities and new modes of exchange emerge, fragile and temporary as they may be, and in which it is no longer easy or simple to determine who is the spectator and who is the photographed subject. Given the current political reality, which is engrained in an extreme visual rights inequality that drastically minimizes Palestinians' political agency, this shift from relying on the redeeming potential of (Israeli) spectatorship to centering on the political potential associated with the ability to manipulate the photographic frame or alter the scene of display/reception is as important as ever.

PART III *Witnessing*

Chapter Five

"Nothing to Look At"; or, "For Whom Are You Shooting?"

The Imperative to Witness and the Menace of the Global Gaze

In this country, we all get filmed. Cameras are running all the time, recording every move we make. Camera people come from all over the world: from France, Italy, Germany and other places. They say we make good news.
—Azza El-Hassan, *News Time* (2001)

The essay film *Nervus Rerum* (Otolith Group, 2008) makes a point of giving us nothing to look at. *We Began by Measuring Distance* (Basma Al Sharif, 2009) closes with the troubling question: "for whom are you shooting us?" Both essay films stand at the heart of this chapter's inquiry into the ethical and political implications of the imperative to witness and to render suffering visible. The immediate historical and political context for this inquiry is the noticeable growth in the number of Human Rights NGOs and global media representatives in the Palestinian Occupied Territories throughout the Oslo period and even more so since the outbreak of the Second Intifada in the early 2000s.[1] Foreign informers' dominant presence has made eyewitness reports of Palestinian suffering the most common mode through which "Palestinians represent themselves to each other and to the international community" (Allen, "Martyr Bodies," 161–62). As Allen notes, Palestinians often rely on "visual proof" like "damaged bodies and images of human suffering" to stage their "claims to a humanity shared in common with the international community" (162). Given the context of an enormously saturated field of (often overdetermined) images and the ubiquity of the international media's gaze, this chapter highlights the problematic nature of visual documentation and witnessing. More specifically, this chapter explores the limitations of the global project of rendering Palestinian suffering visible.

In her documentary film *News Time* (*Zaman al-Akhbar*, 2002), Palestinian director Azza El-Hassan attempts to document the conditions that make it impossible for her to shoot a film in Palestine. The most pressing obstacle she faces, as she notes in a brief essay published with the release of the film, is imposed on her by her own society: "The intensity of the experience [in Palestine] creates a national illusion that . . . if the world knew then it could not remain silent. As a result [people] develop an urge to inform the world. As an artist [I am] expected to mobilize my medium of expression and tell the world 'the truth' . . . to show the world what is happening to us" ("Art and War" 280). El-Hassan explains that while she wanted to make a film about everyday life in Palestine that would not focus on the Occupation, she found herself "a slave of observation and documentation" (280). Lamenting the restricted artistic space available to her as a Palestinian filmmaker, she elsewhere writes, "when you find yourself in a situation where there's great injustice . . . [y]ou're immediately forced into a certain role . . . you have to tell the world what is happening to your people. It is a role that is exhausting and it is also definitely a limiting role artistically" (Muller 1).

French director Jean-Luc Godard echoes this sentiment in *Notre Musique*, an essay film made only two years after *News Time*. "Jews became the stuff of fiction," Godard notes, while "Palestinians make for the stuff of documentaries." In the context of Godard's film, this assertion, much like El-Hassan's, laments the harsh living conditions Palestinians face, which enforce a certain urgency with regard to any act of representation and result in the submission of art and imagination (fiction) to the pressing demands of producing evidence (documentary). But the urgency to provide information and produce evidence of wrongdoing and injustice is only the first part of the problem. El-Hassan also tackles the devastating effects of the invasive presence of international media in Palestine. Thus, she notes that soon after her move to Ramallah she discovered that "practically every corner in town had been featured on a news network" (Muller, "Shifting Roles" 4). Elsewhere she notes that Palestinians, and particularly Palestinian suffering, have become a regular spectacle or news item for international viewers: "Journalists and TV reporters from all over the world [seek] our image. . . . [T]hey think we make good news" (El-Hassan, "Art and War" 281).

For El-Hassan and other Palestinian artists and filmmakers, the issue of being gazed at or becoming the source of sensational news for international viewers is a central concern. Like *News Time*, Ihab Jadallah's eight-minute film *The Shooter* focuses on the international media's excessive presence in Palestine. The film offers a sarcastic image of a crew of foreign journalists who are literally *directing* the Palestinian fighter they are out to film, rendering him into a sensational "news item." *The Shooter* brings this dynamic of exploitation to an extreme by presenting the Palestinian fighter as a performer or actor who follows the guidance and instructions of the foreign news crew. The target of irony is the global gaze that "seems to enjoy gazing at the other [whose] tragedies give them a unique drama in itself" (El-Hassan, "Art and War" 282).

News Time and *The Shooter* highlight the tension between the urge to inform and the desire to avoid becoming a spectacle of sheer voyeurism. When "the act of watching exercised by the world is an act by itself," the call to "reveal" and "inform" is placed under scrutiny (El-Hassan, "Art and War" 281). This tension also informs the two essay films I discuss in this chapter in detail: *Nervus Rerum* (2008), a thirty-two-minute essay film directed and produced by the London-based artistic collaborative the Otolith Group (Kondwo Eshun and Anjalika Sagar)[2] and *We Began by Measuring Distance* (2009), a nineteen-minute essay film directed by the Beirut-based Palestinian director Basma Al Sharif. Both films were made in response to the catastrophic events that took place in Palestine when Israeli occupation forces imposed mass destruction and violence on Palestinians. In these two films, the satire of *The Shooter* and the explicitness of *News Time* are replaced with somber poetic reflection and artistic dissonance, both common features of the loosely defined essay film genre.[3]

For Laura Rascaroli, the "transgressive quality" of the essay film mainly has to do with its "betrayal of the documentary," by which she means the authoritative position of the filmmaker as the author of the text. Documentary film often "convey[s] the ideological position of the filmmaker . . . even when the [film] attempts to make it look like the pure observation of an unaltered reality" (Rascaroli 42). In contrast, the essay film "is a field of experimentation and idiosyncrasy" that "involves the spectator in a dialogue" (Rascaroli 39, 40). The essay film is thus dialogist in essence, despite and perhaps also because of its idiosyncrasy. While the documentary film often begins with uncertainty and leads to authoritative explanation, to paraphrase T. J. Demos, the essay film begins instead with an overdetermined field of representation as its main site of investigation, opening it up, in turn, to paradoxes, skepticism, dialogue, uncertainty, and reflection (128).

Set in the Jenin refugee camp in the West Bank, *Nervus Rerum* is a poetic lament for the loss experienced by the Palestinian inhabitants of the camp before, during, and after the massive Israeli attack on the camp in April of 2002, and for a catastrophe that is both in the past and of the present. The catastrophe marks a specific *event*, but also a *continuous state* of living under the threat of a catastrophe. Filmed in 2009, *We Began by Measuring Distance* was made in part as a direct response to Operation Cast Lead, the massive Israeli military attack on Gaza that took place in the winter of 2008–9 and claimed the lives of over fourteen hundred Palestinians in less than three weeks. But in this case, too, the catastrophic event marks not an arrest or sudden interruption of an otherwise peaceful mundane state, but rather the intensification of a catastrophic reality, which can and may erupt at any given moment.

Ruled by the state of Israel, but as *the exception* to Israeli law, the mundane lives of Palestinians in the Occupied Territories is marked by an extreme *abnormality*: a state of lawlessness lacking any meaningful sovereign protection.[4] The films convey this sense of perpetual loss and the continual threat of violent eruption as they seek to further escape the trap of recirculating familiar and reified images of Palestinian suffering.[5] *Nervus Rerum* achieves this primarily through its avoidance of the testimonial documentary method and by focusing on the spatial contours of the refugee camp (rather than on its inhabitants) as a man-made urban space marked by its nonplace and aberrational status. In *We Began by Measuring Distance*, resisting the circulation of images of suffering (while attempting to nevertheless express an affective outcry) amounts to the film director and her filmed subjects' unwillingness to take up the position of the witness.

These two films must be situated and understood against the immediate political and aesthetic context that is reflected in the dominant documentary practice and cinematic representation of the Palestinian ordeal. This is a cinematic mode of production described by Hamid Dabashi as a "form of visual 'J'accuse'" (Introduction 11). Central to such cinematic practices are eyewitness accounts and other means of providing visual testimony as evidence to the wrongs that the Israeli occupation imposes on Palestinians. The purpose of these films is to inform and provide a witness in order to create "an alternative record for a silenced crime" (Introduction11).[6] The great majority of documentaries made about the occupation since the beginning of the second Palestinian Intifada indeed seem to adopt this cinematic mode, including *Occupation 101* (Sufyan Omeish and Abdallah Omeish, 2002), *Crossing Kalandia* (Sobhi al-Zobaidi, 2002), *This Is Not Living* (Alia Arasoughly, 2001), *I Am Little Angel* (Hanna Musleh, 2000), *Until When* (Dahna Abourahme, 2004), and *Jenin, Jenin* (Muhammad Bakri, 2002).

Both *Nervus Rerum* and *We Began by Measuring* take a radically different standpoint as their point of departure. If the majority of the documentaries mentioned above presuppose that documentary's goal is to inform and make visible an otherwise invisible reality of injustice, the presupposition behind the refusal to provide visual evidence of suffering in *Nervus Rerum* and *We Began by Measuring Distance* is, I believe, not that the world must be given an opportunity to see, but rather that the world spends too much time seeing, and that this seeing secures no political intervention.

Indeed, while Palestinians living in the Occupied Territories are subject to various surveillance practices that render them fully visible to Israeli monitoring eyes, they are also subject to the hypervisibility imposed on them by both the global media and human rights organizations as their suffering becomes a "news item" and an instrument meant to facilitate the ethical response of others. In other words, if the Israeli surveillance visual regime constitutes each and every Palestinian as a suspect and potential terrorist, the human rights and global media visual regimes aim to *rehumanize* the Palestinian (thus rescuing her/him from the labeling force of "the terrorist") primarily by constituting the Palestinian *as a victim* who as such has "no possibility to master a nuanced political position" (Amir and Kotef, "(En)Gendering Checkpoints" 978).[7]

The space reserved for the visualization of suffering is also often constructed as uncivilized insofar as it includes individuals seen as victimized beyond the ability to narrate their loss or politically organize.[8] In turning suffering into a *spectacle*, a specific poetics and style of testimony is created as well—the jiggling camera, the wailing mothers, injured bodies of young children, rubble—all these become familiar images of what is by now considered an authentic delivery of the raw reality of Palestine. One could even say that the problem regarding the visibility of Palestinian suffering is no longer that we are unable to see it (because of Israeli control of global media, for example), but rather that it has become almost the *only* thing we see given the immense growth of human rights organizations and the oppressive presence of the global media in the Palestinian Occupied Territories.

The problem we are facing, then, consists less of making an otherwise invisible catastrophic reality visible (although this seems to be the underlying presupposition guiding Dabashi's description of Palestinian cinema as dominated by a poetics of "traumatic realism"), and more so of challenging the dominant modes of representations through which the very visibility of others' suffering remains nothing but a spectacle, providing at best a momentary source of ethical speculation and, at worst, a source of voyeuristic pleasure (Introduction 12).[9]

It is in this context that we must understand Nervus Rerum's and We Began by Measuring Distance's avoidance of traumatic realism and the testimonial altogether in favor of a poetics of suspense, digression, and visual blocking, or what T. J. Demos has called "opacity."[10] In short, the refusal of both films to render catastrophe visible in the sense of providing visual evidence or testimonial accounts of suffering and destruction is based, I propose, on the recognition that such images fail to provoke a meaningful ethical or political reaction on the part of spectators.[11] Nervus Rerum avoids the testimonial in favor of a visual poetics that mimics the disappearance of evidence as the condition for the film's reflection on the meaning of (everyday) life lived on the perpetual verge of catastrophe. Such conditions of living also imply a certain crisis in representation—a continual deferral and slippage that takes place within the contained, static state of the refugee camp, the very existence of which attests to a historical trauma always already hidden behind and rendered invisible by various traumatic events that manage to become visible only as extreme or exceptional events (for example, a military attack, the demolition of houses, and so on).[12]

Al Sharif's film interrogates the limits of visual images of violence and suffering to solicit any meaningful ethical and/or political reaction from their spectators by the way of their pleasing aesthetic effects. This drastic disbelief in the image translates in the film (a visual medium itself) as a poetic and mournful reflection on the seductive nature of the image and the role of aesthetic gratification in overriding ethical and political answerability. Further, it restores our belief in the power of language (text/narrative) to disrupt the blinding force of the image and force us to see what otherwise remains obscured. Different as they are, both films question the direct link between seeing and knowledge, unfolding a visual language that prevents spectators from easily deciphering or producing knowledge based on their immediate encounters with these images.

Nervus Rerum: The Tired Drunk Ghost of the Camp

In *Nervus Rerum* the idea of speaking truth to power is suspended in favor of the idea of turning one's back on power.
—Kodwo Eshun, "A Trialogue on *Nervus Rerum*"

Nervus Rerum opens with a dark screen that is soon replaced by a frantic moving camera that glides through narrow alleys and focuses momentarily on Arabic graffiti spray-painted on the street walls. The streets are nearly empty, and the few individuals who notice the camera seem to deliberately ignore it. When the camera finally stops moving and focuses on something, it is on an old refrigerator or washing machine. Then, it starts sprinting again. Commenting on the experience of watching the film's opening sequences, Irmgard Emmelhainz emphasized her sense of frustration: "You have the camera focusing on dead commodities such as washing machines, refrigerators, televisions; then linger[ing] on the back of a truck. . . . [T]hen we think it will take us to a [new] site of the camp, but it returns us to the dead commodities, and we realize that we are not being given something to look at" ("A Trialogue" 132). What does it mean to make a film that gives us nothing to look at? In the case of *Nervus Rerum*, this means making a film that draws our attention (by means of negation and absence) to the kind of expectations we have when we are faced with images from/about Palestine. The outcome is a film that proceeds with evident rejection of common documentary practices of exposition (testimonies, visible evidence, factual narrating, voice-over, and so on), and further alludes to the silent violence involved in such practices.

The camera movements in *Nervus Rerum* are frantic. Accompanied by a creepy soundtrack of shrill synthesized sounds, the camera slides through the narrow streets of the camp as if it is trying to capture something: to find a good image. Failing to come up with anything worth focusing on, the camera continues to glide—bumping into walls, circulating the camp, and revisiting the same alleys and objects over and over again. Accounting for this restless movement, Anjalika Sagar describes the camera as the "tired

5.1 | Screen capture from *Nervus Rerum* (Otolith Group, 2008).

drunk ghost of the camp," which keeps creeping around, bumping into people and objects ("A Trialogue" 131). This description effectively conveys the painfully invasive and intrusive camera movement, zooming in and out on random people and objects as it moves rapidly from one angle to another, while at the same time revealing nothing of substance. This fidgety and repetitive movement of the camera (rolled on a Steadicam) captures and highlights the voyeurism and opportunism guiding the documentary zeal through which Palestine and Palestinians are all too often turned into news items (see figure 5.1).

The film's directors, Kodwo Eshun and Anjalika Sagar, account for their avoidance of testimony and sensation in an interview with Irmgard Emmelhainz. "The film does not offer an ethnographic shortcut to empathy," Eshun explains in defense of the camera's "failure" to produce something for us to look at ("A Trialogue" 129). Instead of providing information and testimony, the majority of the people the camera captures explicitly turn away from it, or turn their backs on it, avoiding its scrutinizing lens. In other words, the filmmakers replace the common practice of appealing to spectators' sense of outrage and sympathy (by means of rendering atrocities visible) with a practice that draws attention instead to the violence involved in such common documentary practices. The accusatory mode of documentary filmmaking, as Dabashi writes, "aims at speaking truth to power," whereas the idea of turning one's back on power implies that

5.2 | "Turning one's back on power." Screen capture from *Nervus Rerum* (Otolith Group, 2008).

within the dominate structures of representations and knowledge production it is hardly possible to escape the trap of *reproducing* familiar hegemonic images. Under such circumstances, the only way to articulate a more radical and liberatory position may indeed involve a certain negation of visibility and the refusal to cooperate with the camera's inspection (see figure 5.2).

The outcome of subjects turning away from the camera (even walking away) is that the film not only avoids the testimonial mode of speaking truth to power, but it also documents and renders visible this avoidance. Many of the images include long distant shots of people looking out of a window toward a reality invisible to spectators. Their presence on the screen is often melodramatic and theatrical, calling further attention to the fact that these too are staged scenes. They are out of reach (out of *our* reach), and their turning away from the camera to gaze elsewhere is presented as a staged and manipulated *act of representation* rather than a spontaneous and authentic act of defiance. In other words, highlighting the artificiality of the setting, *Nervus Rerum* draws attention to the presence of the camera as an intruding device *even* as it captures the inhabitants of the camp as disengaged, impenetrable, remote, and pensive noncollaborators who turn their backs on the camera and gaze elsewhere. There is nothing authentic or natural about any of the shots. On the contrary, the film meticulously highlights the manner by which every image is produced, staged, and crafted.

Shot in Jenin in 2007, *Nervus Rerum* systematically avoids images of occupying forces and camp inhabitants' local accounts of experiences of humiliation, destruction, and loss at the hands of Israeli soldiers or Jewish settlers. In the absence of these images and accounts, we become well aware of our own anticipation. We await images of violence, soldiers, tanks, wounded bodies, rubble, and grieving families. We await stories of horror and destruction, but *Nervus Rerum* provides none of the above. Above all, perhaps, we await testimonies. And thus, when we finally see a local resident speaking directly to the camera (the main interviewee is Zacharia Zbeidi, a former leader of the al-Aqsa Brigades), our expectations are shattered yet again when the testimonial voice is *blocked out* and literally silenced. The camera captures Zbeidi's moving lips and body motions, but his words are left unheard and untranslated. Instead, we hear Sagar's mesmerizing voice as she reads excerpts from the works of Brazilian writer Fernando Pessoa and French writer Jean Genet.[13]

There is something truly disorienting and alienating about these silenced interviews (do the interviewees know that their voices are replaced with those of Sagar, Pessoa, and Genet?). This violence of silencing of overwriting calls attention to itself as a means of exposing the violence such silencing *shadows*: that is, the violence involved in the incentive to interview, collect testimony, and produce a good news item, which is the motor behind the great majority of Western media presence in the region. It is important in this regard to highlight the fact that *Nervus Rerum* does not simply silence its interviewees but rather documents, indeed provides visual evidence for, its own act of silencing. Capturing the images of speaking residents while failing to provide them with a voice, the film draws attention to its work as a film—its process of selection, arrangement, and manipulation of images, voices, and the relationships between them. In other words, by including scenes of testimonial collection and interview muted by the film's voice-over, *Nervus Rerum* draws attention to the violence embedded in the act of documenting—a violence that must not be understood in an abstract or general manner, but must rather be situated in the *specific* context of an overdetermined field of representation associated with Palestine and its status in Western media as a fetish spectacle of suffering, violence, and destruction.

Within this field of representation, Palestinians residing in the Occupied Territories have more or less been granted two positions from which they may speak and appear: that of victimization, which manifests in images of wounded unarmed bodies, and that of defiance, which manifests in images of armed freedom fighters.[14] Attempting to escape the conundrum of representation (the choice to speak for or let the oppressed speak for her/ himself), *Nervus Rerum* documents its own silencing mechanism, drawing attention to the film's inevitable violent effects. Elaborating on their decision to silence the testimonies, Eshun and Sagar rely on Édouard Glissant's notion of opacity to suggest that by avoiding "proper interviews," they sought to articulate an ethical and political position that does not do away with alterity and the problem of non: "As he [Zacharia] performs his testimonial address to the camera, he seems to be somewhat withdrawn. We know that he is saying something thoughtful, but what he is referring to is unclear. There is an opacity to his address" ("A Trialogue" 130).[15]

Entering (by invitation) the field of representation dealing with occupied Palestine, *Nervus Rerum* occupies itself with the question of opacity in two fundamental ways. First, the filmmakers appear apprehensive toward the fact that they are (only) guests in the Territory.[16] Coming from the outside into the refugee camp, accompanied by a camera and a small crew, Eshun and Sagar's filming practice attempts to avoid replicating the imperialistic gaze of the master who names, classifies, represents, and re-presents by rejecting the ethnographic gaze that assumes and produces knowledge of the other. Second, in working with Glissant's idea of hiding from power as a mode of resistance (for Glissant, the "right to opacity" ought to be shared by all, but for the oppressed it is a means of survival based on the recognition of a power imbalance), *Nervus Rerum* explores the possibility of creating a cinematic image based on the *refusal to take one's place* within a preexisting, saturated, and overdetermined field of representation.

Promoting a poetics of opacity that veers away from the act of representing (presuming and circulating knowledge of the other) and the act of re-presenting (providing the other, as it were, with the opportunity to speak for her/himself) is never simple. It is perhaps particularly difficult when one is dealing with a medium like film, as it deflects the desire for immediacy so commonly associated with the power of the camera. Eshun and Sangar's decision to *block our vision* can be thought of in terms of disarming the camera. Emphasizing the camera's frantic hunger for images through its movements and sudden fixation on various objects and people, *Nervus Rerum* directs our attention away from the residents of the camp and

5.3 | "Nothing to look at." Screen capture from *Nervus Rerum* (Otolith Group, 2008).

toward its architectural dimension and its spatial arrangement—narrow streets, walls covered with graffiti, posters of martyrs placed on doors and billboards, and exposed cement and half-built housing units—all of which offer us, as it were, nothing to look at (see figure 5.3).

Operating against the idea of visual transparency, *Nervus Rerum* highlights instead the power dynamics involved in the process of representation: what does it mean to render something/somebody visible: to represent or re-present? In a visual economy ruled by a confining set of representations, *opacity* itself, understood as an act of hiding or failing/refusing to make something fully visible, stands for resistance. And yet, as T. J. Demos notes in his insightful essay about *Nervus Rerum*, the embrace of opacity as a strategy of resistance itself is not free of risks. Indeed, it may "end up unintentionally silencing the other, as the unforeseen mimicry of political erasure reenacts the very effect of colonialization" (126). This is not a minor risk, of course, but one must also ask whether the silencing and the hiding of the oppressed, as it appears in *Nervus Rerum*, is more or less dangerous than the silencing imposed on the oppressed through the act of representation (and re-presentation) that relies on the belief in transparency, authenticity, and the political power of visibility.

Nervus Rerum offers no simple answer. When pushed to address this issue by their interviewer Emmelhainz ("*Nervus Rerum*'s mobilization of opacity made me very anxious" 131), Sagar and Eshun defend their choice by arguing that opacity is necessary "in order to complicate normative modes of address" (Emmelhainz and the Otolith Group). Such complication inevitably stands in the way of an ethics of bearing witness, but as such it also serves as a reminder of the conundrum involved in the political promise associated with the victim's right to speak for her/himself. Sagar's thoughtful question addresses this conundrum: "Is it possible for the oppressed, for those that have no space to be visible in the global distribution of the sensible, is it possible for these subjects to appear as *other than* victims or witnesses?" (Demos 128).

This question addressing the limits of the ethics of witnessing as an outline for a politics of representation stands at the heart of Basma Al Sharif's film. Like *Nervus Rerum*, *We Began by Measuring Distance* (2009) adopts some of the key features of the essay film by mixing documentary imagery with other footage and by further accompanying the visual with a poetic narration (a contemplative text written by the director). Whereas *Nervus Rerum* maintains a relative coherence by often synchronizing the texts of Genet and Pessoa with the imagery,[17] *We Began by Measuring Distance* makes no attempt to achieve a cohesive internal logic. In other words, what in *Nervus Rerum* emerges as a narrative about the refusal to represent the misrepresented, which nevertheless remains *as such* a well identified and relatively coherent narrative about this refusal, is replaced in *We Began by Measuring Distance* with a nonnarrative that highlights its own failure/refusal to cohere.[18]

Measuring Distance

There comes a time when one becomes fed up with witnessing things.
—Basma Al Sharif (personal interview)

Shot in the months following the 2009 Israeli invasion of Gaza, *We Began by Measuring Distance* opens with a recognizable array of Palestinian visual icons arranged to suggest a familiar narrative or cultural trope. First we are introduced to images of violence and loss: the sight of a bombarded city is coupled with sounds of approaching sirens and the voice of a screaming young girl who has lost her father. This opening sequence is followed by the image of displacement: women and children sitting by rubble. Finally, the third sequence of images captures the transformation of Palestine

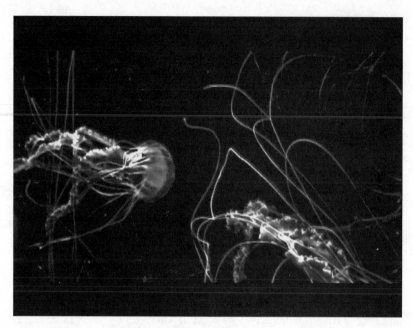

5.4 | Screen capture from *We Began by Measuring Distance* (dir. Basma Al Sharif, 2009).

from a lived place into a concept, image, or memory as we move away from the documentary footage and into the pages of a picture book entitled *Our Homeland*.

It therefore comes as a surprise that the following sequences abandon such readable images altogether in favor of a rich visual and audio collage that completely devastates any straightforward reading of its meaning. Indeed, the initial archival news footage of bombs, sirens, cries of loss, displacement, and rubble (likely, but not certainly, from Gaza)[19] are soon replaced with a rich array of images, including, among others: images of an old forest, an ocean, jellyfish, sea-grass, two people holding a canvas between two trees, and many other less identifiable images. Further frustrating one's attempt to successfully draw meaning out of these images — an interpretative mode the film initially appears to solicit but then renders impossible — is the fact that the narrated text (written by Al Sharif and read by Anas El Tayeb), which serves as the voice-over for most of the film, is profoundly idiosyncratic (see figure 5.4).

Drawing on the language used by Eshun and Sagar, one could argue that *We Began by Measuring Distance* adopts, in its own way, a poetics of opacity.

But, as in the case of *Nervus Rerum*, Al Sharif's own poetics of opacity must be understood neither as the rejection of narrative or of totalizing meaning per se, nor as an academic reflection on the general conditions of the relationship between image and text or image and meaning. More accurately, I contend that it must be understood as a political choice fully grounded in the politics of (visual) representations of the Palestinian ordeal.

Al Sharif began working on the film in the winter of 2008–9, nearly a year *before* Israel launched its massive attack on Gaza. In the midst of making the film, Israel began its grand-scale military Cast Lead operation. Al Sharif, whose extended family resides in Gaza, was living at the time in Cairo and watching, like many others around the world, images from Gaza broadcast on TV news channels and streamed online: "I was horrified by the fact that images of the monstrosity of the [Israeli] operation were broadcast across the globe, and yet nothing happened. The attacks went on as planned and hoards of civilians were massacred as the world sat and witnessed."[20] This constant supply of visual images, exposing violence and destruction, proved ineffective in providing not only the catharsis of political intervention, but also a means of helping one grasp or remotely understand the traumatic reality captured in the images: "We had been fed 24-hour live images from the region, but I could no longer make sense of any of it. The more images I saw the less I knew. Gaza became a cluster of digital pixels."

The crisis of witnessing about which Al Sharif speaks is the crisis of the visual image that has lost its effective political impact. This crisis must itself be further contextualized in relation to the specific field of representation singled out by Sagar and Ashtun in which the oppressed may take the position only of the victim or the witness. "There are a few specific visual icons," Al Sharif notes, "through which people today view Palestinians. . . . The footage I use in the beginning of the film, [the footage] of the veiled women sitting in heaps of rubble, strikes me as one such iconic image: poor helpless women who lost everything and now have no choice but to sit on the ground and listen to the Hamas' empty speeches about liberation." The image remains on the screen for a moment before the voice-over joins in with one single word—"Boredom." This surprising juxtaposition calls attention to the conventional hyperreadability of the image, which has little to do with the image's actual relationship to reality (we do not know who these women are or where and why they are sitting where they are), and a lot more to do with our normative modes of repre-

BOREDOM

5.5 | Screen capture from *We Began by Measuring Distance* (dir. Basma Al Sharif, 2009).

sentations. The voice-over ("boredom") demands we revisit the image. We are asked to consider the photographed women not as ready-made *visual icons* of loss and suffering, but as subjects of a range of unknown and unpredictable states of emotions. What if the women we see in the footage are indeed simply bored? What if this is an image of boredom rather than displacement or loss? This possibility opened by the clash created in the film between the *iconic image* of victimhood (marked by ethnicity and gender), and the word "boredom" (commonly associated with a certain degree of luxury), destabilizes the automatic process of drawing meaning out of the image. It reminds us that images are always read and that we must learn to read *otherwise*. That is to say, we must learn to read images outside of normative conventions of representations in which, for example, veiled Palestinian women sitting on rubble may rarely if ever appear as anything other than victims or witnesses (see figure 5.5).

We Began by Measuring Distance couples its disenchantment with images with a scrutiny of the often automatic and uncritical imposition of meaning onto images. The move from the opening archival news images to the subsequent elaborate sequences of colorful images of jellyfish, sea-grass, and virgin forests, and then back to the news footage of unidentified bombed cities and weeping women with which the film closes highlights the nature of the image, which *as such* (a certain density of pixels, grains, and colors) may or may not engage the spectator; may or may not become politically charged; may or may not become aesthetically pleasing regardless of whether these are images of jellyfish, forests, or bombed-out cities. The film further links this uncertainty with an open deliberation on the ethical and political incentive to witness.

In one scene vision itself is hardly permitted (the screen appears mainly black and gray, and slowly, as more light enters, one is able to see trees, and what appears to be snow or ice), and the narrator's voice-over describes a black cloud descending over an entire city, rendering witnessing literally impossible: "With the arrival of evening, the warmth of the summer was exchanged for a black cloud that descended over the entirety of the mile-high city and surrounded us from the 28th floor. As the days passed . . . we stood witnessing behind our window as a dense fog settled across the body of water below us. We discovered that the entirety of the surroundings had frozen while we were watching." In response to hours of (useless) witnessing, the residents of the city become "more and more agitated" (*gidan, gidan, gidan, gidan, gidan, gidan bi'tawa'tour*).[21]

A similar frustration ("you become fed up with witnessing things") appears to underlie Al Sharif's cinematic choice to limit our own capacity (as spectators of the film) to see or witness. Giving up on the idea of witnessing, the people from the building, the narration tells us, "invent a game of measurement." With this announcement, the film now turns to its central, and longest, sequence: the measuring sequence. The game of measuring begins with random measurements (a circle is measured 360 degrees, a foot is measured 30.48 cm, a shape is measured as triangle, and so on), which are narrated across a black screen. It is soon replaced, however, with more significant measures. The black screen is replaced by the image of a lush green field and two people holding a light blue fabric between two trees, fighting to hold it up straight against a hard-blowing wind. At this point the narrator speaks to the people, directing their movements as they continue to take measurements of "issues more challenging and important." The measurements grow as does the distance between Rome and Geneva, Geneva and Madrid, Madrid and Oslo, Oslo and Sharm El Sheikh, and then begin to shrink as they continue to trace the distances between

5.6 | Screen capture from *We Began by Measuring Distance* (dir. Basma Al Sharif, 2009).

Sharm El Sheikh and Gaza and Gaza and Jerusalem (78 km, 67, 48, 17), culminating in the immeasurable distance between Israel and Palestine.

Replacing the act of witnessing with an obsessive accumulation of quantitative information, Al Sharif explicitly alludes to the iconic status of certain numbers (1917, 1948, 1967, for instance) within the Palestinian narrative of loss, while further highlighting the mechanisms of significations and memorization through which certain names, locations, events, and numbers crystallize into a national narrative.[22] Accordingly, the numbers flicker on the screen—78, 67, 48, 17—and then backward—17, 48, 67, 78—all the way to 2009, watering down, as it were, the symbolic value assigned to these numbers by highlighting the numbers' arithmetical value. This stripping down of the symbol (whether visual or numeric) to its abstract or functional use (the number's arithmetical value, the image's open readable reference) is part and parcel of the film's reflection on common practices of (documentary) representation (see figure 5.6).

The act of measuring meaningful numbers, much like that of witnessing, leads the (invisible) group to despair ("our measurements had left us empty handed"). They therefore decide to go "to a place they have only seen in books" where they would be able "to rest their eyes and ease their minds" and no longer memorize dates or witness horrors. Following the (invisible) group, we enter "the virgin forest": the previously minimal, foggy, and barely visible images are now replaced with bright colorful images of lush green trees, sensual sea-grass blowing in the wind, and colorful fish. The narrator's voice also changes. It is now lower and officious as he switches from the informal Egyptian dialect to standard Arabic (Fus'ha), as would be appropriate for news broadcasting.[23] Light Broadway show–like music is added to the background as a screen fills with bright, high-resolution pictures alternating between images of neon-colored, dancing jellyfish and dazzling images of rockets and bombs landing on cities. Relief comes with the sudden presence of cheerful music replacing the somber voice of the narrator, and bright and clear images replacing our hitherto impaired vision. Like the invisible group, we finally rest our eyes (since we no longer need to labor in order to see) and ease our minds (since we no longer need to decipher the oblique narrative, but can instead enjoy the light music and colorful sights). "I tried as hard as possible to make this scene pleasant to watch," Al Sharif commented in response to my question about her reason for aestheticizing the bombing; "I wanted the audiences to *enjoy* the explosions, to be seduced by it. . . . That is what most images of violence are reduced to . . . colors, pixels, light on the screen" (see figures 5.7 and 5.8).

Like *Nervus Rerum*, Al Sharif's film steers away from the testimonial and from the re-presentation of Palestinian people altogether. In the few scenes where we see Palestinians, they appear—as in the case of the opening archival images of the women sitting by the rubble—as *images*. That is to say, they appear as *preexisting common visual representations* on which the film reflects and whose immediate readability it rejects. For the most part, however, we do not see people at all. We do not see, for example, the young child whose anguished voice pierces through the silence of the film's opening sequence, screaming in terror: "Daddy Daddy! My Daddy! Shoot him, shoot him!" (*Yaba Yaba, Abi, abi, Sawwaruh! sawwarhu!*). While we are made aware of the fact that something horrific has happened, that something horrific *is happening*, we are left to witness something that fails to become, to materialize into an image.[24] We are also made aware of the fact that there is someone there—an addressee who is seeing that which we cannot see; someone who is likely equipped with a camera or a video; someone who is called on to shoot, to document, to witness. But is this act of documenting

5.7 and 5.8 | Screen captures from *We Began by Measuring Distance* (dir. Basma Al Sharif, 2009).

an act of meaningful witnessing, or is it an act of perpetual violence? The film explicitly raises this question by choosing to translate the girl's call "sawwarhu"("film him," or take his picture) to the English subtitle "shoot him." It is no coincidence that the violence involved in this act of documenting/witnessing is explicitly located in the space opened in the act of translating from Arabic to English; from the local to the global; from the actual scene of violence to its mediated image as news item.

The "entire text of the film," Al Sharif noted in an interview, "is written between English and Arabic. It works like a puzzle [between these languages], creating a semblance of a narrative." Wandering between Arabic and English, this "semblance of a narrative" rarely provides information directly related to the images on the screen. On the contrary, for the most part text and image appear to be in a competition for our attention and neither provides sufficient information nor brings us closer to closure. And in the few incidents in which the film deliberately poses a direct link between text/voice-over and image, it further draws attention to its own cinematic work, creating what Trinh T. Minh-Ha has called "the tyranny of meaning" (105).[25]

Highlighting the process of the production of meaning (from image and text), We Began by Measuring Distance draws attention to the limits of conventional documentary methods of representation. Setting up this inquiry in relation to the question of representing the Palestinian ordeal, the film begins by introducing stereotypical visual representations (the image of the women on the rubble, the cover image of the nostalgic "homeland book") and moves toward a further investigation into these images' iconic status and the rejection of witnessing as a privileged mode of representation. In response to my question about her choice of using a male voice with a distinct Egyptian dialect as the voice-over for the film, Al Sharif said she knew from the start that the narrator could not be a woman and certainly could not speak in a Palestinian dialect: "that would have been in contradiction to the film's commitment to finding a voice of belonging [and responsibility] which doesn't simply rely on the documentary, the testimonial, the authentic witness, or the factual."

With what does this great mistrust of the documentary image and of witnessing leave us? The film's final sequence, lasting for approximately three minutes, moves us out of a large fish tank and into an unknown street mirrored behind it. Our vision is again compromised as we vaguely

5.9 | Screen capture from *We Began by Measuring Distance* (dir. Basma Al Sharif, 2009).

recognize the silhouettes of two young boys running, followed by a woman dressed in black. Slowly, the image of the woman becomes clearer, and another woman is seen from behind her, with her hands covering her face. The music stops. The second woman approaches the camera in slow motion, her hands moving away from her face, exposing an expression of extreme distress. Bending down and leaning her head on her hands, she begins screaming. The soundtrack breaks in and out: we hear some screaming, a child calling for his mother, moaning. The woman stares at the camera, then as she turns her back on the camera, we hear her angered question: "for whom are you shooting, for whom?" (*le-min t'sawwarta, le-min?*) (see figure 5.9).[26]

With the woman's turning her back to the camera, we find ourselves back in the discursive territory opened by the Otolith Group's call for replacing documentary practice, which speaks truth to power, with a mode of representation that is based on the turning of one's back on power.

"For whom are you shooting us?"—the troubling question with which *We Began by Measuring Distance* closes—forces us to evaluate the ethical implications involved in the act of documenting and rendering suffering visible: who is rendered visible and for whom? It is not a question we can take lightly. Al Sharif's film opens with the screaming voice of a young girl pleading for someone to film/shoot her dying father and closes with the screaming voice of a woman pleading for the cameraman to stop filming/ shooting. In the middle, and as a *movement between* this opening plea to bear witness and the closing plea to stop filming, the film unfolds its poetic inquiry into the insufficiency of common documentary filmmaking and its failure to account for the violence involved in the act of rendering visible.

With the outbreak of the Second Intifada in the early 2000s, masses of "journalists . . . and TV reporters from all over the world" arrived in the West Bank "together with the Israeli tanks" (El-Hassan, "Art and War" 281). Visual images of Palestinian suffering, injured bodies, and massive destruction have since transformed "the way Palestinians represent themselves to each other and to the international community" (Allen, "Martyr Bodies" 161–62). Relying on the misguided assumption that once confronted with *visual proof* of injustice and human suffering the world would act, many Palestinians and pro-Palestinian human rights organizations have also joined the forces of the global media in producing eyewitness accounts of Palestinian suffering and Israeli atrocities. While such practices of documentation surely contributed to the growing visibility of Palestinians in the West, the actual political merit of the widespread circulation of such suffering imagery remains questionable.

Given the enormously saturated field of images of suffering and destruction associated with the Palestinian plight today, one must begin to question the fetishized status of Palestine as image. This I believe is also the context for understanding *Nervus Rerum*'s and *We Began by Measuring*'s contention with the problematic nature of the act of documentation itself. The films' shared refusal to provide visual evidence or inform viewers must be understood as a refusal to play into this model of knowledge production, which reifies Palestinians as a news item or, to quote Godard, allows them to be nothing but "the stuff of documentaries."

Chapter Six

Shooting War

On Witnessing One's Failure to See (on Time)

To awaken is . . . to awaken only to one's repetition of a previous failure to see in time.
—Cathy Caruth, *Unclaimed Experience*

Whereas the previous chapter centered on the imperative to witness and the refusal to bear witness on the part of Palestinians, this chapter focuses on the conditions of seeing and witnessing on the part of Israeli soldiers as perpetrators of war violence. Analyzing two Israeli films about the 1982 Lebanon War, *Waltz with Bashir* (*Vals im bashir*, Ari Folman, 2008) and *Lebanon* (*Levanon*, Samuel Maoz, 2009), this chapter approaches the question of witnessing by examining the perpetrator's ability to generate an effective ethical and political viewing position based on the documentation of one's own failed witnessing. If the problem addressed in the previous chapter concerns the demand imposed on Palestinians to serve as eyewitnesses of and informers on their own suffering, the question tackled in this chapter focuses on the challenges facing the perpetrator when attempting to bear witness to his own failure to see others' suffering.

Taking the lead from Freud's *Beyond the Pleasure Principle* (1920), I advance a reading of combat trauma in terms of a failed witnessing or a momentary blindness, suggesting that we read the visual narratives of *Waltz with Bashir* and *Lebanon* as two different cinematic articulations of such a failure to see (on time). Next, the chapter ponders the ethical position associated with the scopic relationship generated in and through these films: between perpetrator and victim and also between spectators of the films and the historical subjects portrayed within them. Specifically, I ask: What does it mean to render visible one's own trauma, understood as a failure to see?

And what, if any, ethical position of spectatorship can be modeled on the witnessing of such failed vision?

Trauma, War, War Films

War films, by which I mean films that center on the spectacle of combat and the battlefield, tend to focus on the experience of soldiers. We usually see war from their point of view. In cases in which war (or its outcomes) are celebrated, soldiers appear heroic and their acts of destruction and violence are glorified. In cases in which war (or its outcomes) are critiqued, the spectacle of violence remains central, but the soldiers are portrayed as vulnerable men caught up in a situation they cannot fully control. At the heart of these cinematic narratives one finds the heroic dream shattered and replaced with narratives about the soldiers' traumas, which center on death: witnessing the death of friends, fearing the prospect of one's own death, and, significantly, taking part in the killing of others.[1]

One of Freud's main sources for elaborating his theory of trauma and repetition compulsion in *Beyond the Pleasure Principle* is soldiers' postcombat experience. Upon observing the fact that soldiers returning from World War I often became fixated in dreams on the terrifying and violent experiences they appeared to otherwise forget, Freud concludes that an involuntary compulsion to repeat lies at the heart of all traumatic experiences. It is with regard to both soldiers' and large-scale accident survivors' dreams that Freud describes trauma as a phenomenon always divorced from the event and experienced *in delay* in the form of a compulsive repetition. Significantly for Freud, the traumatized individual is not the firsthand victim of physical harm, but rather *the survivor* of such harm, who, in the process of escaping injury, bears witness to violence. Freud's examples of the train accident survivor and the soldier returning from war both involve an act of witnessing that is best understood in terms of a hole or a gap in experience. The stimulus is too overwhelming to experience in real time, and the witnessed traumatic event leads to a momentary shutdown of all sensory organs, most notably the eyes. Trauma survivor witnessing is thus more accurately a *failed witnessing*. The cause for the traumatic repetitions and reenactments exhibited by trauma victims is precisely this failure: the traumatized survivor is compelled to revisit the scene via images and dreams so as to finally *see* what s/he has failed to see at the time of the event. Accordingly, and quite tragically, to awaken from a traumatic vision is to awaken "to one's repetition of a previous failure to see in time" (Caruth 100).

The central place Freud gives to the shutdown of the sensory organs (the failure to experience trauma by witnessing violence at the time of the event) is translated, I argue, into a scopic relationship between witness and victim, and between past and present, as well as between reality and fantasy. Indeed, it can be argued that trauma is *innately scopic* and that it is accessible only insofar as it appears in the form of images of an otherwise missed (unseen) event. In other words, trauma may only be experienced in delay through one's compulsion to see what s/he has failed to see, and this experience inevitably involves coming to terms with one's previous failure to see *on time*.[2]

This mechanism, which transplants experience from the event to its image, and from the past to the present, makes this particular mode of trauma (associated most noticeably with posttraumatic stress disorder, or PTSD) pertinent to cinematic war representations. Narrated and filmed from the perspective of veterans or soldiers, many of the critical war (or antiwar) films focus on the experience of being present at the scene of violence yet failing to wake up, as it were, so as to prevent the catastrophe. The drama reenacted in such films thus follows, to a great degree, the paradoxical nature of trauma, understood by Freud as an experience of having simultaneously seen too much and (hence) seen nothing.

I will soon return to this paradox as I ponder the possibilities and limitations associated with the question of ethically filming and watching war. But first we must briefly quarrel with a more fundamental objection, namely that there is in effect "no such thing as an antiwar film," as Francois Truffaut has famously stated. Truffaut of course meant that there is something *inherently violent* to the visual cinematic representation of war that makes a cinematic *critique* impossible. A similar argument is advanced by Keith Solomon in his reading of *Apocalypse Now*, the emblem of the American antiwar war films: "the very nature of cinema has the tendency to turn war into spectacle," he writes, concluding that the most critical "antiwar film" "is at best ambivalent about war and at worse . . . celebrates it" (25). Solomon further suggests that spectators of such films are lured by seductive spectacle of violence and inevitably positioned at an explicitly *uncritical* position vis-à-vis the violence projected on the screen, thus becoming "tacit supporters of war's imperial project" (25).

In light of these concerns, I discuss *Lebanon* and *Waltz with Bashir* as critical (indeed *antiwar*) war films, which *as such* do not escape the allure of the spectacle but rather mobilize it, drawing attention to their ability (as cinematic texts) to manipulate and seduce their viewers. My reading of these films in other words by no means denies the fact that as spectators we are invited (indeed seduced) to find pleasure in the sights of violence and destruction. The critical stance I am alluding to is articulated *within* rather than *outside* the principle of the spectacle, which is also to say that it is articulated *within* and not *outside* the principle of pleasure.

Perpetrators, Victims, and the Ethics of Representation

If we follow the scopic relationship that trauma establishes between the witness of violence and its direct victim, we must conclude that it is marked by the agonizing and inescapable sign of an ethical failure. Indeed, the traumatized individual appears to be caught in a vicious cycle of *repeated failed witnessing*, or, to put it differently, s/he is traumatized precisely because s/he cannot overcome her/his (original) failure to see, and her/his repeated attempts to do so only make visible the unhappy fact that such seeing, if and when it takes place, is always already too late.[3]

The traumatized individual may not be able to escape this horrific fate of repeated failures, but the question that shall occupy us for the rest of this chapter still remains: is there a way to render this failure *visible for others* so that they may witness this failure to witness and translate it into a valid and productive ethical and political stance? To put it differently: Could the passing on of a story about failed witnessing and blindness have a productive effect, awakening others and opening their eyes *to see* what otherwise might continue to go unnoticed?

Both *Waltz with Bashir* and *Lebanon* center on the first stages of the 1982 Israeli invasion of Lebanon, which has come to be known in Hebrew as "the first Lebanon war" (*milchemet levanon ha-reshona*) and in Arabic as "the invasion" (*Alijtiyah*). Ultimately lasting nearly twenty years, the war was initially planned as a short-term military action, named Operation Peace for Galilee (*mivtsa shlom hagalil*), that aimed to destroy the Palestinian Liberation Organization (PLO) and Syrian military infrastructure in southern Lebanon and thereby to prevent further rocket attacks into northern Israeli towns. Israel's initial goal was achieved swiftly, resulting in the evacuation of more than fourteen thousand PLO combatants in August that year. But the events that followed the killing of the newly elected and Israeli-backed president of Lebanon, Bashir Gemayel, by the Syrian Social National Party, led to a serious escalation. Following the assassination, Israeli forces occupied West Beirut and authorized the entrance of a force of approximately 150 Phalangists (members of the Lebanese Christian Militia) into the Palestinian Sabra and Shatila refugee camps. This resulted in the Sabra and Shatila Massacre, in which the Phalangists slaughtered an undetermined but clearly great number of civilians. Israeli troops facilitated the massacre by surrounding the camps and monitoring all entrances and exits.[4] Israeli forces remained in southern Lebanon, in what Israel designated as the security zone, to fight the Hezbollah militia that took the place of PLO militants. Thus, despite Israel's immediate success in eradicating PLO bases from Lebanon, the Israeli invasion eventually resulted in an increased militarization of local Lebanese militias, and in the establishment of the powerful Hezbollah movement. In 2000, Israeli forces finally withdrew from southern Lebanon, where Hezbollah has since assumed full military control.[5]

I offer this selected and brief background mainly in order to emphasize the specific nature of a war that was experienced within Israel and by the Israeli forces first as a swift success and then as a lingering and daunting failure. This narrative of premature celebration followed by a great sense of (often denied) defeat provides material for cinematic projections of a drama of declined heroism and camaraderie, along with the strong melancholic overtones of a war gone wrong. It has often been suggested that the 1982 Lebanon War has become Israel's Vietnam: the decisive moment through which the ideas of Israeli exceptionalism and high moral standards lost their authority not only in the international community, but more significantly within Israeli society itself.[6] In other words, the Lebanon War marks a crucial shift or break in the perception of war within Israeli society. If the concept of a nation in war was previously successfully rendered within Israeli society in terms of self-defense and situated within broader narratives of both victimhood (a small nation under attack from the entire Arab world) and extreme omnipotence (a small nation overcoming the aggression of the entire Arab world), the 1982 Israeli invasion into Lebanon made such national myths impossible to sustain. This crisis—the urge to come to terms with it, and perhaps even the need to somehow overcome it—is,

I believe, greatly responsible for the fact that five Israeli feature films had already been made about the war prior to the recent release of *Lebanon* and *Waltz with Bashir* (hereafter referred to as wwb).[7]

Like the great majority of earlier Israeli war films (about Lebanon or other wars), wwb and *Lebanon* provide narratives focusing almost exclusively on the experience of Israeli soldiers accounting for their haunting memories, their friendships, their pain, their fear, their losses, and their coming to terms. Unsurprisingly, both films have been accused of joining a long Israeli repertoire of shooting and crying narratives, which center on the humanity or sensitivity of the Israeli soldier in the service of legitimizing Israel's moral superiority. While several critics have advanced such a reading (Shmulik Duvdevani, Naira Antoun, Rachel Shabi, Ursula Lindsey), the most elaborate critique along these lines comes from Slavoj Žižek. Like a great number of contemporary American antiwar films, these two Israeli films, Žižek contests, are at fault for two related reasons. First, in focusing on *personal narratives* (memories and experiences of individual soldiers) *Lebanon* and wwb (like the 2008 American *The Hurt Locker*, by Kathryn Bigelow) reproduce a spectacle of horror devoid of any meaningful political or historical analysis. The personal narrative, in other words, evades critiquing the greater structure that informs the driving ideological mechanism of the (Israeli, imperial) war machine. Second, the focus on the personal narrative legitimizes "the re-focus on the perpetrator's traumatic experience," thus resulting in the troublesome "humanization of the soldier" (Žižek, "A Soft Focus").

In the context of broader critiques of Israel's international public relationship ("Brand Israel" being a case in point), one could certainly see how the attempt to present Israeli soldiers as suffering from bad conscience can be seen as working in service of this sort of state propaganda. Without outright dismissing such accusations, I nevertheless argue that a closer and more patient engagement with the films suggests a profoundly more intriguing and critically productive understanding of their potential political significance.

While it is undeniably true that wwb and *Lebanon*, like many other antiwar war films (German, British, American, Israeli, and others), focus almost exclusively on the psychological experience of the soldiers rather than on the suffering of their victims, I would like to suggest that such deliberation is not in itself necessarily an indication of the films' ethical bankruptcy. Along these lines, I would argue that the question that appears to stand at the center of the critical reception of these films—namely "who is the (real) victim of the war?"—may not be the most productive question for determining these films' critical potentiality.[8]

Although never openly stated, a misguided assumption nevertheless underlies Žižek's and others' ethical condemnation of the films, which assume that within the visual economy of suffering one must first clearly distinguish between perpetrators and victims (a quasi-task in itself when it comes to war) before a politically and ethically responsible representation can occur. This assumption further implies that one must avoid "humanizing" the soldier, since we are warned that identifying with his position inevitably stands in the way of forming a responsibly critical analysis of violence, historical trauma, and loss.[9] Humanization of the soldier is dangerous, Žižek concludes, because of an "emphasis on the gap between the person's complex reality" and the role s/he is forced to play historically. This gap *secures our empathy* toward the perpetrator and evades the soldier's responsibility as well as our own: "we are there with our boys, identifying with their fears and anguishes instead of questioning what they are doing at war in the first place" ("A Soft Focus on War"). But are these two positions necessarily mutually exclusive, as Žižek would have us believe? Can we not consider soldiers as individuals who are victims of a war machine (itself dictated by nationalist ideology and capitalist imperialism), while we further ask, "what they are doing at war in the first place?" Writing more specifically about the Israeli case, Žižek goes on to say: "The 'humanization' of the soldier . . . is a key constituent of the ideological (self)presentation of the Israeli Defense Forces (IDF). The Israeli media loves to dwell on the imperfections and psychic traumas of Israeli soldiers, presenting them neither as perfect military machines nor as super-human heroes, but as ordinary people who, caught into the traumas of history and warfare, commit errors and can get lost as all normal people can" ("A Soft Focus on War"). But are they not? While I have no dispute with Žižek regarding Israeli media's role in circulating the image of the Israeli soldier as innocent and clueless, I nevertheless question the logic of his objection: Are we to conclude that the soldiers are not ordinary people? Are we to assume they are categorically different from "us" or that their crimes are ones that we "ordinary people" would have not committed under similar circumstances?

The critique of the humanization of the soldier becomes particularly alarming when juxtaposed and read against the heated debated surrounding the release of Hany Abu-Assad's film *Paradise Now* (al-Jannah al-ān, 2005). The film follows the last forty-eight hours in the lives of two young men from the West Bank who have volunteered to carry out a suicide attack in Tel Aviv. The film was celebrated by many but was also scrutinized by several critics on the grounds that it portrays a sympathetic image of Palestinian suicide bombers as normal people who are just like us. Israeli novelist, journalist, screenwriter, and celebrity Irit Linor, for example, writes: "Who are the suicide bombers in the film? They are no more than innocent victims of an occupation devoid of reason or purpose. . . . [T]hey are innocent heroes and likable killers. . . . The message of *Paradise Now* is simple: We're all people, even mass murderers. You see, anyone has the potential to blow up children and babies in a restaurant. It can happen to anyone, like dandruff. . . . Hany Abu-Assad sells us a humanity whose outer characteristics we find palatable: young heroes, sweet families. . . . The film's message is clear: if these people can become murderers—then clearly so could I" ("Anti-Semitism Now"). The symmetry of these polar reactions (it is bad to humanize Israeli soldiers who we must think are opposed to ordinary people, and it is bad to humanize Palestinian suicide bombers who we must not think are like us) calls attention to the critical discourse's ethical limits when it comes to the question of humanizing of the perpetrator. In both Linor's and Žižek's critiques, the concern over the humanization of the bad guys in effect betrays the critics' investment in their *dehumanization*. A narrative that focuses on the pain, thoughts, fears, and fantasies of those who become suicide bombers is thus deemed immoral for humanizing mass murderers, whereas a cinematic representation that focuses on the anguish, confusion, and pain of Israeli soldiers is considered, for similar reasons, "perverse" (Antoun, "Review"). I believe the limits of this critical framework are apparent. Consequently, against this mode of critique I would like to advance an alternative reading of the films that locates the question of their ethical appeal not in their commitment to adequately account for the suffering of others, but rather in their ability to mobilize cinematic language so as render visible and interrogate one's own ethical failure: one's own (ongoing) failure to see (on time).

Engaging with the films, my aim, then, is not to create a hierarchy of war victims (citizens versus soldiers, Palestinians and Lebanese versus Israelis, and so on), but rather to begin to articulate, together and through the films, an ethical stance that avoids the victim/perpetrator dyad. The ethical position of spectatorship to which I refer is not based on setting the picture straight, as it were, by differentiating (real, ultimate) victims from the so-called lesser ones. More accurately, it refers to a self-reflective position generated in response to the films' direct engagement (both thematically and formally) with the question of seeing in its relationship to power, deception, violence, and ethics.

Waltz with Bashir: *Animating War*

WWB is an animated docudrama that follows protagonist (modeled on the director) Ari Folman's attempt to recover his absent memories of the 1982 Lebanon War, in which he participated as a young soldier. Aside from its last scene, which introduces videotape footage of the victims and survivors of the Sabra and Shatila Massacre, the film is animated and composed of a collage of memories, fantasies, dreams, and monologues belonging to the various people Folman (the character) interviews as part of his attempt to retrieve his lost memories. Interviewees include several soldiers who served alongside Folman, journalists who reported from the war, and a couple of psychotherapists with whom Folman explores the nature of memory and PTSD.

WWB's surrealist meditation on memory and forgetting expands the cinematic conventions of both the great majority of war films and the great majority of documentaries. The film's uniquely animated format and compelling visual rendition of traumatic memories received much critical attention and for the most part was highly regarded as an effective commentary on the limits of traditional documentary filming conventions.[10] But the film has also been scrutinized for transforming the historical reality it seeks to reconstruct and document into an unreliable narrative about memory, hallucination, and fantasy. It has been further suggested that the blurry reality depicted in the film, along with the failure of the protagonist and his friends to see clearly through their distorted memories, serves an excuse for the director's failure to produce a responsible critique of the Israeli involvement in the Sabra and Shatila Massacre. Along these lines, Anthony Quinn writes: "Folman stresses the slippery, unreliable nature of memory, but is that actually a way of ducking his own responsibility?" ("Review"). Israeli poet and acclaimed critic Yitzhak Laor has advanced the most extreme of such critiques, suggesting that "thanks to the film's use of the childish genre of the comics [Folman was able] to infantilize not just the soldiers he depicts, but also the viewers" ("Dor shalem"). Since nothing is real and everything is simply comic and fantasy, Laor concludes that even the horrid footage images at the end of the film "look like nothing more than a comic flashback" ("Dor shalem").[11]

Contrary to such accusations, I contend that WWB's use of animation functions primarily to draw attention to the film's act of representation. Unlike the photographed image, used most commonly to advance documentary narratives and gain authorship over the truth, the affectivity of animation, to borrow Sheila Sofian's words, lies in its being "more transparent in its construction" (9). In the case of WWB, this becomes particularly noticeable since the animation is seemingly realistic (the film uses rotoscoping as its technique of animation), yet the movements of the characters are slightly slowed down and are hence not in full synchronization with the characters' speech. The drawn bodies seem somewhat stiff and their movements overaccentuated: "an eye moves back and forth inside its lid, a brow raises, fingers intermittently tap on the cheek, lips and eyelids open and close. . . . [E]ach movement and each space between the movements are seen" (Schlunke 957). WWB draws attention to this excess of representation, making us aware of the fact that we are watching a slightly off version of reality. When this off version, which makes up the bulk of the film, is juxtaposed in the closing scene with photographed television footage of the massacre in the Sabra and Shatila camps, we must ask ourselves about the meaning of this sudden transition. Does the replacement of the animated image with the photographed footage stand for "a clash" between the "dreamlike imagery" and the "ugly truth of urban warfare," as Ali Jaafar suggests ("Live Action")? Or does it, on the contrary, draw attention to the inability to draw a clear distinction between the two? WWB, I believe, leaves this question purposefully open in order to invite another question: What does it mean to *finally* see? And what, if anything, is made visible in the transition from the animated images (the stuff of dreams) to the photographed footage (as encore to reality)?

A fairly common reading of this transition suggests that it stands for the final recovery of Folman's memory. The final scene, toward which the whole film leads, is thus read as a moment of closure: a moment in which the protagonist finally remembers his repressed past, a moment in which he finally sees" what he has failed to see for so many years—his role as an Israeli soldier who witnessed the massacre and did nothing to stop it. Reading this as a moment of working through, most critics have concluded that WWB follows a healing narrative, a working through that results in the protagonist finally remembering or seeing clearly.[12] Suggesting otherwise, I contest that WWB is not about the recovery of memory, but rather about the persistence of forgetting. Further, I contend that the film is not simply about the personal forgetting that results from postcombat stress disorder, but, more precisely, about collective amnesia.

The sudden break from the language of animation (the protagonist's hallucinatory dreams, the surreal visions of war, and the conflicting and fragmented memories of Folman's friends), which takes place in the film's final images of photographed footage of the carnage, marks a startling transition from fantasy to reality. Unlike the hazy dreams, which make up the bulk of the film, the photographs index a reality beyond dispute. And yet, when the camera returns from the footage of the massacre to the animated face of the protagonist—breathing heavily as he stares with eyes wide open at the victims and survivors of the camps—we are invited to ask: Does he (finally) see? Does he in fact remember his position as a witness who failed to witness in the past, or does he continue to fabricate his own memories, reminding us that if he failed to witness then he surely is failing to witness now?[13]

While the film does not provide clear-cut answers to these troubling questions, the fact that it leaves them open forces on us (and perhaps most urgently on Israeli viewers) a more difficult question: Do *we* (finally) see? The film's closing scene, marked by the abrupt transition from the animated images to the photographed footage, I suggest, does not stand for closure in the form of overcoming trauma. Quite the contrary, it represents the *first and only traumatic moment* visualized through the entire film—a moment capturing (on-screen) the protagonist's own witnessing of his (past) failed witnessing. As for us, the question is asked: What does it mean for us to see these images? Have we not, like Folman, seen them already in the past, perhaps as we were watching the news back in 1982? And if so, are we too called on to witness our own failure to witness on time?

To further understand the parallel the film draws between its protagonist's position and that of its spectators, we must take a closer look at how the film cinematically represents war and its effects on those who experience it. As a general theme, like *Apocalypse Now* (Francis Ford Coppola, 1979) before it, WWB highlights the fact that war operates as a blinding mechanism, a violence too unreal to be experienced as real. War, the film suggests, can only be experienced by those who manage to survive it: as a dream, a spectacle, or better yet, a movie.

Ambiguous flashbacks, delirious images, impressionistic pictures of war, and dream-like visions of violence make WWB a captivating movie to watch. Indeed, the film's ability to visually mimic the stuff of dreams (rather than capture reality in its so to speak "light-of-day" clarity) is greatly responsible, I believe, for the film's wide appeal. But the film does not simply present enticing images of war and spectacular violence. Rather, it further interrogates how the technology of modern warfare facilitates its virtual phantasmatic experience and renders it similar to the experience of watching a film.[14] The film indeed overflows with both verbal and visual references to the optic and cinematic nature of modern warfare. In one scene, for example, the camera follows the movements of another camera located on top of a helicopter. Following a car on a video board, the camera aims and then attacks it with missiles. Crosshairs at the center of the digitalized image appear on the screen, aiming at the car below. Time and again missing the car, the explosions result in collapsed buildings, trees set on fire, and more destruction, but the target—the little car—continues to move forward. The whole scene looks like a video game: one of those familiar and frustrating games in which one has to nail down a small moving object as various tunnels and other obstacles block the way or delay visibility (see figure 6.1).

In another scene, Folman speaks to a psychoanalyst who specializes in combat PTSD. She tells him about one of her old patients, an amateur photographer, who made it through an entire war emotionally unaffected by the horror thanks to his ability to "see everything through an imaginary camera." He spent most of the war, she says, "looking for great scenes." For him, war was like "watching a movie," until one day his imaginary camera breaks and he goes crazy. Finally, in a scene narrated by the Israeli reporter Ron Ben-Yishai, Ben-Yishai and his cameraman are following the Israeli troops as they try to escape the bullets shot at them from the nearby buildings: "Women, children, and old people were gathered in the balconies watching the gun battle [between the Palestinians on the upper floors and the Israeli soldiers on the ground] as if it was a film." Commenting

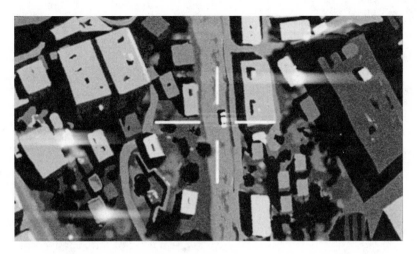

6.1 | Screen capture from *Waltz with Bashir* (dir. Ari Folman, 2008).

on the gathering people for looking at war "as if it was film," this report carries a certain irony because as Ben-Yishai speaks we see a flashback of his cameraman crawling on the floor with a big TV camera on his shoulder, trying to escape the bullets as he continues to shoot war for the Israeli TV broadcast.

"War is a symptom of delirium operating in the half-light of trance, drugs, blood, and unison," writes Paul Virilio; "it can never break free from the magical spectacle because its very purpose is to produce that spectacle" (*War and Cinema* 7–8). The only way war can be seen and experienced by those who manage to survive it, WWB seems to suggest, is through the lens of an imaginary camera. There is, in other words, no war without the spectacle of war, and the two are, in the final analysis, one and the same. To document one's failure to see (on time), then, is also to document war's *blinding impact*: a blinding that renders the horror a mere spectacle (see figure 6.2).

WWB's protagonist, we must recall, first enters the film unaware and clearly untroubled by his lack of memories of the war. It is not until he listens to his friend Boaz's confession about his repeated nightmare associated with the war that the protagonist realizes there is something disturbing about the fact that he has absolutely no recollections from Lebanon, or that, as he puts it, "Lebanon is simply not in my system" (*zeh lo basystem sheli*). It is this sudden realization that eventually unleashes Fol-

6.2 | Screen capture from *Waltz with Bashir* (dir. Ari Folman, 2008).

man's own enigmatic dream-memory, which he spends the remainder of the film trying to decipher and which serves as the repeated visual sequence of the film. Young Folman floats in a golden-black ocean next to two other young men and to the sound of the eerie soundtrack (composed and mixed by Max Richter). The three emerge from the water, skinny and naked, but still armed; slowly they put on their soldiers' uniforms and begin walking from the beach toward an empty street. At this point the dream-memory is always cut off.

Knowing that his unit must have been among those stationed in Beirut in 1982, Folman suspects that his dream has something to do with the massacre but cannot figure out what the connection may be. Determined to find out, Folman interviews friends who served with him, hoping someone else shares his enigmatic dream. He discovers that no one does, but that they all have their own surreal memories and dreams. The film opens with Boaz's vivid dream of a horde of ravenous dogs speeding through an empty boulevard—their eyes red with fever, their teeth exposed, and saliva dripping from their mouths. They run manically until they stop just below his window and wait for him, ready to tear him apart. Boaz, who recounts the dream to Folman, knows exactly what it is about: "I remember each and every one of the 26 dogs I killed in Lebanon," he says. "The dogs are there for revenge,'" Boaz determines. Yet other memories and visions presented throughout the film are less explicitly legible, instead emphasizing the difficulty involved in drawing a clear line between reality and fantasy, memory and dream, and event and image. For example, Carmi, another friend Folman interviews, recalls that he and the rest of his combat unit were sent to Lebanon on a luxurious "love boat" cruise. The soldiers dance and drink all night until Carmi finds himself in the arms of a huge blue naked woman who takes him with her to the ocean, rescuing him from the bomb that soon after falls on the boat and sets all the other soldiers on fire. Carmi tells Folman he realizes that none of this could have in fact happened, and that they were most likely sent on "an old commando boat." Still, he says, that's how he sees it in his mind: "that is what I remember."

Throughout the film, the animated scenes depicting the war expose Israeli soldiers experiencing war as if it were a summer camp or a field trip: they sunbathe by the beach, sing war songs as they ride their tanks, watch porn, and, with the same degree of blasé, they bomb buildings from their helicopters and shoot in all directions from their tanks. There are a few scenes within the fragmented animated narrative in which a momentary realization of the danger and horror of war is realized in real time, but for the most part even direct interaction with death is revisited as an experience that never took place *as such*. Thus, in one of the early flashbacks, Folman is ordered by an officer "to collect all the dead and wounded and dump them somewhere by the big light." Initially stunned by the officer's brutal language, Folman repeats his words *"dump them?"* "Yes, dump them," the officer repeats. Folman, who follows the order, soon realizes how easy it is: "we dropped them there, washed off the blood, and drove back, shooting. We didn't see a thing, we were just shooting at whatever." Soon after, when he is confronted by another soldier who asks him what they should do now, Folman responds: "What else? Shoot!"

Shoot, dump, bomb, sing, jump, run, shoot, dump, bomb. This is the rhythm of war in WWB. Indeed, the film does not shy away from highlighting the fact that war is laden with infantile masculine fantasies, and that the spectacle of violence and destruction is itself strongly tied to questions of masculine performance or failure. In her fierce attack on the film, Antoun accuses it of depicting Israeli soldiers as "young men going off to war, fantasizing about women, wondering at how to prove their masculinity, licking the wounds of being dumped by girlfriends, [and] singing songs with upbeat tunes about bombing Beirut." One could of course agree with Antoun that such depictions are insensitive to the victims of the Israeli

6.3 | Screen capture from *Waltz with Bashir* (dir. Ari Folman, 2008).

violence and that as such they function as renewed sites of injury. But one might also suggest that such insensitive depictions are simply more candid images of war insofar as they account for the aspects of war we would all rather forget: not the perceivable violence and the horror, but the pleasure and the seduction of the spectacle of destruction, all of which are summarized by veteran William Broyles's oft-quoted words: "the beauty of war is what veterans refer to as 'eye-fucking'" ("Why Men Love War") (see figure 6.3).

If WWB provides a critical cinematic representation of war (that is, if it can be considered a sincere antiwar war film), it is certainly not because the film presents a strong critical stance and a public condemnation of Israel's role in facilitating the Sabra and Shatila Massacre, a task the film only partially achieves.[15] WWB does not provide a reliable historical analysis of, or teach us anything we didn't already know about, the 1982 war, nor about Israel's reasons for invading Lebanon in the first place. Rather, what makes WWB an important antiwar war film is that it offers an uncompromising interrogation of war's seductive spectacular character. In doing so, it further forces us to reflect on the analogy forged between our own position as spectators of the (war) film and the position of the soldier, whose blindness and forgetfulness ("Lebanon is not in my system") is by no means coincidental or personal, but rather structural.

In this regard, it is worth emphasizing the fact that Folman (the character) never successfully remembers or finds out where he was at the time of the massacre. Indeed, the footage we see at the end of the film does not represent (as it is commonly suggested) the images he actually saw at the time, but rather the images that he, like us, and many others around the globe, saw on our TV screens in the aftermath of the horror. To read the film along the lines of a personal confession (that is, to read it as a story about an Israeli veteran coming to terms with his repressed memories of the 1982 war) is to miss that the troubling questions the film raises about blindness, ethical failure, and forgetfulness are ultimately not about Folman but about ourselves: about our blindness, our failure, and our forgetfulness.

Indeed, the film resists the logic of separation advanced by Žižek and others in relation to the soldier/perpetrator (his blindness, his aggression, his seduction, and so forth). It demands that we form a position of ethical spectatorship not by removing ourselves, but rather by considering the implications of forming an analogy between our own position (as spectators) and that of the perpetrator whose failure we are called on to witness. We are called on to witness the perpetrator's failure not in order to condemn, excuse, or forgive it, but rather in order to, first and foremost, give an account of ourselves.

Lebanon structures an analogy between spectator/perpetrator similar to WWB's analogy between our position as spectators and the position of the protagonist as a failed witness. However, Lebanon does so by interrogating the relationship between the manipulative effects of the filming camera and that of war machinery on the visual field. Centering the drama on the soldier's eye, Lebanon calls attention to the ability of the eye (ours, as well as the soldier's and the filmmaker's) to be trained so as to select what it sees to the point of becoming blind to the suffering of others. The possibility of shooting an antiwar film becomes in this case an explicit question about the possibility of rendering visible an account of the eye's malaise.

Lebanon: Seeing through the Gun Sight

Lebanon's spectatorship experience is drastically different from that of WWB. The latter offers viewers a true cinematic tour de force that unfolds a visual orgy of light, motion, and color, accompanied by a club-like upbeat soundtrack, as part of its attempt to highlight war's spectacular and seductive nature. Lebanon, by sharp contrast, severely compromises our audio-visual field, limiting it to the suffocating space of the inside of a dreary tank and the sound of the tanks' rotating arm-gun's grinding, mechanical, ear-piercing squeaks. In short, whereas WWB makes war look and sound like an acid hallucination trip (the film explicitly compares the battlefield and the dance club), *Lebanon*'s rendition of war is more akin to a visceral nightmare. Shot almost in its entirety from within the confined space of the tank, and mainly as a series of close-ups with some single shots lasting for over twenty minutes, *Lebanon*, to put it simply, is an oppressive film to watch.

There are several other differences between the films. While WWB traces the temporal gaps between event, memory, and image to explore the *belated* experience of war's traumatic impact, *Lebanon* seeks to mimetically revive and reconstruct a detailed account of a real-time war experience. *Lebanon* aims, in other words, to capture (on camera) the traumatic events that escape the protagonist but that can nevertheless be made visible to the film's spectators. These different tasks, along with the different temporal orders they follow, are further accompanied by radically different aesthetics and visual grammar. Briefly stated, WWB explores the cinematic nature of war, and how its spectacular, markedly artificial, and mediated features prevent it from ever being experienced as something other than a movie or a video game. In a manner more akin to the film conventions of the antiwar war film, *Lebanon* on the other hand seeks to capture the destructive psychological reality of war as a spectacle of growing violence, loss, confusion, and insanity.

Differences aside, the films share a critical interrogation of the potentials and the limits of the *cinematic medium itself* to faithfully and responsibly "take us through" what is inherently war's *unwitnessable* reality. Each film compares and contrasts the cinematic apparatus and the modern battlefield, as well as film spectators' position and the ethically compromised soldier's position. If WWB forges this analogy by tracing the "derealization of military engagement," to borrow Paul Virilio's words, *Lebanon* does so by aligning our vision with that of the gun sight, in accordance with Virilio's dreadful maxim: "I see therefore I kill" (quoted in Rotbard, "Wall and Tower: The Mold of Israeli Adrikhalut").

WWB can be understood to directly contend with the war film genre, particularly thanks to its use of *animation* as a means of critically recirculating some familiar cinematic icons of popular American antiwar films.

Yet, although *Lebanon* does not explicitly interrogate the genre of the war film itself, it nevertheless invites us to read its critique of war as inseparable from its deliberation on our own cinematic experience of war. Indeed, as in WWB, *Lebanon*'s interrogation of war is intimately linked to an interrogation of the cinematic apparatus as it concerns the conditions of both shooting and watching war. What cinema captures and documents, as far as the experience of war is concerned, is none other than the ability of war (like cinema) to manipulate and severely alter one's visual field. In other words, shooting war becomes the process of calling attention to the visual manipulations involved in both the act of shooting and the act of shooting a film about shooting.

Like WWB, *Lebanon* is based on the director's personal memories of his service as a young Israeli soldier in Lebanon in 1982. Whereas WWB accounts for the first few days of the war, leading up to the massacre in the refugee camps, *Lebanon* tells the much more narrow story of the war's first four hours as experienced by tank gunner Shmulik (modeled after the director) and three other soldiers enclosed with him. The soldiers in the tank are told in the opening scene that their mission is simply to back up a group of Israeli paratroopers after the Israeli air force has already bombed the area: "the Air Force has already wiped out this place; all we need to do now is go through the town and make sure there are no terrorists left behind. Nice, quick and easy." Things go wrong, as they often do in war. A miscalculation leads the tank into an urban war zone controlled in parts by Syrian forces, Lebanese Christian militia, and Palestinian fighters. A missile soon hits the tank, oil leaks all over its walls, and the engine stops working. From this moment on, our eyes face the dark close-up shots of the tank's interior walls and the soldiers' filthy faces. Only a few glimpses of the bleak and bloody reality outside the tank, as seen through the limited perspective of its gun sight, occasionally interrupt these images (see figure 6.4).

Lebanon did not enjoy the same international exposure as WWB, but it did attract some of the same criticism, namely, that the film disproportionally focuses on the trauma of the Israeli soldiers rather than on their innocent victims' suffering. Rachel Shabi, for example, finds fault with the fact that the film makes the "the grisly killing machine, the Israeli tank, appear as a source of terror for the soldiers inside it, rather than for the people outside it" ("Ajami and Lebanon"). Film director Elia Suleiman (discussed in chapter 2) makes a similar argument, explaining his refusal to watch the film:

6.4 | Screen capture from *Lebanon* (dir. Samuel Maoz, 2009).

"I did not see *Lebanon* and don't want to see [it]. To think of a film from the point of view of a tank barrel is already so inhumanly positioned. This is when film can reveal itself scandalously" ("The Other Face"). But in their rush to condemn the film for its focus on the soldiers, or on the reality *in-side* rather than *outside* the tank, these and other critics have failed to recognize that *Lebanon* is not simply (or even primarily) a film about the suffering Israeli soldier. More accurately, it is a film about the *becoming of the soldier*, that is to say, a film about the gradual transformation of a soldier into an integral and inseparable part of the grisly killing machine.

"War alters the body," *Lebanon* director Samuel Maoz recalls, "it is a physical experience. . . . First you lose your sense of taste, you don't need to eat, [then] you suddenly hear everything sharp and clear . . . and if you survive—and most who died, died in the first day—after the second day you become a soldier of the war"(Enlarger). What does it mean to become a soldier of war? Shot from within the tank, *Lebanon* invites us to follow what appears to be an inescapable metamorphosis in the face of violence, fear, and danger. Unfolding a narrative of the becoming-soldier, the film visualizes the radical physical and mental changes that take hold of the men in the tank. Indeed, as the film progresses, the soldiers become increasingly enmeshed with the machine. It becomes more and more difficult to distinguish between tank and soldiers as their sweat and blood mixes with the tank's leaking oil and as their dirt-covered faces come to resemble the tank's gray walls. The changes that take place in the process of the becoming-soldier moreover involve the deterioration of vision: a partial blindness produced and cultivated by weapon machinery.

More than anything else, *Lebanon* is about (failed) vision and the hijacking of the eye by military (and cinematic) devices. In other words, it is a film that accompanies its inquiry into the horrific nature of war with a deliberate focus on *the eye*. There are several eyes explored on the screen via close-up shots: pained and angered eyes of dead victims' relatives looking directly into the gun sight of the tank, the terrified eyes of a Syrian prisoner who is brought into the tank, the eyes of the soldiers in the tank, and, most prominently, the jittery eye of Shmulik, the Israeli soldier and protagonist of the film, which is attached to the tank's gun sight throughout the greater part of the film. Focusing on Shmulik's eye as it follows the reality outside of the tank through the gun's crosshair and the periscope, *Lebanon* is about war as *seen through and marked on* the aiming eye (see figure 6.5).

The film opens with Shmulik's failure to follow his commanding officer's order to shoot at a car of Palestinian militants. As the movie progresses, we follow Shmulik's increasing ability to aim and shoot: at first hesitant, and then mechanical. Close-up shots of his eye trace this transformation. At first, opened wide, the eye nervously twitches, failing to fixate on a target. Gradually, it loses its sparkle and becomes fixated—a mere extension of the gun sight. By the end of the film, Shmulik's eye is glued to the periscope and his vision no longer escapes the limited frame of the target overlaid with the crosshairs. As his fellow soldiers in the tank lose their sanity, give in to fear, or die, Shmulik becomes a killer. His militarized gaze functions as a site of convergence, aligning the eye of the soldier, the eye of the tank, and the eye of the film's spectator.[16] Depending on where he directs the tank's arm-gun, Shmulik's eye provides the only reality made available to the spectator. And, like Shmulik, whatever we see on the screen *is already* overlaid with the crosshair; it already appears as a potential target.

For Virilio, "war is cinema, and cinema is war" (*War and Cinema* 26). Elsewhere, he notes, "cinema means pulling a uniform over our eyes . . . stepping up an eye regime that leads to an eye disease" (*Open Sky* 97). Depicting the damaging effects of cinema on the eye in *military terms*, Virilio concludes that cinema and war are equally responsible for creating what he describes as a modern eye disease on an epidemic scale. Limiting our vision to a reality overlaid with the crosshairs, *Lebanon* maximizes the converging

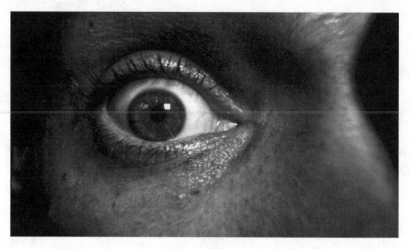

6.5 | "The aiming eye." Screen capture from *Lebanon* (dir. Samuel Maoz, 2009).

points between the camera (the one filming *Lebanon*) and the tank's gun. But the film does not simply reaffirm the analogy Virilio makes between war and cinema. More accurately, the film is best understood as an attempt to wrestle with this overlap and to defy its overdetermined conclusions. While the film certainly draws attention to the similarities between cinema and war, more specifically between our position as spectators of the violent images projected on the screen and the position of the soldier looking at reality though his gun sight, it eventually uses the analogy in order to generate a critical mode of spectatorship. Via this critical mode exposing the cinematic camera's manipulative work, the blinding mechanism that generates the military gaze may become visible.

Indeed, insofar as the film aligns our gaze with Shmulik's aiming eye, it does so while further making us aware of the presence of the camera within the tank and while reminding us that the reality we see is itself an outcome of a successful manipulation of vision. This critical position is enabled primarily by the fact that every slight movement of the camera is accompanied by a squeaking mechanical sound that accentuates the movement and renders it visible. In other words, drawing us into the tank to see through the gun sight what war really looks like, the film nonetheless makes us aware of the cinematic apparatus involved in this manipulation. Thus, a critical gap emerges in our relation to the camera and the perspective of the gun sight it forces us to see through *even* as these two collide in the images of

6.6 | Screen capture from *Lebanon* (dir. Samuel Maoz, 2009).

violence and destruction projected on the screen. In short: we don't just see *like*, or *through*, Shmulik's gun-sight position, we also see that we are *forced into* this limited viewpoint.

The double vision generated in *Lebanon* (seeing like the soldier, but also seeing the manipulation involved in the production of this visual field) allows spectators to realize our position as witnesses of failed seeing. As we follow Shmulik's eye (the eye is the real protagonist of the film), we are made aware of the fact that it loses its ability to see beyond the manipulative frame of the periscope. But as we witness the growing captivity of the soldier's eye, we are not asked, as some critics suggest, to identify with the tank, nor with the soldier situated inside the grisly machine. More accurately, we are asked to recognize the danger involved in the militarization of vision, and we are warned about the relative ease with which the eye (the soldier's and also our own) can be manipulated and trained to select what it sees to the point where others become targets and where the ability to see amounts to the ability to kill (see figure 6.6).

Visualizing Failure: Seeing, Blindness, Witnessing

At the heart of both WWB and *Lebanon*, I have argued, one finds a visual narrative about compromised seeing that correlates to a narrative of ethical failure. As viewers, we are called on to witness this failure, to reflect on the dangerous outcomes of drifting into gun-sight outlook, and to question our own gaze: seduced, tantalized, distressed, or blinded by the spectacle of violence. In the tension between the reflective gaze (reflecting on its own operation of looking) and the witnessing gaze (directed at the eye's failure to see), we may begin to delineate the possibility of ethical spectatorship.

This mode of spectatorship calls on us to reexamine our position of spectatorship in direct relation to the soldier's indisputably compromised ethical position. If we are asked to hold back judgment, it is not in the name of identification or empathy (with the perpetrators), but in the service of reflecting on our own answerability as the precondition for casting ethical judgments of others. Finally, although this invitation to self-reflection may be articulated in general ethical terms, I contend that it carries particular prominence to Israeli viewers. Indeed, against the popular perception of these films as universal condemnations of war targeted equally at all viewers, I argue that the greater political significance of these films is found in their inward address to Israeli viewers, who, like the filmmakers themselves, belong to a hypermilitarized society largely oblivious to its own ongoing blindness.[17]

If war is experienced through an imaginary camera (WWB), and if it further trains the eyes to see others only as targets (Lebanon), the only hope of restoring vision for a nation constituted on heroic myths of self-sacrifice, security exceptionalism, and national revival lies in its breaking away from such limited sight to witness its long years of distorted vision and blindness. Both WWB and Lebanon extend this invitation to look closely at one's own failure to see. The final outcome, however, remains in the eyes of the spectators.

Closing Words

Visual Occupations opens with an inquiry into Israeli blindness, characterized by the visible invisibility in present-day Israel of the Palestinian Nakba, the Palestinian catastrophe of 1948, and follows with a chapter about the absurd experience of Palestinian invisibility, which occurs in his own homeland for Elia Suleiman's cinematic protagonist, E.S. While the book's first two chapters focus on the Israeli visual field, the following two chapters shift attention to the visual field that dominates the interactions between Israelis (citizens) and Palestinians (noncitizens) within the Occupied Territories. Chapters 3 and 4 examine surveillance and the military gaze, further interrogating various artistic interventions' capacity to redirect and undermine those modes of power. Finally, the book's last two chapters focus on what I call "the crisis of witnessing." Through a close engagement with several Palestinian and Israeli films, these final two chapters probe the ethical and political limitations of the eyewitness accounts and visual testimonies that humanitarian and global media typically rely on to document and decry atrocities.

The book as a whole targets the colonial visual arrangement that currently grants unequal visual rights to Israelis and Palestinians (Occupiers and Occupied). Denaturalizing vision and questioning the pre-givenness of any dominant visual order, *Visual Occupations* suggests that identifying, mobilizing, and manipulating sites of ambiguity and gray zones is key to bringing about political change. Marked as they are by the barely visible, the visibly invisible, and the *disappeared*, such skewed visual arrangements are often associated with failure: the failure to see, the failure to appear, the failure to bear witness, or the failure to provide visual evidence. Yet, the book suggests, such failures must also be considered political and ethical potentialities of seeing and appearing *differently*, thereby generating alternative ways of seeing and new modes of appearance. Still, the massive scope of reshaping this visual field requires more than new ways of seeing or appearing; it further involves, as the book's individual chapters sought to demonstrate, a refusal to *take one's place in a predetermined visual field*. This refusal includes tactics of deliberately declining to appear as a victim, declining to exchange gazes under conditions of extreme visual inequality, declining to bear witness, or refusing to be seen.

As I argue throughout the book, matters of visibility (the condition of being seen), vision (seeing or failing to see), and visuality (the distribution of power determining who can see what and how) never reflect a single, coherent, or predetermined political function. Most often, visibility and access to sight ensure political empowerment, but this is not always the case. At times, these positions tip the balance toward oppressive power relations. There is, in other words, *nothing intrinsic to vision and visibility that marks them as either emancipatory or suppressive*. In the case of Israel/Palestine, as in the case of other militarized conflicts involving civilian occupation, state surveillance, competing narratives of loss, and ongoing violence, questions concerning the political life of vision must be considered along a *plurality* of scenarios and circumstances whose sum inevitably escapes any single formulaic visuality narrative.

The readings I advance in this book are accordingly not designed to provide an overarching argument about the nature of the conflict's visuality (nor of the Israeli Occupation for that matter), but more precisely to highlight the complexity and multiplicity of positions and forces involved in the creation and sustainability of the dominant visual configurations of this conflict, which, given their complexity, are also open to manipulation and reconfiguration.

My faith in the ability to mobilize (failed) vision as a political instrument of change may strike some readers as overly optimistic. I do not deny the fact that *Visual Occupations* advances a certain optimistic view by articulating the possibility of altering what is, without doubt, a bleak political reality. This optimism, however, is neither celebratory nor secured—it is grounded neither in a modernist belief in the political transformative capacities of art, nor in an abstract perception of historical progress or human nature. Rather, and far more modestly, it is a *cautious optimism* that primarily originates from my ongoing conversations with many Palestinians and Israelis, which make me genuinely believe there are enough of us out there who wish to see otherwise; enough of us out there who wish to see and be seen in a different-looking future.

....

I initially ended the afterword with these hopeful words. But as the book was going through production, Israel and Hamas entered the twenty-seven days of fighting, resulting (at the moment of writing) in over eighteen hundred Palestinian casualties and sixty-seven Israeli casualties. While I wrote *Visual Occupations* out of an urgent sense of necessity as well as a conviction that change is not just necessary but also possible, the unfathomable magnitude of the recent Israeli offense on Gaza, and the gross number of Palestinian casualties, made it almost impossible for me to uphold this sense of optimism, tentative and cautious as it may be.

Given the magnitude of the disaster we now face in Gaza and what seems to be a bleak ongoing future of violence and war, I decided to end instead with some preliminary thoughts about the enormously harmful impact of the fast growing new technologies of war. Yesterday's gun, tank, and checkpoint—the means of violence and destruction discussed in this book—are now rapidly replaced with long-range missles and, more significantly, with drones. The visual field generated by such remotely piloted aircrafts is one that maximizes the visibility of potential targets (rendering everything and everyone that appears in the crosshair *as a target*) while drastically minimizing the visibility of casualties for both the pilots operating the drones from afar and the external viewers of the aftermath, the majority of whom view only recorded images of the attack seen from a bird's-eye-view. This remote vision "from above" renders the very act of looking at, or "seeing," violence fully detached from anything that could be associated, even remotely, with an act of witnessing in any ethical sense. Indeed the aircraft attacks, many of which are posted online (plenty of them can be found on the IDF's official webpage), conceal more than they reveal. The distant, black-and-white images of aiming, followed by remote sights of explosions, offer absolutely no visual evidence of carnage, suffering, destruction, or loss. On the contrary, these images, so precise, are nevertheless profoundly detached, numbing, and blinding.

In light of the centrality of these new war techniques (in Israel's war on Gaza but also in Pakistan, Afghanistan, Iraq, Yemen, and other places where the United States uses drones to attack regularly), and given that drones have already become a popular new "field of study," enticing students to enroll in "America's newest, and possibly best paying, major" (Johnson, "New Drone Studies Major"), I believe that any future work on the relationship between vision and violence, or visibility and militarism, will have to engage in a close critical study of drones, not just as a dangerous mass-killing weapon, but also as a destructive and manipulative new *mode of visualization*: one that eliminates the possibility of witnessing, while rendering those who are subjected to live *under the drones* completely invisible despite their hypervisibility. I close here, then, on this somewhat less optimistic note as I present this daunting if urgent task for others to pursue.

Notes

Introduction

The Haraway quotation appears on p. 146 of "Situated Knowledge."

1. DAAR (Decolonizing Architecture Art Residency) is an art and architecture collective and a residency program based in Beit Sahour, Palestine. The founding members of the collective include Sandi Hilal, Alessandro Petti, and Eyal Weizman. Numerous artists and architects have taken part in various projects installed by DAAR since its establishment in 2007. See "Vision," http://www.decolonizing.ps/site/visibility/.

2. Built by the British Mandate army during the mid-1930s Arab Revolt, Oush Grab is located on the highest hill at the southern entrance to the Palestinian city of Beit Sahour, east of Bethlehem. After 1948 the area became a military base of the Jordan Legion, and after 1967 it became an Israeli military base. From 1967 through 2006, when the Israeli military abruptly evacuated the base, many of the Palestinian houses surrounding the camp were destroyed, and inhabitants of Beit Sahour had to endure the ongoing invasive lighting projected onto the town from the military watch tower located at the summit of the hill just above. After the evacuation in 2006 (also resulting in the demolition of many Palestinian homes and the destruction of other Palestinian property), the camp was left in rubble aside from a few concrete buildings that were left standing at the summit. As of February 2010, the Israeli army reoccupied the summit and preparations for the construction of a new watchtower were put in place, thus effectively placing the entire renovated area (and the Bethlehem area at large) under direct Israeli militarized surveillance.

3. The origin of the phrase "a land without a people for a people without a land" is in fact not Zionist or Jewish but Christian. It was coined and propagated by nineteenth-century Christian clergymen advocating for the Jewish return to the land of Israel as part of the fulfillment of biblical prophecy. The first Zionist use of the term came only in the early twentieth century when Israel Zangwill wrote in the New Liberal Review that "Palestine is a country without a people; the Jews are a people without a country." For a detailed account of the history of the phrase and its critique see Diana Muir, " 'A Land without a People for a People without a Land.' "

4. In a long interview from 1998, Ben Tsion Netanyahu, father of the Israeli Prime

Minister Benjamin Netanyahu, was quoted saying the same thing (Shavit, "Ben Tsion Netanyahu").

5. Yehouda Shenhav advocates a similar argument in *Beyond the Two State Solution* (2012), asserting that the traditional analytic framework for thinking about the conflict—a position, which he ascribes to the Israeli Zionist liberal left, that advocates for a return to 1948 borders and an end to the corrupting occupation—has been based on a sharp division between 1948 and 1967. Shenhav highlights the ways in which this conception is based on a historical distortion or "myth" by which Israel violent colonial formulation is done away with.

6. The term used frequently by scholars preoccupied with the politics of vision is "visuality." The field of "visuality studies" emerged as a distinct field of inquiry in the early 1990s. Pioneering studies in the field include Teresa Brennan and Martin Jay, *Vision in Context*; Jonathan Carry, *Techniques of the Observer*; Hal Foster, *Vision and Visuality*; Rosalind Krauss, *The Optical Unconsciousness*.

7. In his study of photojournalism of the Israeli Occupation, visual sociologist Nathansohn concludes that almost all the photographs published in Israeli newspapers "reveal nothing" we don't already know about the Israeli Occupation. Nathansohn's analysis focuses on photographs taken by Israeli journalists, but his critique can certainly be extended to include the great majority of journalistic photographs and images circulating around the globe. The main problem Nathansohn identifies is the need for "immediacy" associated with photojournalism. "The process through which visual knowledge 'becomes news,'" he notes, is greatly responsible for this reproduction of the "familiar" (127). The more familiar a certain visual icon is, the less time is needed for the viewer to read it. News reports tend to favor such familiar images, which ensure the immediacy of the news. The paradoxical outcome is that images that are meant to inform us instead tend to regenerate already familiar settings, thus hardly informing us of anything new.

8. There are numerous books and essays dedicated to the issue of media coverage and media wars in the context of the Israeli-Palestinian conflict. Among these are Mike Berry and Greg Philo, *More Bad News from Israel*; Norman Finkelstein, *Image and Reality of the Israel-Palestine Conflict*; Stephanie Gutmann, *The Other War: Israelis, Palestinians and the Struggle for Media Supremacy*; and Marda Dunsky, *Pens and Swords: How the American Mainstream Media Report the Israeli-Palestinian Conflict*.

9. "Le regard qui voit est un regard qui domine," Michel Foucault, *Naissance de la clinique*, 38. My translation.

10. I am of course speaking in a general manner. I am well aware of the fact that not all Israelis and not all Palestinians see alike and that even within the broader collective/national field of visions one finds different positions and different ways of seeing. The point I am emphasizing, however, is that the governing principle of partition functions as the key element in the distribution of the seeable, thus radically separating Israeli Jews and Palestinians within radically different visual regimes.

11. The phenomena known as "the glorification of death" is presented as a distinctly Islamic culture of death by a wide array of journalists and so-called specialists in Israel and throughout the Western world. It is often part of a broader theoretical framework

that emphasizes a so-called clash of civilizations setting apart Judeo-Christian values from the tradition of Islam. While the first is described as committed to life and free will, the latter is associated with the worship of death and submission to a greater power (God, state rulers, and so on). The father of this theoretical framework and the main source of its academic legitimacy is American professor of Near Eastern studies Bernard A. Lewis. See, for instance, Bernard Lewis, *What Went Wrong? The Clash between Islam and Modernity in the Middle East* (2003), and *The Crisis of Islam: Holy War and Unholy Terror* (2003). Also see Alan Dershowitz, "Does Oppression Cause Suicide Bombing?"

12. For more on the visual representation of Israeli female soldiers see Chava Brownfield-Stein, "Visual Representations of IDF Women Soldiers," and Eva Berger and Dorit Naaman, "Combat Cuties: Photographs of Israeli Women Soldiers."

13. See McClintock, "Slow Violence and BP Coverups." Azoulay and Ophir make a similar distinction between what they call "spectacular violence" and "suspended violence" ("The Monster's Tail" 3). Finally, Nadera Shalhoub-Kevorkain's writing on Palestinian women living under Israeli Occupation further highlights the role of gender and sexuality in the uneven distribution of visibility insofar as violence is concerned. How certain modes of recognizable violence render other ones invisible is her main inquiry with regard to what she calls the "invisibility of violence against women in conflict zones" ("Palestinian Women," 17).

14. The quote is attributed to IDF spokesperson Arye Shalicar (Shabi, "Anger over Ex-Israeli Soldier's Facebook Photos"). Michael Freund advanced a similar position in the *Jerusalem Post*: "the young soldier's bad taste and unsound moral judgment may speak volumes about Aberjil herself, but say nothing about the organization to which she belonged" (Freund, "Washing Dirty Laundry in Public").

15. Following the event, the Israeli human rights organization Breaking the Silence posted their own Facebook pictures of numerous Israeli soldiers posing next to captive Palestinians, declaring that they are aware of many similar photographs taken by Israeli soldiers: "Many Israeli soldiers spend much of their three years of military service in the West Bank, manning checkpoints, and conducting security operations against Palestinians. This is the sort of thing they see every day. When you become used to this sort of behavior, it does not seem a bad thing to photograph it" ("Facebook Photos of Soldiers Posing with Bound Palestinians").

16. Accounting for such split arrangements of space, Israeli architect Eyal Weizman coined the term "politics of verticality." Weizman describes how the same terrain is traveled in two radically separate layers, as if two parallel realities exist: a top one allocated to Jews and a bottom one to Palestinians (Weizman, "The Politics of Verticality").

17. Israel has so far (as of July 2013) completed over 60 percent of the planned Wall's construction. Of this portion, 85 percent is built behind the Green Line (1967 borders) and deep into Palestinian land in the West Bank.

18. Rachel, the wife of Jacob, son of Isaac, is one of the most central female figures in Judaism. Her tomb is located just north of Bethlehem. It is a small building with a white dome, which can no longer be seen as it is completely hidden behind a huge bunker-like structure with guard towers and barbed wire. The way into the tomb (via Jerusalem) is also surrounded with high concrete walls. This is all particularly ironic given that Jewish

women who are unable to give birth are supposed to visit the tomb, which is believed to be a spiritual site and a source of inspiration and future fertility.

19. According to the company, the idea behind the commercial was to contrast the "concrete wall of insult, ugliness and humiliation with beauty, femininity and fashion" (Bennet, "Fashionable Protest").

20. From his early writings on the birth of modern medical discourse to his later writings on various modern disciplinary practices, Foucault highlights the centrality of vision as a means of subjecting and normativizing. In *Discipline and Punish*, Foucault turns to Jeremy Bentham's Panopticon, an architectural structure designed in the eighteenth century as an ideal prison, as an example for what he considers a much wider phenomenon of internalized self-discipline, which characterizes all aspects of modern society. Bentham's Panopticon is an architectural structure of surveillance, comprised of ring-shaped buildings in which all cells face a central watchtower. The goal of the Panopticon is to ensure the complete and ongoing visibility of the prisoners in the cells while further ensuring the invisibility of the guard. Surveillance thus takes the form of an omnipresent invisible gaze. While Bentham's Panopticon serves as Foucault's starting point, he eventually concludes that rendering subjects visible by means of ongoing yet mostly invisible surveillance forces functions as a means of control and discipline in modern times *independent* of particular architectural devices.

21. Ariella Azoulay and Adi Ophir, also referring back to Agamben, advance a very similar argument in "The Monster's Tale." Also see Adi Ophir, "A Time of Occupation."

22. Witnessing and testimony became central critical terms and the subject of numerous books and essays since the late 1980s, increasingly so in the late 1990s and throughout the 2000s. Among the key works in the field of cultural studies are Shoshana Felman and Dori Laub's *Testimony: Crises of Witnessing in Literature, Psychoanalysis, and History* (1992); Georgio Agamben's *Remnants of Auschwitz: The Witness and the Archive* (1999); Kelly Oliver's *Witnessing: Beyond Recognition* (2001); Didier Fassin and Richard Rechtman's *Empire of Trauma: An Inquiry into the Condition of Victimhood* (2009).

23. Breaking the Silence is the first Israeli NGO of its kind, but the practice of collecting and disseminating soldiers' eyewitness accounts and testimonies of atrocities has a much longer history in the context of Israel, beginning with confessional narratives of the 1948 war (notably two of S. Yizhar's most famous short stories "The Prisoner"[Hashavoi] and "Khirbat Khizeh"), and growing after the 1967 war. A famous text in this regard is the book *The Seventh Day: Soldiers Talk about the Six-Day War* by Avraham Shapira, which was published shortly after the war and in which a group of Israeli soldiers' collective testimonies describe the brutal acts they carried out during the war and the conquest of the Palestinian land. In the past few years, several documentary films including testimonies of Israeli soldiers confessing to atrocities committed by themselves or other fellow soldiers have also been released, among them most notably *To See If I'm Smiling* (Tamar Yarom, 2007) and *Z32* (Avi Mograbi, 2008).

24. Seeing is never a simple act of perception but always already a *reading practice* in the sense that "What is 'seen' is always already in part a question of what a certain racist episteme produces as the visible" (Butler, "Endangered/Endangering" 17).

Chapter One: Visible Invisibility

Azmi Bishara quotation translated by the author. Published in Hebrew.

1. For a comparison between Israel's incomplete settler colonial erasure of the past inhabitants of the land in comparison to other more coherently successful settler colonial projects, see Patrick Wolf's "Settler Colonialism and the Elimination of the Native" (2006) and "Structure and Event: Settler Colonialism, Time, and the Question of Genocide " (2008), as well as Lorenzo Veracini's *Israel and Settler Society* (2006) and "Historylessness: Australia as a Settler Colonial Collective" (2007).

2. In the 1950s, Israel's policy toward the remaining ruins of depopulated villages was mainly focused on the elimination of any visible signs that would "serve as a reminder to the Palestinian refugee problem" (Kadman 30). In the 1960s and 1970s, erasure of ruins was still prevalent, but a competing trend of preservation emerged and was informed by the idea that the return of Jews to the promised land meant not just the redemption of the people but also the redemption of the land. Within this mindset, the redemption of the land meant, among other things, "a revival of the landscape which has been said to be destroyed and neglected by the previous inhibiters of the land" (Kadman 38). The bitter irony is that Jews were said to preserve and redeem the ruins that Palestinians were said to have left behind and neglected.

3. In her landmark study of the Israeli artist colony Ein Hod, built in 1953 over the ruins of the Palestinian village Ein Houd, Susan Slyomovics explores the way in which Palestinian ruins have been carefully preserved by the Jewish artists but have been emptied of their actual historical status, instead becoming symbolic markers of "both primitive and ancient features of the landscape" (51).

4. The incorporation of the ruins of Palestinian villages into the Israeli landscape by means of resignification has been the topic of several studies to date, including Walid Khalidi, *All That Remains: The Palestinian Villages Occupied and Depopulated by Israel in 1948* (1992); Meron Benvenisti, *Sacred Landscape: Buried History and the Holy Land since 1948* (2000); Susan Slyomovics, *The Object of Memory* (2000); and Noga Kadman, *Erased from Space and Consciousness* (2008).

5. This is particularly true for the leading artistic school Ofakim chadashim (New Horizons) established in Israel in 1948. Members of the group included Yosef Zritsky, Marcel Janco, Avigdor Stimatsky, Yitzhak Desinger, and Yekheszel Shtriman.

6. The figure of the "deserted village" (*ha-kfar ha-natush*) appears in poetry as well, often representing the narrator's sense of being haunted by memories. See, for example, Ḥaim Gouri's collection *Ha-boker sh-le-macharat* (The Morning-After Poems) (1954) and Hannan Hever's anthology *Al Tagidu Be-Gath: Ha-Nakba ha-Falastinit ba-shirah ha-Ivrit 1948-1958* (Tell It Not in Gath: The Palestinian Nakba in Hebrew Poetry 1948–1958), and earlier poems by Avot Yeshurun.

7. I use the term *allegorical* here in the sense assigned by Walter Benjamin, whose landmark study *The Origin of German Tragic Drama* (1977) has long set the tone for understanding ruins not just in their materiality, but also as a poetic device, a mode of representation, interpretation, and sensibility that emphasizes dissonances and breaks that Benjamin associates especially with the baroque (178–80). Yet, one must also keep in

mind that the ruin in itself "is neither symbol nor allegory but an object of contestations over meaning, memories, histories, and the form in which meaning is presented" (Lloyd, "Ruination" 269). In other words, the question is not about the nature of the ruin as such but about the meaning we ascribe it or the mode of representation in which it appears before us. It is only when the ruin marks an *unobservable* element, a break, or a disturbance that undoes the image of coherence in "the landscape of the present" that we can ascribe to it an allegorical mode of thinking and way of seeing (269).

8. Freud seems to advance this point in highlighting the double meaning of the German word *heimlich*, standing for both belonging and familiar *and* concealed and invisible. Thus, he writes: "In general we are reminded that the word *heimlich* is not unambiguous, but belongs to two sets of ideas, which without being contradictory are yet very different: on the one hand, it means that which is familiar and congenial, and on the other, that which is concealed and kept out of sight" ("The Uncanny," 199).

9. Abraham and Torok suggest, departing from Freud, that haunting occurs not as a result of the actual "return of the repressed," but rather as an outcome of an ongoing failure or inability to face the repressed, resulting in the creation of secrets and the cryptic burial of the repressed trauma within the self (*The Shell and the Kernel*). The legacy of such encryption, they suggest, is found in the transmission of transgenerational trauma, which is buried and sealed with shame. The crypt is therefore where the violent past is kept, simultaneously revealed and hidden.

10. All translations are mine unless otherwise stated, and all references from the novella refer to the Hebrew original, although the novella was recently published in English. See S. Yizhar, *Khirbet Khizeh*, translated by Nicholas de Lange and Yacob Dweck. The title of the English translation uses the common but mistaken Hebrew pronunciation of the Arabic words *hirbah't hize*, thus transliterating the title as *Khirbet Khizeh*. I use this transliteration only when referring to the title of the book in order to avoid confusion. In all other cases I use the correct Arabic transliteration.

11. According to Anita Shapira, the novella, published in September 1949, had sold a total of 4,354 copies by April 1951, which is an undeniably impressive number considering the small number of Hebrew readers of the Jewish Israeli collective (the *yeshuv*) at that time (10). Since 1964 the novella has been incorporated into the Israeli national high school curriculum as a required text.

12. For a great number of critics the main task was to reconcile the violence described in the novella with the principles of Zionist nationalism and universal humanism. See, for instance, Anita Shapira (especially 5–10), and Baruch Kurzweil, *Ben chazon le-ven ha-absurdi*.

13. While some critics suggested that the violence involved in the establishment of the state of Israel and described in the novella is the least of possible evils, others have suggested that the novella ought to be read allegorically and as a universal statement, rather than as a political commentary on any particular sociohistorical or political reality. For allegorical readings of the text, see Dan Miron's "S. Yizhar: Some General Observations," and Gershon Shaked's "Eretz Yisrael ha-yafa shel ha-milim."

14. I borrow this phrase from William Shakespeare's *Hamlet* (Act 1, scene 5, line 190).

15. Derrida opens his deliberation on haunting in *Specters of Marx* with a commentary on Shakespeare's *Hamlet*. He writes, "as in Hamlet, the Prince of a rotten state, every-

thing begins by the apparition of a specter. More precisely by the waiting for this apparition. The anticipation is at once impatient, anxious, and fascinated" (4). "The future,"
Derrida writes a few pages later, "comes back in advance: from the past, from the back"
(10). For Derrida, haunting, or the condition of being haunted, marks not a simple "return of the past" (as in Freud's unveiled repressed) but a temporality that is out of joint—
the return of the future as an anticipation of a returned haunting past and the return of
the past as an anticipated future.

16. All translations from the Hebrew are my own unless otherwise mentioned. Page
numbers refer to the Hebrew edition. English translation of the text is available; see A. B.
Yehoshua, *Three Days and a Child*, translated by Miriam Arad, 131–74.

17. Keren-Kayemeth LeIsrael–Jewish National Funds is an organization established
in 1901 with the goal of carrying out major foresting activities in historical Palestine.
The Hebrew website for the organization includes an elaborate account of various foresting activities divided by decades and locations (not all sections appear on the English
KKL–JNF website). The years 1950–65 seem particularly dense with foresting activities around the mountains surrounding Jerusalem. For details, see: http://www.kkl.org
.il/kkl/hebrew/nosim_ikaryim/al_kakal/history/asorkkl/asorim.x; and the English site:
http://www.kkl.org.il/eng/about-kkl-jnf/our-history/.

18. For more readings on the central role of forest planting within the making of
the Israeli national collective memory, see Carol Bardenstein's "Threads of Memory and
Discourses of Rootedness: Of Trees, Oranges and the Prickly-Pear Cactus in Israel/Pales-
tine," and Shaul-Efraim Cohen's *The Politics of Planting: Israeli-Palestinian Competition for Control of Land in the Jerusalem Periphery* (1993).

19. See, for example, Mordechai Shalev's "Ha-aravim ke-pitaron sifruti" ("The Arabs
as Literary Solution"), Shaked's "Eretz Yisrael," Yael Zerubavel's "The Forest as a National Icon: Literature, Politics, and the Archeology of Memory," and Hannan Hever's
"Rov ke-mi'ut le'umi be-siporet yisra'elit me-reshit shnot ha-60."

20. In several new literary works by young Israeli novelists, the plot centers on the
quest to expose and identify Palestinian ruins concealed under Israeli structures and
landmarks. But in these cases we are no longer speaking about a poetics of haunting
(secrets, the return of the repressed, symptomatic blindness) but about something that
is more akin to a search for historical justice and restoration. Among these works are,
most notably, Tomer Gardi, *Eaven, niyar* (*Stone, Paper*) (2012); Alon Hilu, *Achozat a'ddjani*
(*The House of Dajani*) (2008); and Eshkol Nevo, *Arba'a batim ve-ga'agu'a* (*Homesick*) (2004).

21. I am of course using "crypt" in reference to Abraham and Torok's theory of transgenerational trauma. The refusal to mourn, resulting in the creation of a "psychic tomb"
(22) in the form of a secret passed from one generation to another that harbors the undead ghosts. An "entombment" (16) that makes the living themselves become more
like "living dead." This idea is developed primarily in their chapter dedicated to Freud's
"Mourning and Melancholia" (125–39) and in the following chapter, "The Lost Object-
Me" (139–56).

22. Describing ruins caused by human violence as sites haunted by a traumatic past,
Dylan Trigg writes that "the formal features of the ruin are situated in an ambiguous
zone, whereby what remains is defined by what is absent" (95).

23. The village Suba was conquered during the 1948 war. The ruins of the depopulated village remained intact for the most part and have blended into the landscape of the mountain. Signs placed by JNF along the walking paths nearby ignore the visible ruins.

24. Several other Israeli artists, particularly from the 1990s and 2000s, center on the image of the ruins of evacuated Palestinian villages in an attempt to revisit the melancholic and picturesque status of these ruins in earlier Israeli landscape paintings. These include works by photographer Shoka Glutman and painters Dina Shenhav, David Reeb, Ruth Shlus, and Avner Ben-Gal, among others.

25. Zritsky lived in Kibbutz Tsuba in the early 1970s and painted the view from his studio. He completed numerous paintings of the hills of Tsuba between 1970 and the mid-1980s.

26. The phrase "A land without a people for a people without a land" was coined and propagated by nineteenth-century Christian clergymen advocating for the Jewish return to the land of Israel as part of the fulfillment of biblical prophecy. The first Zionist use of the term came only later, in the early twentieth century, when Israel Zangwill wrote in the *New Liberal Review* that "Palestine is a country without a people; the Jews are a people without a country." For more details see Diana Muir, "'A Land without a People for a People without a Land.'"

Chapter Two: From Invisible Spectators to the Spectacle of Terror

The epigraph to this chapter appears in "Situated Knowledge," 64–65.

1. "Palestinian citizens of Israel" refers to Palestinians who remained in Palestine after 1948 and became citizens of Israel soon after. In Arabic these Palestinians are known as the Arabs "of the inside" (*min al-dakhil*). In Hebrew these Palestinians are referred to as "the Arab inhabitants" (*ha-toshavim ha-aravim*) or as "Israeli Arabs" (*Aravim Israelim*). I use the term "Palestinian Israelis" to mark the national identity and the citizenship status of this population. By comparison, the majority of the Palestinians living in East Jerusalem hold the status of "permanent residents" of Israel, but they are not for the most part granted Israeli citizenship. There has been, however, a strong indication that a growing number of Palestinian residents of East Jerusalem are seeking (and in some cases gaining) Israeli citizenship. See Riman Barakat, "Quietly East Jerusalem Palestinians Acquiring Israeli Citizenship."

2. The trilogy comprises three chronicles: *Chronicle of a Disappearance* (1996), followed by *Divine Intervention*, which is subtitled *A Chronicle of Love and Pain* (2002), and, finally, *The Time That Remains* (2009), which is subtitled *Chronicle of Present Absentee*. The latter was released after the completion of this chapter. It also differs in many ways from the previous two in that it follows a more conventional narrative format typical of a docudrama.

3. While the great majority of Palestinians living within the 1948 borders are Israeli citizens, their citizenship status is managed by various displacement mechanisms that severely restrict their civil rights. Consider, for example, the fact that nearly 300,000 Palestinian Israeli citizens are still known today as "present absentees." After their families fled their homes in 1948, they became recognized as present in Israel but absent from

their property, meaning that they are permanently denied any right to family property even though they supposedly enjoy equal rights as citizens. In addition, close to 100,000 Bedouin Israeli citizens live today in unrecognized villages whose names do not appear on any official Israeli map. These villages receive no state services, as they do not officially exist. For a detailed account see Joseph Schechia, "The Invisible People Come to Light."

4. Derrida notes that while the specter remains invisible, we nevertheless continue to feel it watching: "we feel ourselves observed, sometimes under surveillance by it even before any apparition" (101).

5. Signed in 1993, the Oslo Accords mark the first and most supported internationally recognized attempt to resolve the Israeli-Palestinian conflict. The optimistic state of mind during the years immediately following Oslo gave bloom to a flowery rhetoric of coexistence, particularly in regard to the relationship between Jewish and Palestinian citizens of Israel. In reality, however, this rhetoric of coexistence amounted to little more than a financially driven and short-lived collaborative attempt to transform Palestinian villages in Israel into new and somewhat exotic tourist sites for Jewish Israeli visitors. Contrary to the promising rhetoric, and perhaps even to some original good intentions, the impact of the Oslo Accords on the daily reality of Palestinian citizens of Israel (and most certainly on Palestinians living in the Occupied Territories) has been devastating. While the negative impact of the Oslo Accords on the Palestinian population within the Occupied Territories has been discussed in detail (see, for example, Eyal Wiezman's *Hollow Land: Israel's Architecture of Occupation* [2007], Saree Makdisi's *Palestine Inside Out: An Everyday Occupation* [2008], and Nathan Brown's *Palestinian Politics after the Oslo Accords: Resuming Arab Palestine* [2003]), significantly less attention has been given to the negative impact of the Accords on Palestinians residing within the pre-1967 Israeli borders. According to Cook "before Oslo, Israel was chiefly interested in containing and controlling the minority. After Oslo, it has been trying to engineer a situation in which it can claim to no longer be responsible for the Palestinians inside Israel with formal citizenship" (Cook, "The Decline"). A special report prepared by Adalah (the legal center for Arab minority rights in Israel) also suggests worsening economic and overall living conditions of 1948 Palestinians: "while many Palestinian Israeli citizens [initially] believed that their situation would improve with the signing of the Oslo Accords, they [soon enough] found themselves excluded from the peace process, and their civic and socio-economic status unilaterally neglected and declined" ("Historical Background").

6. This sense of radical invisibility and ongoing disappearance is similarly brought to life in the 2004 novel *Let It Be Morning (Va-yehi boker)* by Palestinian Israeli writer Sayed Kashua, which elaborates on the option of, without consulting with Palestinian Israeli citizens, exchanging Palestinians residing within Israel for so-called Jewish land in the West Bank. For a full account, see my essay "To Be or Not to Be an Israeli Arab: Sayed Kashua and the Prospect of Minority Speech Acts."

7. For an excellent essay on the ghettoized architecture of Nazareth, see Samir Srouji, "Nazareth: Intersecting Narratives of Modern Architectural Histories." For a Deleuzian reading of Suleiman's "ghettoized" rendition of space and characters, see the fine essay by Patricia Pisters entitled "Violence and Laughter: Paradoxes of Nomadic Thought in Postcolonial Cinema."

8. The scene sparked major controversy in the Arab world, where the film was eventually banned. Commenting on this regretful incident, Suleiman notes, "They misunderstood the irony of the use of the Israeli flag in the final scene and accused me of being a Zionist collaborator" ("A Breakdown of Communication").

9. This division between the male and female protagonists is accompanied by several other divisions: passivity and activity, observation and participation, the mundane and the fantastic. For an important critique of Suleiman's poetics of gender and sexual difference, see Anna Ball, "Between a Postcolonial Nation."

10. Recently writing about the outcome of the fall 2000 mass demonstrations in support of Palestinians in the Occupied Territories that took place in various Palestinian Israeli towns, Budour Youssef Hassan notes that despite the tragic outcome of these demonstrations (with the Israeli police claiming the lives of thirteen Palestinian Israeli citizens), they nevertheless mark an important and publically commemorated historical transition for the majority of Palestinians living in Israel: "For the first time, we as 1948 Palestinians (Palestinians with Israeli citizenship) felt relevant. . . . We did not just watch the news and comment about a Palestine so close, yet so far away from us. We actually *made the news*" ("The Second Intifada," my emphasis).

11. To date, and contrary to the recommendations made by the Or Commission after examining the events, no indictment was brought against any of the officers involved in the shooting. For detailed reports of the events of October 2000 and the following attempts to initiate a legal investigation of the police, see Adalah's website.

12. In a study conducted in 2006 by Israeli psychologist Daniel Bar-Tal, the events of October 2000 appear to have had a great impact on the negative stereotypic status of Palestinian Israeli citizens among the Israeli Jewish population. Out of the 847 Israeli Jewish participants in the study, close to 40 percent recommended banning Palestinian Israeli political parties. Out of them, 72 percent agreed that the best definitions for Palestinian citizens of Israel were "fifth column" and "enemy of the state," 57 percent agreed with the definition "terrorists," and 48 percent agreed with the definitions "barbarians" and "beasts" (*Living with the Conflict*, 237).

13. The trope of an impossible love between a Palestinian from Israel and a lover from the Occupied Territories is also at the heart of Hany Abu-Assad's *Rana's Wedding* ('*Urs Rana* 2002). For more on the Palestinian cinematic trope of weddings as a mode of resistance to the occupation and its relation to the checkpoint as a site of divide/unification, see Nadia Yaqub, "The Palestinian Cinematic Wedding."

14. Suleiman's early film *Introduction to the End of an Argument* (1990), produced with Jayce Salloum, could be considered an early version of a similar practice of citation parody described by Ella Shohat and Robert Stam in terms of how it "hilariously deconstructs mass-media orientalism" (*Unthinking* 13).

15. A different and more interesting interpretation is advanced by Anna Ball, who argues that the film's fantastic scenes of victory and revenge do not express a collective Palestinian fantasy as much as a distinctively *male* fantasy. According to Ball, the figure of the resilient Palestinian femme fatal stands for "Suleiman's wish-fulfilling fantasy" and is modeled on a familiar and somewhat reactionary national imagination in which the male subject (the film's protagonist and the film director) is "a dreamer" and "a visionary," while the female character functions as "the object of [his] national fanta-

sies" and a figure who displays traditional feminine qualities "of the sensuous, erotic, and intimate: the realms of romantic fantasy" ("Between a Postcolonial Nation" 18, 24).

16. In his review of the film, Dennis Grunes writes: "Suleiman has made a very fine film [that] is visually exciting. But . . . his spectacular scene of Jewish slaughter is way out of his control, especially in terms of its more dire implications. Regrettably, the relentless Palestinian killing of innocent Jews is the reality that Suleiman fails everywhere to acknowledge" ("Divine Intervention").

17. Haim Bresheeth similarly notes the centrality given to cinematic references, including the syntax of cinema, in Divine Intervention. He writes: "A pumped-up balloon—with obvious cinematic references—but also a pastiche of Arafat connects the hopes of Palestine to the symbol of its identity, the Al Aqsa mosque, which gave its name to the Second Intifada. . . . This mélange—Arafat, Suleiman, his 'superwoman' girlfriend, musical and action extravaganza, Christ's crown of thorns, the Intifada—provides the elements in a narrative rich with cinematic references" ("The Nakba Projected" 502).

Chapter Three: The (Soldier's) Gaze and the (Palestinian) Body

1. Sharif Waked lives and works in Haifa and Nazareth. While his work has long been appreciated in Palestine, Israel, and elsewhere in the Middle East, he has more recently gained a broader international recognition thanks to his video work To Be Continued (2009), which is now part of the Guggenheim's permanent collection in New York.

2. There is now a vast body of work dedicated to the evolution of the Israeli checkpoints and the changing nature of the so-called modernized terminals. See, among others, Eyal Weizman's chapter on the checkpoints in his Hollow Land: Israel's Architecture of Occupation; Yehudit Kirstein Keshet, Checkpoint Watch: Testimonies from Occupied Palestine; Elisha Efrat, The West Bank and Gaza Strip: A Geography of Occupation; Daniela Mansbach, "Normalizing Violence"; Hagar Kotef and Merav Amir, "Between Imaginary Lines"; and Ayelet Maoz, "The Privatization of the Checkpoints."

3. For a detailed analysis, see Irus Braverman's excellent essay "Civilized Borders." Also see Shira Havkin's "The Reform," describing in detail the complex process of privatization involved in the management of the checkpoints since 2005.

4. For more on security exceptionalism, see Gil Merom's "Israel's National Security and the Myth of Exceptionalism."

5. Numerous critics have elaborated on the gendered nature of nationalism (Anthias and Yuval-Davis, Women-Nation-State; MacKinnon, Towards a Feminist Theory of the State; and Mayer, Women and the Israeli Occupation, to mention but a few), and several have explored the intimate ties between modern masculinity and nationhood (Mosse, The Image of Man; Mayer, Gender Ironies of Nationalism; and Nagel, "Masculinity and Nationalism"). Others have elaborated on the heteronormativity of the nation-state, revealing the how the coherence of the nation depends not only on an economy of gender differences (the idea that men and women have different and unequal positions and that they fulfill distinct roles within the nation/family), but also on a continual performance of normative sexualities and the casting out of so-called non-national sexualities and bodies (Berlant, The Queen of America; Warner, The Trouble with Normal; Puar, Terrorist Assemblages; and Axel, The Nation's Turtured Body). Both Amal Amirah and Joseph Massad have written specifically

about the masculine prefiguration of the Palestinian national narrative (Amirah, "Between Complicity and Subversion"; Massad, "Conceiving the Masculine").

6. That this cultural trope is reminiscent of the early Zionist articulation of Jewish national redemption is bitterly ironic. Accounting for Zionism as a gendered ideology, Daniel Boyarin has convincingly argued that, from its inception, Zionism has been concerned with the need to *regenerate* Jewish masculinity and redeem it from its historical ties to effeminacy and homosexuality, no less than with the need to establish a Jewish national territorial center. The (anti-Semitic) idea that the Jewish man was inherently queer (effeminate, prone to homosexuality, physically weak, unhealthy, and contaminating), Boyarin argues, has haunted the project of modern Jewish emancipation and culminated in the Zionist commitment to creating a *new* manly and heterosexual Jew. Zionism, he therefore concludes, is a masculinist ideology based on internalized anti-Semitism and homophobia. Others have since elaborated on these ideas, tracing the rejection of the prototypical weak, effeminate, and diasporic *Ostjuden* figure in favor of a new muscular and national Jew, while further arguing that the threat of homosexuality (that is, the fear of becoming, *yet again*, associated with homosexuality) continues to dominate contemporary Jewish Israeli culture, even in its most chauvinistic and triumphant moments, feeding its obsessive preoccupation with militarization and heterosexualization. See Boyarin, *Unheroic Conduct: The Rise of Heterosexuality and the Invention of the Jewish Man*; Mayer, "From Zero to Hero: Nationalism and Masculinity in Jewish Israel"; Yosef, "Homoland: Interracial Sex and the Israeli-Palestinian Conflict in Israeli Cinema"; and Gluzman, "Longing for Heterosexuality: Zionism and Sexuality in Herzl's *Altneuland*."

7. As Joseph Massad notes, the Israeli soldier is portrayed either as the dangerous aggressor who has "raped the land" (from the Palestinian point of view), or as the protector/lover who has "saved/fertilized the land" (from the Israeli point of view) ("Conceiving the Masculine" 467–77). In both cases, the Israeli soldier is perceived as a heterosexual man whose masculinity (directed at the feminine land) is greater than that of the Palestinian. For a related argument, see Kawash, "Nation, Place, and Placelessness: Identity, Body, and Geography in the Case of Palestine."

8. Susan Sontag has famously argued, "while it's not true that Camp taste is homosexual taste, there is no doubt a peculiar affinity and overlap . . . not all homosexuals have Camp taste. But homosexuals, by and large, constitute the vanguard and the most articulate audience of Camp" ("Notes on Camp").

9. The fantasy of the sexy terrorist is explicitly elaborated on in the Israeli film *The Bubble* (dir. Eytan Fox, 2006). But while Waked works *with* and *against* the fantasy, exposing its role as part of a broader system of colonial control, Fox's film appears to uncritically embrace the fantasy. Indeed, the narrative of a homosexual bond between an Israeli soldier and a young Palestinian man seems to be modeled on this fantasy from beginning to end. For an elaborate reading of *The Bubble* along these lines see Stein, "Explosive: Scenes from Israel's Gay Occupation."

10. For a reading of the occupied Palestinian body through the lens of Georgio Agamben's notion of "bare life," see Enns, "Bare Life and the Occupied Body."

Chapter Four: Visual Rights and the Prospect of Exchange

The Handel quotation that serves as the epigraph is from "Notes on the Senses," 160.

1. Azoulay develops these ideas at length in her 2006 book *Ha-amana ha-chevratit shel ha-tsilum*. MIT Press released an English translation of the book in 2008 as *The Civil Contract of Photography*.

2. Rula Halawani is an internationally renowned Palestinian photographer based in East Jerusalem. Halawani began her career as a photojournalist, making a break with photojournalism and shifting to alternative modes of photography in the late 1990s. In 2000 she founded the photography program at Birzeit University, where she currently teaches.

3. For a more detailed discussion of these changes, see the previous chapter.

4. Both quotations are taken from a personal interview with the author (Jerusalem, May 22, 2013).

5. Azoulay in part developed this argument in her 2007 exhibit and following book publication *Ma'ase Medina: Historiya metsulemet shel ha-kibush 1967–2007* (*Act of State: A Photographic History of the Occupation, 1967–2007*). Curated by Azoulay, the exhibit included over six hundred photographs collected from several Israeli state archives and taken by Israeli photographers between 1967 and 2007, in addition to long textual comments written by Azoulay.

6. Photography has been repeatedly accused of failing to turn seeing into an effective ethical reflection or political intervention. John Berger, for example, has argued that the violence captured in photographic images of war results in an inevitable depoliticized reaction on the part of the spectators, whose confrontation with the images of horror only result in her/his sense of "personal moral inadequacy" (280). Roland Barthes has similarly expressed concern over the ability of photographs to produce a political reaction in their viewers, suggesting that "photographs that are meant to shock us have no effect at all" (71). Growing ever more suspicious of the medium, Allan Sekula has suggested that photography "has contributed much to spectacle . . . to voyeurism, to terror, envy and nostalgia, and only a little to the critical understanding of the social world" (57); and Susan Sontag famously concluded that "photography has done at least as much to deaden consciousness as to arouse it" (*On Photography* 21).

7. I elaborate on this humanitarian framework and its reliance on visual evidence of suffering in the following chapter.

8. Personal interview with the artist (Jerusalem, May 22, 2013).

9. Jarrar has since gained international recognition for his project *Live and Work in Palestine*. The project involves Jarrar's performative act of taking the role of a state representative and stamping the passports of foreigners visiting the Palestinian Occupied Territories. The stamp, created by Jarrar, carries the slogan "State of Palestine." The project has now expanded to include staged appearances of Jarrar and his stamp worldwide. For more, see the Facebook page linked to the project: http://www.facebook.com /lawi.pal. Jarrar is currently working on producing "sport goods" from cement parts he manages to remove from the separation wall.

10. Jarrar's exhibit was the second event in the "30 Days against Checkpoints Campaign," which was organized by the Nablus-based group HASM (Palestinian Body for Peace, Dialogue, and Equality). In the first action at Hawara checkpoint, on January 14, 2007, Palestinian youth dressed up as Native Americans and displayed banners linking the fate of the indigenous peoples of America and Palestine.

11. Jarrar conveyed this information to me during my interview with him on December 2, 2010.

12. In his interview with me, Jarrar mentioned that when faced with the demand to look at the photographs and take responsibility for the their wrongdoing ("Look what you are doing to us!") most soldiers simply looked away. One soldier responded, however, saying, "What do you want from me? I am not in that picture!" It was hard to tell, Jarrar explained, "if he was being cynical. It almost felt like he believed what he was saying: he wasn't in the picture, so all this was not his fault" (Ramallah, September 2011).

13. These are the words of Dorit Herskkovits, member of the grassroots organization Machsom Watch, as quoted in Ruthie Ginsburg, "Taking Pictures over Soldiers' Shoulders" 27.

14. Quotes taken from a personal interview with the artist via Skype (recorded December 12, 2010).

15. Quotes taken from a personal interview with the artist (Ramallah, September 2011).

Chapter Five: "Nothing to Look At"; or, "For Whom Are You Shooting?"

1. Lori Allen notes that in the 2000s, "human rights and other NGOs flourished [in the West Bank] as the Israeli occupation took on a new rhythm. . . . It soon became clear that there was a common collective recognition of human rights, and the state-in-the-making, as a performance. . . . '[H]uman rights' was a pretense, a façade that everyone recognized as such but was feigning to keep up nevertheless" ("New Texts Out Now," *Jadaliyya*). In her recently published book, *The Rise and Fall of Human Rights*, Allen provides a detailed ethnographic account of this process, which she astutely describes as the "NGOization of political activism" and the emergence of the "Human Rights Industry" in Palestine, tracing it from the early 1990s to the present (97).

2. "Homeworks 4: A Forum on Cultural Practices" commissioned the film. The Homeworks Forum, organized by Ashkal Alwan (Lebanese Association for Plastic Arts), is a multidisciplinary project that brings together artists, writers, and intellectuals to present their work every eighteen months in exhibition and performance venues throughout Beirut. Homeworks 4 (April 12–20, 2008) invited participants to contemplate the theme of representing disaster and catastrophe.

3. The essay film genre incorporates text and image and follows what can be loosely defined as an essay format. The genre is commonly characterized by its own fragmentation and the avoidance of closure. Most film scholars agree that the attempt to define the essay film have so far been only *partially* successful mainly because of the hybrid form of the genre itself, which crosses between fiction and nonfiction cinema, and between cinematic and noncinematic qualities. For work on the classification of the essay film (also known as the cinematic essay), see Nora Alter, "The Political Im/perceptible

in the Essay Film: Farocki's *Images of the World and the Inscription of War*"; Phillip Lopate, "In Search of the Centaur: The Essay-Film"; Michael Renov, *The Subject of the Documentary*; and Laura Rascaroli, "The Essay Film: Problems, Definitions, Textual Commitments." Among the originators of this cinematic genre are Chris Marker, Alain Resnais, Agnès Varda, and Jean-Luc Godard. Later known directors working in the genre include Chantal Ackerman, Werner Herzog, Harun Farocki, and Isaac Julian.

4. For more on the state of exception in this particular context, see David Lloyd, "Settler Colonialism and the State of Exception: The Example of Israel/Palestine"; Sari Hanafi, "Explaining Spacio-cide in the Palestinian Territory: Colonization, Separation, and State of Exception"; and Adi Ophir, Michal Givoni, and Sari Hanafi, eds., *Power of Inclusive Exclusion: Anatomy of the Israeli Rule in the Occupied Palestinian Territories*.

5. In her conversation with the Otolith Group, Irmgard Emmelhainz commends the film's avoidance of "current documentary representations of the Palestinian ordeal," the ineffectiveness of which are attested to by the circulation of the term "Pallywood" (Emmelhainz and the Otolith Group 129). The term "Pallywood" was coined by Boston University professor Richard Landes following the controversy surrounding the authenticity of video recording of the death of twelve-year-old Mohammad al Durah, who was shot by Israeli soldiers in 2000. Some critics alleged the video was staged.

6. The underlying presupposition guiding this mode of documentation is that a direct connection exists between suffering and political entitlement, as well as between seeing or witnessing suffering and political action/intervention. These assumptions are well grounded in the post–World War II discourse of international human rights in which witnessing operates as "the idiom in which individuals speak back to power" (Givoni 149). Associated with the *exposure* of otherwise unreported, invisible, or undermined atrocities, "witnessing" and "providing testimony" became "the primary ethical configuration of the age of globalism" (Givoni 162).

7. Amir and Kotef convincingly argue that within the Israeli public and militarized discourse the Palestinian body is imagined along strict gender divisions: while the *masculinized* Palestinian body signifies terror and danger (the mark of the potential suicide bomber, the terrorist, the body on the verge of explosion), the *feminized* Palestinian body (prefigured most explicitly in the body of the woman giving birth at the checkpoints) symbolizes helplessness, suffering, and complete subjection. This artificial dichotomy through which the Palestinian body is constructed as either terrorist/victim makes for the complete occupied subject: the subject who lacks a valid political agency or a nuanced political judgment ("[En]Gendering Checkpoints" 978–79).

8. Writing about the barbaric zone constructed by the visualization of suffering, Pramod Nayar writes: "the visuals of Darfur's refugee camps, the survivor tales from 26/11 . . . sufferings of patients in hospitals construct space we are forced to watch suffering . . . those who cannot speak who are consigned by their suffering to spaces beyond speech and self representation . . . are given names, faces, and are recreated as individualized sufferers" (152).

9. A relevant argument is presented in Susan Sontag's *Regarding the Pain of Others*.

10. See throughout Demos, "The Right to Opacity: On the Otolith Group's *Nervus Rerum*."

11. For a related discussion, see Libby Saxton's essay "Fragile Faces," in which she

brings Levinas' philosophy of ethics to bear on Claude Lanzmann's monumental documentary *Shoah* and on Lanzmann's refusal to visualize the traumatic past.

12. The existence of a refugee camp, of course, is due to the creation of the Palestinian refugee problem in 1948. Since 1948, Palestinians in the West Bank and Gaza have lived under occupation and endure the daily violence of such exceptional conditions. When events such as the violent Israeli military attack that took place in Jenin in 2002 erupt and receive media attention, they are seen as violent eruptions of otherwise a nonviolent daily reality. What remains invisible and hidden, then, is the ongoing violence that marks daily life in a refugee camp, which fails to appear as violence.

13. Other parts of the testimony are blocked out by the eerie synthesized soundtrack written by British musician Ryan Teague.

14. The division between victim and fighter brings to mind Gayatri Spivak's argument about the Sati, in which she demonstrated the manner by which the subaltern is always framed and understood through the tension between the two positions: victimhood and resistance. See "Can the Subaltern Speak?"

15. For Glissant, "opacity" stands for the fundamental unknowability of the Other: a fundamental refusal or failure to become the object of knowledge. This refusal/failure, he maintains, is first and foremost a *visual matter*. The colonial history he unfolds in his discussions about the Caribbean is one in which knowledge is inscribed by means of visual classifications and naming. The violence inherent in the gaze of the colonialist master is the violence of assuming knowledge of the Other from a position of power: the power to classify and represent. The key, then, for escaping the invasive violence of (colonial) oppression lies in hiding: hiding, as it were, from the intruding eyes of the master and escaping the trap of being positioned in one's own designated place within the master's system of classification and representation. My understanding of Glissant's "opacity" as a form of *anticolonial resistance* is not so much a resistance to cultural assimilation (a reading Celia M. Britton advances in *Edouard Glissant and Postcolonial Theory: Strategies of Language and Resistance*) as it is resistance to taking one's place within a predetermined system of representation, which is, as such, subjected to a preexisting hierarchal power dynamic.

16. Unlike the majority of documentary filmmakers working in Palestine, Eshun and Sagar arrived at the scene with their camera *as outsiders*. To begin with, as Britons, their position as filmmakers is closer to that of foreign media news crews. In other words, coming to film the refugee camp and its inhabitants as British filmmakers places Sagar and Eshun in a complicated position vis-à-vis the goal of producing knowledge, and it is from this complicated position that they set out to interrogate the limits of ethnographic filmmaking.

17. At times the matching between text and image slips into an overbearing didacticism. Many of the paragraphs chosen from Pessoa's and Genet's texts focus on the obscurity of images and their complex relationship to the Real. Other paragraphs focus on the relationship between life and death: "What we call life is the slumber of our real life, the death of who really are" or "we are dead when we think we're living; we start living when we die." Sagar reads Pessoa as the camera slides through the narrow streets of the refugee camps, stopping at times on posters of shahids (martyrs). The message here is too obviously stated: life in the refugee camp is sometimes closer to death, while

death offers the only opening to life. Similar didactic uses of the narrative run through the film, as in the section in which Sagar reads Genet's contemplation on images: "the image shows what it shows, but what does it hide?" Here the lines remind us a little too explicitly of the danger involved in our naïve trust in images or in the camera's capacity to document in the sense of transcribing truth (the danger *Nervus Rerum* as a whole is seeking to escape in its rejection of the testimonial mode of filmmaking).

18. It is worth noting the similarities in titles between Al Sharif's film, *We Began by Measuring Distance*, and the earlier experimental video by Mona Hatoum, *Measures of Distance* (1981). To the best of my knowledge, there is no direct intertextual relationship between these two works, which, although similar in title, otherwise significantly differ.

19. Al Sharif has confirmed that the image was taken from footage she received from a news agency during the Cast Lead operation, and so one is inclined to identify the women and children as Gazans. We never find out whether the images are in fact from Gaza, but, as Al Sharif notes, this does not necessarily matter: "the very proximity of the event to the images has already shifted how all other news footage would be read. The [Israeli] bombs render all footage [of destruction] Gazan."

20. Interview with the artist conducted via several e-mail exchanges between October 27, 2010, and November 19, 2010. All subsequent quotes from Al Sharif refer back to this interview.

21. It is important to note that the Arabic word (here in the Egyptian colloquial) *betwattar* means (emotional) "tension" and implies a sense of nervousness, restlessness, anxiety, and agitation that seems to escape the English translation "stressed."

22. "Growing up," Al Sharif comments, "I was bombarded with facts, figures, numbers, dates, names of leaders, places, cities, and events. . . . [A]s I grew older the collection grew more confusing: dates got mixed up with events and cities with treaties. . . . I wanted to return to the numbers' 'pure' arithmetic value."

23. The text accompanying the "Virgin Forest" sequence is from the introduction of a report entitled "Ecological Characteristics of Old-Growth Douglas-Fir Forests," from the U.S. Department of Agriculture. It is the only part of the narrative that Al Sharif did not write.

24. The soundtrack for this opening scene comes from news footage of a girl named Huda Ghaliya, whose family was shelled on a Gaza beach in 2006. News crews arrived before the ambulances and found the girl running from one deceased family member to another. The story made headlines, and the visual footage soon became iconic. Al Sharif's refusal to show the images has partially to do with what she describes as the short life span of horror images, especially in Gaza, where perpetual violence quickly brings about the replacement of "one iconic image with another."

25. Thus, for example, when the narrator announces that the group of people conducting the various measurements "took [their] measurements elsewhere / to find a distance between two points, to fix our text to," the text the narrator refers to soon appears in the frame as a subtitle, situated between the two trees where the fabric is held. Similarly, when he contests that the "distance is a bit too short," this distance may refer to the distance between the two trees seen in the frame, or indeed to the length of the subtitle.

26. The voice-over footage, like the visual images of the woman, is constructed from video belonging to independent Egyptian newscast footage, likely from Gaza. Al Sha-

rif translates the plea of the woman, which in Arabic literally means "for whom are you filming [us]?" to "for whom are you shooting [us]," in accordance with her translation of the first scene in the film in which the young girl pleas for the camera to film/shoot her father.

Chapter Six: Shooting War

The epigraph to this chapter is from *Unclaimed Experience*, 100.

1. This depiction appears to be true for iconic American Vietnam films such as *Platoon* (Oliver Stone, 1986) and *Apocalypse Now* (Francis Ford Coppola, 1979), as well as more recent films about the war in Iraq such as *The Hurt Locker* (Kathryn Bigelow, 2008) and *StopLoss* (Kimberly Peirce, 2008). It is also true for some of the landmark German films about WWII, for example, *Das Boot* (*The Boat*) (Wolfgang Petersen, 1981) and *Der Untergang* (*Downfall*) (Oliver Hirschbeigel, 2004), and for many Israeli "antiwar war films," such as *Echad Mi'Shelanu* (*One of Us*) (Uri Barbash 1989), *Kippur* (Amos Gitai, 2000), and *Bufor* (*Beaufort*) (Joseph Cedar, 2007).

2. Perhaps more than any of Freud's readers, Lacan emphasizes the scopic nature of trauma and the correlation between the failure to see (on time) and ethical failure, which for Lacan constitutes the site of trauma. The traumatized person is traumatized, Lacan suggests, precisely because s/he is forced to over and over again revisit her/his previous failure to see. See Lacan, "Touché and Automaton," in *The Four Fundamental Concepts of Psychoanalysis*. For a later articulation of this similar idea see Elizabeth A. Brett and Robert Ostroff, "Imagery and Posttraumatic Stress Disorder: An Overview."

3. Commenting on Lacan's infamous reading of the burning child dream, originally introduced and analyzed by Freud in *The Interpretation of Dreams*, Caruth offers a similar understanding of trauma and repetition compulsion. In the dream, a child calls on his sleeping father to wake up and see him burning ("Father, don't you see that I am burning?"). This call, which comes from within the father's own unconscious, does indeed wake him up. However, "as a response to the child's request, the plea to be seen," this awakening only repeats a previous failure to see on time: "waking up in order to see, the father discovers that he has once again *seen too late* to prevent the burning" (100).

4. The estimated number of victims ranges from seven hundred to eight hundred according to Israeli military intelligence, up to two thousand victims according to various reports given by the Lebanese authorities, and to over three thousand according to Israeli journalist Amnon Kapeliouk in his published report *Sabra et Chatila: Enquête sur un massacre*.

5. Israeli invaded Leadon for the second time in July 2006 following a Hezbollah attack on an Israeli patrol, which occurred on the Israeli side of the border with Lebanon, and the abduction of two Israeli soldiers. The 2006 Lebanon War, known in Arabic as the July War (*Harb Tammuz*) and in Hebrew as the Second Lebanon War (*Milchemet Levanon ha-shniya*) lasted for thirty-four days (from July 12 to August 14) and ended with both sides (Israel and Hezbollah) claiming victory.

6. See Kirsten E. Schulze, "Israeli Crisis Decision-Making in the Lebanon War: Group Madness or Individual Ambition?"

7. They are *Shtie etsbaot mitsidon* (Ricochets) (Eli Cohen, 1986); *Onat ha-duvdevanim* (Cherry Season) (Haim Bouzaglo, 1991); *Gmar gavi'a* (Final Cup) (Eran Riklis, 1991); *Yossi ve Jager* (Yossi and Jagger) (Eytan Fox, 2002); *Bufor* (Beaufort) (Yosef Sidar, 2007). It is interesting to note that in contrast to the great number of films made about the Israeli military presence in Lebanon not a single Israeli feature film has been made about the Israeli occupation of the West Bank and Gaza.

8. This question appears to frame and limit the discussion of the films in the great majority of reviews. For example, see John Rosenthal ("*Waltz with Bashir*, Nazi Germany"); Hillel Halkin ("The Waltz with Bashir"); Natalie Rothschild (*Waltz with Bashir: Post-Zionist Stress Disorder*); and Ursula Lindsey ("Shooting Film and Crying").

9. Against this narrow view one can find a vast literature on the particularly dubious position of the soldier as both perpetrator and victim, also known in the professional literature as "victimizer victims." See, for example, Kali Tal, *Worlds of Hurt: Reading the Literatures of Trauma*; Omar Bartov, "Defining Enemies, Making Victims: Germans, Jews, and the Holocaust"; and Gabriele Schwab, *Haunting Legacies: Violent Histories and Transgenerational Trauma*.

10. For instance, see Robert Moses Pealsee ("It's Fine as Long as You Draw"); Ohad Landsman and Roy Bendor ("Animated Recollection"); Andrew Wright ("More Than Ink"); Reuben Ross ("Waltz with Bashir and Persepolis").

11. One must note Laor's own infantilization of animation as a genre. He mentions *Bambi* and *Fritz the Cat* but ignores the important tradition of the political graphic novel (including Art Speigelman's *Maus*, and Joe Sacco's *Footnotes in Gaza*) and, even more specifically, the tradition of the animated documentary cinema that includes *Drawn from Memory* (Paul and Sandra Fierlinger, 1991), *Pro and Con* (Joanne Priestly and Joan Gratz, 1992), and *Ryan* (Chris Landreth, 2004).

12. For readings along these lines, see Raz Yosef, "War Fantasies: Memory, Trauma and Ethics in Ari Folman's *Waltz with Bashir*"; Garrett Stewart, "Screen Memory in *Waltz with Bashir*"; and Natasha Jane Mansfield, "Loss and Mourning: Cinema's 'Language' of Trauma in *Waltz with Bashir*."

13. The latter possibility is explicitly articulated in the film in a somewhat didactic manner when Folman's psychologist tells him how easy it is to manipulate one's memory and how mysterious memory can be: "It is quite fascinating," he recounts, "how easy it is to install memories into people's minds. . . . You simply show them an image and then tell them a narrative about their own past in relation to that image. Initially they may claim not to remember, but eventually, as they look at the image through the narrative they hear, they come to remember. They even give details of events they never experienced or saw."

14. In the works of Jean Baudrillard and Paul Virilio we find an elaborated concern with the growing aestheticization and consumption of images of war, violence, terror, and other horrors. With the advancement of technologies in both the fields of war and cinema, these critics suggest, war becomes more susceptible to spectacle such that the gap between reality and image—war and its screen representation—gradually disappears. See Paul Virilio, *War and Cinema: The Logistics Of Perception*, and Jean Baudrillard, *Simulacra and Simulation*.

15. The critique voiced in the film pales in comparison to the one presented in 1982

by the Kahan committee, which was set up by the Israeli government to examine the role of Israel in the massacre. The latter has concluded that Israeli forces were indirectly responsible for the massacre and that Ariel Sharon alone was personally responsible and should resign from his then-position as Israel's defense minister.

16. While the film invites this conflation of perspectives, there is no doubt that the varied positions of the viewers further determine their ability/willingness to see with Shmulik, as it were. In other words, it is likely that this cinematic manipulation, which conflates the position of the camera with that of the Shmulik's weaponized camera, would yield different results (or fail to work at all) depending on viewers' initial resistance or ability/willingness to see things from the perspective of an Israeli soldier.

17. It is important to note in this regard that while both films were immediately successful in Europe and the United States, their reception in Israel was significantly more ambivalent and met with a fair degree of public resistance and suspicious critique. It is indeed important to distinguish between the significant role these films have within the Israeli public and culture, as agitators of political consciousness, and their status in the context of the greater international market.

Bibliography

Abraham, Nicholas, and Maria Torok. *The Shell and the Kernel: Renewals of Psychoanalysis.* Trans. Nicholas T. Rand. Chicago: University of Chicago Press, 1994.

Abramson, Larry. "Larry Abramson on Art, Society and the Relationship between Them." *Art in Process: Israeli Artists on Art and on Themselves.* October 24, 2011. http://art-in -process.com/he/2011/10/abramson-he/. [Hebrew]

———. "Ma ha-nof rotse, we-ma chaser lo?" ["What Does the Landscape Want and What Is It Missing?"] *Ma'arav* June 8, 2010. http://maarav.org.il/archive/?author=206. [Hebrew]

Abu-Remaileh, Refqa. "Palestinian Anti-narratives in the Films of Elia Suleiman." *Arab Media and Society* 5 (2008): 1–29. http://www.arabmediasociety.com/?article=670.

Agamben, Georgio. *Homo Sacer: Sovereign Power and Bare Life.* Trans. Daniel Heller-Roazen. Stanford, CA: Stanford University Press, 1998.

———. *Remnants of Auschwitz: The Witness and the Archive.* Trans. Daniel Heller-Roazen. New York: Zone, 1999.

Ahmed, Sara. *Queer Phenomenology: Orientations, Objects, Others.* Durham, NC: Duke University Press, 2006.

Allen, Lori A. "Martyr Bodies in the Media: Human Rights, Aesthetics, and the Politics of Immediation in the Palestinian Intifada." *American Ethnologist* 36, no. 1 (2009): 161–80.

———. "New Texts Out Now: Lori Allen, *The Rise and Fall of Human Rights: Cynicism and Politics in Occupied Palestine.*" Interview. *Jadaliyya,* July 10, 2013. http://www.jadaliyya .com/pages/index/12832/new-texts-out-now_lori-allen-the-rise-and-fall-of-.

———. "Pain, Touch, Pressure, Temperature: Rula Halawani's Intimacies of Occupation." *ArteEast Virtual Gallery.* ArteEast: The Global Platform for Middle East Arts, n.d. http://www.arteeast.org/virtualgallery/apr05_halawani/arteeast-vg-halawani-2 .html.

———. *The Rise and Fall of Human Rights: Cynicism and Politics in Occupied Palestine.* Stanford, CA: Stanford University Press, 2013.

Al Sharif, Basma. Personal interviews. October 27 and November 19, 2010.

Alter, Nora M. "The Political Im/perceptible in the Essay Film: Farocki's *Images of the World and the Inscription of War.*" *New German Critique* 68 (1996): 165–92.

Amicha, Yehuda. *Elegya al kfar natush.* [*Elegy on an Abandoned Village.*] *The Selected Poetry of Yehuda Amichi.* Newly revised and expanded edition. Trans. Chana Bloch and Stephen Mitchell, 42–43. Berkeley: University of California Press, 1996.

Amir, Merav. "Borders beyond Territory: Population Management through Border-Making and the Borders of Israel." PhD diss., Tel Aviv University, 2011.

Amir, Merav, and Hagar Kotef. "Between Imaginary Lines: Violence and Its Justifications at the Military Checkpoints in Occupied Palestine." *Theory, Culture and Society* 28, no. 1 (2011): 55–80.

———. "(En)Gendering Checkpoints: Checkpoint Watch and the Repercussions of Intervention." *Signs: Journal of Women in Culture and Society* 32, no. 4 (2007): 973–96.

Amireh, Amal. "Between Complicity and Subversion: Body Politics in Palestinian National Narrative." *South Atlantic Quarterly* 102, no. 4 (2003): 747–72.

An-Na'im, Abdullahi A. "Toward a Cross-Cultural Approach to Defining International Standards of Human Rights: The Meaning of Cruel, Inhuman or Degrading Treatment or Punishment." *Human Rights in Cross-Cultural Perspectives: A Quest for Consensus.* Ed. A. An-Na'im, 19–43. Philadelphia: University of Philadelphia Press, 1995.

Anthias, Floya, and Nira Yuval-Davis, eds. *Women-Nation-State.* London: Macmillan, 1989.

Antoun, Naira. "Review of Waltz with Bashir." *Electronic Intifada,* February 19, 2009. http://electronicintifada.net/content/film-review-waltz-bashir/3547.

Apel, Dora. "On Looking: Lynching Photographs and Legacies of Lynching after 9/11." *American Quarterly* 55, no. 3 (2003): 457–78.

Arendt, Hannah. *The Human Condition.* Chicago: University of Chicago Press, 1958.

———. *The Origins of Totalitarianism.* New York: Harcourt, 1951.

Asad, Talal. "On Torture, or Cruel, Inhuman, and Degrading Treatment." *Social Suffering.* Ed. Arthur Kleinman, Veena Das, and Margaret Lock, 285–308. Berkeley: University of California Press, 1997.

Atherton, D. Kelsey. "University of Nevada Students Could Soon Earn Degrees in Drone Studies." *Popular Science,* June 26 2013. http://www.popsci.com/technology/article/2013-06/industry-urges-nevada-start-drone-degree-programs.

Aufderheide, Patricia. "An Interview with Elia Suleiman." *Visual Anthropology Review* 13, no. 2 (1997–98): 74–78.

Avni, Ronit. "Mobilizing Hope: Beyond the Shame-Based Model in the Israeli-Palestinian Conflict." *American Anthropologist* 108, no. 1 (2006): 205–14.

Axel, Brian Keith. "The Diasporic Imaginary." *Public Culture* 14, no. 2 (2002): 411–28.

Azoulay, Ariella. *The Civil Contract of Photography.* Trans. Rela Mazali and Ruvik Danieli. Cambridge, MA: MIT Press, 2008.

———. *Death's Showcase: The Power of Image in Contemporary Democracy.* Trans. Ruvik Danieli. Cambridge, MA: MIT Press, 2003.

———. "Determined at Will." *Chic Point: Fashion for Israeli Checkpoints,* 134–54. Exhibition Catalog. Tel Aviv: Andalus, 2007.

———. *Ma'ase Medina: 1967–2007; Hakdama.* [*Act of State: 1967–2007; Introduction.*] *Etgar: Magazine politi ve-tarbuti,* January 15, 2008. http://www.etgar.info/he/article__169. [Hebrew]

Azoulay, Ariella, and Adi Ophir. "Back to Basics: Israel's Arab Minority and the Israeli-Palestinian Conflict." International Crisis Group, Middle East Report 119, March

14, 2012. http://www.crisisgroup.org/~/media/Files/Middle%20East%20North%20 Africa/Israel%20Palestine/119-back-to-basics-israels-arab-minority-and-the -israeli-palestinian-conflict.pdf.

―――. "The Monster's Tail." *Against the Wall: Israel's Barrier to Peace.* Ed. Michael Sorkin, 2–27. New York: New Press, 2005.

Ball, Anna. "Between a Postcolonial Nation and Fantasies of the Feminine: The Contested Visions of Palestinian Cinema." *Camera Obscura: A Journal of Feminism, Culture, and Media Studies* 23, no. 3 (2008): 1–33.

Banbaji, Amir. "Yehoshua be-re'i ha-sifrut ha-ivrit." ["Yehoshua's Place in Hebrew Literature."] *Intersecting Sights: New Critical Essays on A. B. Yehoshua.* Ed. Amir Banbaji and Nitza Ben-Dov, 14–29. Tel Aviv: Ha-kibuts ha-me'uchad, 2010. [Hebrew]

Barakat, Riman. "Quietly East Jerusalem Palestinians Acquiring Israeli Citizenship." +972 *Magazin,* May 20, 2012. http://972mag.com/quietly-east-jerusalem-palestinians-are -becoming-israeli-citizens/46298/.

Bardenstein, Carol. "Threads of Memory and Discourses of Rootedness: Of Trees, Oranges and the Prickly-Pear Cactus in Israel/Palestine." *Edebiyat* 8, no. 1 (1998): 1–36.

Bar-Tal, Daniel. Lechyot im hasikhsokh: Nitoach psikhologi chevrati shel ha-chevra ha-yehudit be-yisrael. [Living with the Conflict: Socio-psychological Analysis of the Israeli-Jewish Society.] Jerusalem: Carmel, 2007. [Hebrew]

Barthes, Roland. "Shock-Photos." *The Eiffel Tower and Other Mythologies.* Trans. Richard Howard, 71–74. New York: Hill and Wang, 1979.

Bartov, Omar. "Defining Enemies, Making Victims: Germans, Jews, and the Holocaust." *American Historical Review* 103, no. 3 (1998): 771–816.

Baudrillard, Jean. *Simulacra and Simulation.* Trans. Sheila Faria Glaser. Ann Arbor: University of Michigan Press, 1995.

Baum, Dalit, and Ruchama Marton. "Transparent Wall, Opaque Gates." *Against the Wall: Israel's Barrier to Peace.* Ed. Michael Sorkin, 212–23. New York: New Press, 2005.

Benjamin, Walter. *The Arcades Project.* Ed. Rolf Tiedemann. Trans. Howard Eiland and Kevin McLaughlin. Cambridge, MA: Belknap/Harvard University Press, 1999.

―――. *The Origin of the German Tragic Drama.* London: Verso, 1977.

―――. "The Work of Art in the Age of Mechanical Reproduction." *Illuminations.* Ed. Hannah Arendt, 217–52. New York: Schocken, 1969.

Benn, Aluf. "Sharon's Real Legacy—Keeping the Arabs Out of Sight." *Ha'aretz,* January 13, 2010. http://www.haaretz.com/print-edition/opinion/sharon-s-real-legacy -keeping-the-arabs-out-of-sight-1.261361.

Bennet, James. "Fashionable Protest, Lost in Translation." *New York Times,* March 4, 2004. http://www.nytimes.com/2004/03/04/world/fashionable-protest-lost-in-translation .html.

Benvenisti, Meron. *Sacred Landscape: The Buried History of the Holy Land since 1948.* Trans. Maxine Kaufman-Lacusta. Berkeley: University of California Press, 2000.

Berda, Yael. "The Bureaucracy of the Occupation in the West Bank: The Permit Regime 2000–2006." Jerusalem: Van Leer Institute in Jerusalem and ha-kibuts ha-me'uchad, 2012. [Hebrew]

———. "The Erotics of the Occupation." Trans. Hillel Dayan. *www.Gate48.org*. www
.gate48.org/pdf/ruination2.pdf.

Berger, Eva, and Dorit Naaman. "Combat Cuties: Photographs of Israeli Women Soldiers in the Press since the 2006 Lebanon War." *Media, War and Conflict* 4, no. 3 (2011):
269–86.

Berger, John. "Photographs of Agony." *Selected Essays*. Ed. Geoff Dyer, 279–81. New York:
Pantheon, 2001.

Berlant, Lauren. *The Queen of America Goes to Washington City: Essays on Sex and Citizenship*.
Durham, NC: Duke University Press, 1997.

Berry, Mike, and Greg Philo. *More Bad News from Israel*. London: Pluto Press, 2011.

Birney, Earle. "Can. Lit." *The New Oxford Book of Canadian Verse in English*. Ed. Margaret
Atwood. Toronto: Oxford University Press, 1982.

Bishara, Azmi. *Al-Hajiz: Shazaya riwaya al-kitab al-awwal—Wajd fi bild al-hawajiz*. [*The Checkpoint: Book One—Wajd in the Land of Checkpoints*.] Beirut: Riad El-Rayyes Books, 2004.
[Arabic]

———. "Ben makom le-merchav." ["Between Place and Space."] *Studio* 37 (1992): 6–9.
[Hebrew]

Bishop, Ryan. " 'The Threat of Space': A Discussion between Bashir Makhoul and Gordon
Hon." *Theory, Culture and Society* 29, nos. 7–8 (2012): 324–40.

Boyarin, Daniel. *Unheroic Conduct: The Rise of Heterosexuality and the Invention of the Jewish Man*.
Berkeley: University of California Press, 1997.

Braverman, Irus. "Civilized Borders: A Study of Israel's New Crossing Administration."
Antipode 43, no. 2 (2010): 264–95.

Brenez, Nicole. "Visual Oxymoron." *Chic Point: Fashion for Israeli Checkpoints*, 166–72. Exhibition Catalog. Tel Aviv: Andalus, 2003.

Brennan, Teresa, and Martin Jay, eds. *Vision in Context: Historical and Contemporary Perspectives on Sight*. New York: Routledge, 1996.

Bresheeth, Haim. "The Nakba Projected." *Third Text* 20, nos. 3–4 (2006): 499–509.

———. "A Symphony of Absence: Borders and Liminality in Elia Suleiman's *Chronicle of
a Disappearance*." *Framework* 43, no. 2 (2002): 71–84.

Bresheeth, Haim, and Haifa Hammami. "Introduction: Palestine and Israel." *The Conflict
and Contemporary Visual Culture in Palestine and Israel*. Spec. issue of *Third Text* 20, nos.
3–4 (2006): 281–84.

Brett, Elizabeth A., and Robert Ostroff. "Imagery and Posttraumatic Stress Disorder: An
Overview." *American Journal of Psychiatry* 142, no. 4 (1985): 417–24.

Britton, Celia M. *Edouard Glissant and Postcolonial Theory: Strategies of Language and Resistance*.
Charlottesville: University Press of Virginia, 1999.

Brown, Nathan. *Palestinian Politics after the Oslo Accords: Resuming Arab Palestine*. Berkeley:
University of California Press, 2003.

Brownfield-Stein, Chava. "Visual Representations of IDF Women Soldiers and 'Civil
Militarism' in Israel." *Militarism and Israeli Society*. Ed. Gabriel Sheffer and Oren
Barak, 304–28. Bloomington: Indiana University Press, 2010.

Broyles, William. "Why Men Love War." *Esquire*, November 1984. http://public.wsu.edu
/~hughesc/why_men_love_war.htm.

The Bubble. [*Ha-buah*.] Dir. Eytan Fox. Israel, 2006. DVD. [Hebrew]

Buck-Morss, Susan. *The Dialectics of Seeing: Walter Benjamin and the Arcades Project.* Cambridge, MA: MIT Press, 1991.

Butler, Judith. "Endangered/Endangering: Schematic Racism and White Paranoia." *Reading Rodney King/Reading Urban Uprising.* Ed. Robert Gooding-Williams, 15–22. New York: Routledge, 1993.

———. *Frames of War: When Is Life Grievable?* New York: Verso, 2009.

Cadava, Eduardo. "Lapsus Imaginis: The Image in Ruins." *October* 96 (2001): 35–60.

Campbell, David. "Constructed Visibility: Photographing the Catastrophe of Gaza." Symposium: The Aesthetics of Catastrophe, Northwestern University, Chicago, June 5, 2009. Unpublished conference paper.

"Capt. Barak Raz Responds to Shameful Photos Uploaded by Discharged IDF Soldier." *Israeli Defense Forces Blog,* August 17, 2010. http://www.idfblog.com/2010/08/17/capt -barak-raz-responds-to-shameful-facebook-photos-uploaded-by-discharged-idf -soldier-17-aug-2010/.

Careccia, Grazia, and John J. Reynolds. "Al-Nu'man Village: A Case Study of Indirect Forcible Transfer." *Al-Haq,* November 2006. http://www.alhaq.org/attachments /article/182/Al-Numan%20Village_2.pdf.

Carry, Jonathan. *Techniques of the Observer: On Vision and Modernity in the Nineteenth Century.* Cambridge, MA: MIT Press, 1990.

Caruth, Cathy. *Unclaimed Experience: Trauma, Narrative, and History.* Baltimore: Johns Hopkins University Press, 1996.

Cellcom. 2009 TV commercial. *Youtube.* Uploaded July 13, 2009. https://www.youtube .com/watch?v=AH02uc1vB4k.

Chic Point: Fashion for Israeli Checkpoints. Dir. Sharif Waked. Israel/Palestine, 2003. DVD.

Chouliaraki, Lilie. *The Spectatorship of Suffering.* London: Sage, 2006.

Chronicle of a Disappearance. [*Segell ikhtifa.*] Dir. Elia Suleiman. Israel/Palestine, 1996. DVD. [Arabic, Hebrew]

Cohen, Shaul-Efraim. *The Politics of Planting: Israeli-Palestinian Competition for Control of Land in the Jerusalem Periphery.* Chicago: University of Chicago Press, 1993.

Cohen, Stanley. *States of Denial: Knowing about Atrocities and Suffering.* Cambridge: Polity Press, 2001.

Connell, R. W. *Masculinities.* Berkeley: University of California Press, 1995.

Cook, Jonathan. *Disappearing Palestine: Israel's Experiments in Human Despair.* London: Zed Books, 2008.

———. "The Decline of Israel and the Prospects for Peace." *New Left Project,* March 10, 2010. http://www.newleftproject.org/index.php/site/article_comments/the_decline _of_israel_an_prospects_for_peace/.

———. "What Future for Israel's Palestinian Citizens?" *Electronic Intifada,* March 19, 2005. http://electronicintifada.net/v2/article3696.shtml.

DAAR, "Vision." *Glossary section. www.decolonizing.ps/site.* www.decolonizing.ps/site/visibility.

Dabashi, Hamid, ed. *Dreams of a Nation: On Palestinian Cinema.* New York: Verso, 2006.

———. "In Praise of Frivolity: On the Cinema of Elia Suleiman." *Dreams of a Nation: On Palestinian Cinema.* Ed. Hamid Dabashi, 131–60. London: Verso, 2006.

———. "Introduction." *Dreams of a Nation: On Palestinian Cinema.* Ed. Hamid Dabashi, 7–16. New York: Verso, 2006.

Dauphinee, Elisabeth. "The Politics of the Body in Pain: Reading the Ethics of Imagery." *Security Dialogue* 38, no. 2 (2007): 139–55.

Davidovitz, Miri. "Miri Davidovitz, Israeli Photographer, at the Separation Wall for Comme il Faut Catalog 2004." *YouTube*. March 26, 2011. http://www.youtube.com /watch?v=Hdub5LoK6yQ.

Demos, T. J. "Recognizing the Unrecognized: The Photographs of Ahlam Shibli." *Photography between Poetry and Politics: The Critical Position of the Photographic Medium in Contemporary Art*. Ed. Helen Westgeest and Hilde Van Gelder, 123–42. Leuven: Leuven University Press, 2008.

———. "The Right to Opacity: On the Otolith Group's *Nervus Rerum*." *October* 129 (2009): 113–28.

Derrida, Jacques. *Specters of Marx: The State of the Debt, the Work of Mourning, and the New International*. Trans. Peggy Kamuf. New York: Routledge, 1994.

Dershowitz, Alan. "Does Oppression Cause Suicide Bombing? Some Overprivileged Muslims Support a Culture of Death While Impoverished Tibetans Celebrate Life." *Jerusalem Post*, May 21, 2004, 17.

———. "Worshippers of Death." *Wall Street Journal*, March 3, 2008. http://online.wsj .com/article/SB120450617910806563.html.

Divine Intervention. [Yadon Ilaheyya.] Dir. Elia Suleiman. Palestine, 2002. DVD. [Arabic]

Donnelly, Jack. *International Human Rights*. Boulder, CO: Westview, 1993.

Dragon, Zoltán. "Derrida's Specter, Abraham's Phantom: Psychoanalysis as the Uncanny Kernel of Deconstruction." *AnaChronisT* 11 (2005): 253–69.

Dunsky, Marda. *Pens and Swords: How the American Mainstream Media Report the Israeli-Palestinian Conflict*. New York: Columbia University Press, 2008.

Duvdevani, Shmulik. "Ha-korban she-ba-tank yenatsach." ["The Victim in the Tank Shall Win."] *Ynet*, September 14, 2009. Accessed Nov. 19 2009. http://www.ynet .co.il/articles/0,7340,L-3790700,00.html. [Hebrew]

"Eden Aberjil Facebook Photos Controversy: Israeli Ex-soldier Says She Didn't Humiliate Palestinians." *Huffington Post*, August 17, 2010. http://www.huffingtonpost .com/2010/08/17/eden-aberjil-facebook-pho_n_684611.html.

Efrat, Elisha. *The West Bank and Gaza Strip: A Geography of Occupation*. New York: Routledge, 2006.

El-Hassan, Azza. "Art and War." *Unplugged: Art as the Scene of Global Conflicts*. Ed. Gerfried Stocker and Christine Schöpf, 280–83. Ostfildern: Hatke Kanz, 2002. Accessed October 14, 2011. 90.146.8.18/en/archiv_files/20021/E2002_280.pdf.

———. "News Time." *Unplugged: Art as the Scene of Global Conflicts*. Ars Electronica Festival Program, 280–83, September 7–12, 2002. http://90.146.8.18/en/archives/festival _archive/festival_catalogs/festival_artikel.asp?iProjectID=11789.

Emmelhainz, Irmgard, and the Otolith Group. "A Trialogue on *Nervus Rerum*." *October* 129 (2009): 129–32.

Enlarger, Steven. "A Tank-Eye View of an Unpopular War: Interview with Samuel Maoz." *New York Times*, July 30, 2010. http://www.nytimes.com/2010/08/01/movies /011ebanon.html.

Enns, Diane. "Bare Life and the Occupied Body." *Theory and Event* 7, no. 3 (2004). Theory _and_event/v007/7.3enns.html.

"Erasing the Nakba." Al Jazeera, May 17, 2012. http://www.aljazeera.com/indepth/opinion/2012/05/201251591926951514.html.

Eshel, Amir. "Layered Time: Ruins as Shattered Past, Ruins as Hope in Israeli and German Landscapes and Literature." Ruins of Modernity. Ed. Julia Hell and Andreas Schönle, 133–50. Durham, NC: Duke University Press, 2010.

"Facebook Photos of Soldiers Posing with Bound Palestinians Are the Norm." Ha'aretz, August 17, 2010. http://www.haaretz.com/news/diplomacy-and-defense/facebook-photos-of-soldiers-posing-with-bound-palestinians-are-the-norm-1.308582.

"Fashion on Israel's Frontline." BBC News Online, March 4, 2004. http://news.bbc.co.uk/2/hi/middle_east/3531149.stm.

Fassin, Didier. "The Humanitarian Politics of Testimony: Subjectification through Trauma in the Israeli-Palestinian Conflict." Cultural Anthropology 23, no. 3 (2008): 531–55.

Fassin, Didier, and Richard Rechtman. Empire of Trauma: An Inquiry into the Condition of Victimhood. Princeton, NJ: Princeton University Press, 2009.

Faulkner, Simon. "The Most Photographed Wall in the World." Photographies 5, no. 2 (2012): 223–42.

———. "Photography, Citizenship and the Israeli Occupation." Media, Communication and the Spectacle Conference, European Communication Research and Education Association, Erasmus University, Rotterdam. November 2009. Conference paper.

———. "What Are You Looking At?" Programma (September 1, 2009): 128–35.

Felman, Shoshana, and Dori Laub. Testimony: Crises of Witnessing in Literature, Psychoanalysis, and History. New York: Routledge, 1992.

Finkelstein, Norman. Image and Reality of the Israel-Palestine Conflict. 2nd ed. New York: Verso, 2003.

Foster, Hal, ed. Vision and Visuality: Discussions in Contemporary Culture. London: New Press, 1998.

Foucault, Michel. Naissance de la clinique. Paris: Presses Universitaires de France, 1963.

———. Discipline and Punish: The Birth of the Prison. Trans. Alan Sheridan. New York: Random House, 1977.

Freud, Sigmund. Beyond the Pleasure Principle. Trans. James Strachey. New York: W. W. Norton, 1961.

———. "The Uncanny." Writings on Art and Literature, 193–233. Stanford, CA: Stanford University Press, 1997.

Freund, Michael. "Washing Dirty Laundry in Public." Jerusalem Post, August 18, 2010. http://www.jpost.com/Opinion/Columnists/Article.aspx?id=185196.

Gana, Nouri. "Reel Violence: Paradise Now and the Collapse of the Spectacle." Comparative Studies of South Asia, Africa, and the Middle East 28, no. 1 (2008): 20–37.

Gardi Tomer. Eaven, niyar. [Stone, Paper.] Tel Aviv: Ha-kibuts ha-me'uchad/Sifriyat ha-po'alim, 2012. [Hebrew]

Gertz, Nurith, and George Khleifi. "Between Exile and Homeland: The Films of Elia Suleiman." Palestinian Cinema: Landscape, Trauma, and Memory, 171–89. Edinburgh: Edinburgh University Press, 2008.

———. "Palestinian 'Roadblock Movies.'" Geopolitics 10, no. 2 (2005): 316–34.

Giles, Frank. "Golda Meir: 'Who Can Blame Israel?'" *Sunday Times* (London), June 15, 1969, 12.

Ginsburg, Ruthie. "Taking Pictures over Soldiers' Shoulders: Reporting on Human Rights Abuse from the Israeli Occupied Territories." *Journal of Human Rights* 10, no. 1 (2011): 17–33.

Givoni, Michal. "Witnessing/Testimony." *Mafte'akh: Leftist Review of Political Thought* 2e (winter 2011): 147–68.

Gluzman, Michael. "Longing for Heterosexuality: Zionism and Sexuality in *Altneuland*." *Theory and Criticism* 11 (1997): 145–62.

Goodhand, Jonathan. "Research in Conflict Areas: Ethics and Accountability." *Forced Migration Review* 8 (2000): 12–15. http://www.fmreview.org/FMRpdfs/FMR08/fmr8 .4.pdf.

Gordon, Avery. *Ghostly Matters: Haunting and the Sociological Imagination.* Minneapolis: University of Minnesota Press, 1997.

Gordon, Neve. *Israel's Occupation.* Berkeley: University of California Press, 2008.

———. "On Visibility and Power: An Arendtian Corrective of Foucault." *Human Studies* 25, no. 2 (2002): 125–45.

———. "Erasing the Nakba." *Al Jazeera English*, May 17, 2012. http://www.aljazeera.com /indepth/opinion/2012/05/201251591926951514.html.

Gouri, Ḥaim. *Ha-boker sh-le-macharat.* [*The Morning-After Poem.*] *Shirei chotam.* [*Late Poems.*] Tel Aviv: Ha-kibuts ha-me'uchad, 1954. [Hebrew]

———. "Yarid ha-Mizrach." ["Oriental Fair."] *Ha-shirim.* [*The Poems.*] Tel Aviv: Ha-kibuts ha-me'uchad, 1998. [Hebrew]

Gregory, Derek. *The Colonial Present: Afghanistan, Palestine, Iraq.* Oxford: Blackwell Publishing, 2004.

———. "Palestine and the 'War on Terror.'" *Comparative Studies of South Asia, Africa, and the Middle East* 24, no. 1 (2004): 183–95.

Grunes, Dennis. "*Divine Intervention* (Elia Suleiman, 2001)." February 15, 2007. http:// grunes.wordpress.com/2007/02/15/divine-intervention-elia-sulieman-2001/.

Guillermo, Luis, and Vasco Uribe. "Rethinking Fieldwork and Ethnographic Writing." Trans. Joanne Rappaport. *Collaborative Anthropologies* 4 (2011): 18–66.

Gutmann, Stephanie. *The Other War: Israelis, Palestinians and the Struggle for Media Supremacy.* San Francisco: Encounter Books, 2005.

Habibi, Emile. *Al-Mutasha'il: al-waq'i al-ghariba fi ikhtifaa' Said abi al- nahs al-mutasha'il.* [*The Strange Events related to the Disappearance of the Ill-Fated Sa'id, the Pessoptimist.*] Beirut: Dar Ibn Khaldun, 1974. [Arabic]

Haider, Sabah. "'A Different Kind of Occupation': Interview with Elia Suleiman." *Electronic Intifada*, February 1, 2010. http://electronicintifada.net/content/different-kind -occupation-interview-elia-suleiman/8654.

Halawani, Rula. "Arts and Politics in Palestine through My Photographs." *ArteEast Virtual Gallery.* ArteEast: The Global Platform for Middle East Arts, spring 2005. http://www .arteeast.org/2012/03/08/arts-and-politics-in-palestine-through-my-photographs/.

Halawani, Rula, and Rema Hammami. "Lifta: The Cipher of the Landscape—A Photographic Essay." *Jerusalem Quarterly* 37 (2009): 98–103.

Halberstam, Judith. "Shame and White Gay Masculinity." *Social Text* 84–85 (2005): 219–33.

Halkin, Hillel. "The *Waltz with Bashir* Two-Step." *Commentary* 127, no. 3 (2009): 46–51.

Halper, Jeff. "The Key to Peace: Dismantling the Matrix of Control." Israeli Committee against Home Demolitions, n.d. http://www.icahd.org/node/100.

Hanafi, Sari. "Explaining Spacio-cide in the Palestinian Territory: Colonization, Separation, and State of Exception." *Current Sociology* 61, no. 2 (2013): 190–205.

———. "Spacio-cide: Colonial Politics, Invisibility and Rezoning in Palestinian Territory." *Contemporary Arab Affairs* 2, no. 1 (2009): 106–21.

Handel, Ariel. " 'Kaze re'eh ve-chasel': He'arot al ha-chushim ve-al tafkidiehem bashtachim ha-kvushim." ["Notes on the Senses and Their Functions in the Occupied Territories."] *Theoria ve-bikoret* 28 (2006): 157–73. [Hebrew]

Haraway, Donna. "Situated Knowledge: The Science Question in Feminism and the Privilege of Partial Knowledge." *Feminist Studies* 14, no. 3 (1988): 575–99.

Hass, Amira. "You Can Drive Along and Never See an Arab." *Ha'aretz English Edition*, January 22, 2003. http://www.haaretz.com/print-edition/opinion/you-can-drive-along -and-never-see-an-arab-1.21522.

Havkin, Shira. "The Reform of Israeli Checkpoints: Outsourcing, Commodification and Redeployment of the State." *Les Etudes du CERI* 174 (2011): 1–37.

Hedges, Chris. "What War Looks Like." *New York Times Sunday Book Review*, May 20, 2009. http://www.nytimes.com/2009/05/24/books/review/Hedges-t.html?_r=0.

Hesford, Wendy S. *Spectacular Rhetorics: Human Rights Visions, Recognitions, Feminisms*. Durham, NC: Duke University Press, 2011.

Hever, Hannan, ed. *Al Tagidu Be-Gath: Ha-Nakba ha-Falastinit ba-shirah ha-Ivrit 1948–1958*. [*Tell It Not in Gath: The Palestinian Nakba in Hebrew Poetry 1948–1958*.] Tel Aviv: Sedek, 2010. [Hebrew]

Hever, Hannan. "Rov ke-mi'ut le'umi be-sifrut yisra'elit me-reshit shnot ha-60." ["The Majority as a National Minority in Hebrew Literature since the Early 1960s."] *Hasipur ve-hale'om: Qri'ot biqortiyot be-qanon ha-sifrut ha-ivrit*. [*Narrative and Nationality: Critical Readings of the Literary Hebrew Canon*.] Tel Aviv: Resling, 2007. [Hebrew]

Hilu, Alon. *Achozat a'djani*. [*The House of Dajani*.] Tel Aviv: Yedi'ot sefarim, 2008. [Hebrew]

Hirsch, Joshua. *After Image: Film, Trauma and the Holocaust*. Philadelphia: Temple University Press, 2004.

"Historical Background: Oslo Accords." *Adalah: The Legal Center for Arab Minority Rights in Israel*, n.d. http://adalah.org/eng/?mod=articles&ID=1478.

Hochberg, Gil. "A Poetics of Haunting: From Yizhar's Khirbeh to Yehoshua's Ruins to Koren's Crypts." *Jewish Social Studies* 18, no. 3 (2013): 55–69.

———. "Edward Said: 'The Last Jewish Intellectual': On Identity, Alterity, and the Politics of Memory." *Social Text* 24, no. 2 87 (2006): 47–65.

———. *In Spite of Partition: Jews, Arabs and the Limits of Separatist Imagination*. Princeton, NJ: Princeton University Press, 2007.

———. "Soldiers as Filmmakers: On the Prospect of 'Shooting War' and the Question of Ethical Spectatorship." *Screen* 54, no. 1 (2013): 44–61.

———. "To Be or Not to Be an Israeli Arab: Sayed Kashua and the Prospect of Minority Speech Acts." *Comparative Literature* 62, no. 1 (2010): 68–86.

Holt, Maria. "Palestinian Women, Violence and the Peace Movement." *Development, Women, and War: Feminist Perspectives*. Ed. Haleh Afshar and Deborah Eade, 109–32. London: Kumarian, 2003.

Hutcheon, Linda. *The Politics of Postmodernism*. New York: Routledge, 2002.

"Inequality Report." *Adalah: The Legal Center for Arab Minority Rights in Israel*. March 2011. http://adalah.org/upfiles/2011/Adalah_The_Inequality_Report_March_2011.pdf.

Isin, Engin, and Greg Nielsen, eds. *Acts of Citizenship*. London: Zed Books, 2008.

Jaafar, Ali. "Live Action Doc Leaps to Animation: Ari Folmer's 'Waltz with Bashir' First Israeli Toon." *Variety*, May 30, 2008. http://www.variety.com/article/VR1117986665?refCatId=3152.

Jarrar, Khaled. "Artist Profile." *Palestine Monitor*, August 17, 2009. http://www.palestinemonitor.org/spip/spip.php?article1042.

Jay, Martin. *Downcast Eyes: The Denigration of Vision in Twentieth-Century French Thought*. Berkeley: University of California Press, 1993.

Johnson, Penny, and Eileen Kuttab. "Where Have All the Women (and Men) Gone? Reflections on Gender and the Second Palestinian Intifada." *Feminist Review* 69 (2001): 21–43.

Johnson, Robert. "New 'Drone Studies' Major Has Graduates Starting at $120,000 a Year." *Business Insider*, March 28, 2012. http://www.businessinsider.com/new-college-major-in-drone-studies-has-graduates-pulling-in-up-to-200k-a-year-2012-3.

Kadman, Noga. *Be-tsidei ha-derekh u-be-shulei ha-toda'a: Dechikat ha-kfarim ha-arviyim shhitroknu be-1948 me-hasiach ha-yisraeli.* [*Erased from Space and Consciousness: Depopulated Palestinian Villages in the Israeli Zionist Discourse.*] Jerusalem: November Books, 2008. [Hebrew]

Kapeliouk, Amnon. *Sabra et Chatila: Enquête sur un massacre*. Paris: Seuil, 1982.

Kaplan, Danny. *Brothers and Others in Arms: The Making of Love and War in Israeli Combat Units*. New York: Southern Tier Editions/Harrington Park Press, 2003.

Kashua, Sayed. "The Palestinian Novelist Sayed Kashua on Dual Belongings and His Compositions in Hebrew." *Al Nahar*, July 14, 2004. [Arabic]

———. *Let It Be Morning (Va-yehi boker)*. Trans. Miriam Shlesinger. New York: Grove Press, Black Cat, 2006.

Katz, Sheila Hannah. "Adam and Adama, 'Ird and Ard: Engendering Political Conflict and Identity in Early Jewish and Palestinian Nationalisms." *Gendering the Middle East*, ed. Deniz Kandiyoti, 85–107. Syracuse, NY: Syracuse University Press, 1996.

Kawash, Samira. "Nation, Place, and Placelessness: Identity, Body, and Geography in the Case of Palestine." *Croatian Journal of Ethnology and Folklore Research* 40, no. 1 (2003): 37–48.

Keren Kayeneth LeIsrael-Jewish National Fund (KKL-JNF). http://www.kkl.org.il/eng/about-kkl-jnf/our-history/. http://www.kkl.org.il/kkl/hebrew/nosim_ikaryim/al_kakal/history/asorkkl/asorim.x.

Keshet, Yehudit Kirstein. *Checkpoint Watch: Testimonies from Occupied Palestine*. London: Zed Books, 2006.

Khalili, Laleh. "Palestinians: The Politics of Control, Invisibility, and the Spectacle." *Manifestations of Identity: The Lived Reality of Palestinian Refugees in Lebanon*, ed. Muhammad Ali Khalidi, 125–45. Beirut: Institute for Palestine Studies, 2010.

Khalidi, Walid, ed. *All That Remains: The Palestinian Villages Occupied and Depopulated by Israel in 1948*. Washington, DC: Institute for Palestine Studies, 1992.

Klein, Uri. "Khronika shel hitbagrut." [A Chronicle of Maturation.] *Akhbar Ha-ir*, May 25, 2009. http://www.mouse.co.il/CM.articles_item,1142,209,36320,.aspx. [Hebrew]

Kleinman, Arthur, and Joan Kleinman. "The Appeal of Experience: The Dismay of Images; Cultural Appropriations of Suffering in Our Times." *Social Suffering*, ed. Arthur Kleinman, Veena Das, and Margaret M. Lock, 1–23. Berkeley: University of California Press, 1997.

Koren, Yeshayahu. *Levaya ba-t'sohorim*. [*Funeral at Noon*.] Tel Aviv: Ha-kibuts ha-me'uchad, 2008. [Hebrew]

Krauss, Rosalind. *The Optical Unconsciousness*. Cambridge, MA: MIT Press, 1993.

Kuntsman, Adi. "The Soldier and the Terrorist: Sexy Nationalism, Queer Violence." *Sexualities* 11, nos. 1–2 (2008): 142–70.

Kuntsman, Adi, and Rebecca L. Stein. "Digital Suspicion, Politics, and the Middle East." *Web Exclusive: The New Arab Spring*. Spec. issue of *Critical Inquiry*, August 8, 2011. http://criticalinquiry.uchicago.edu/digital_suspicion_politics_and_the_middle_east/#_ednref.

———. "Another War Zone: New Media and the Israeli-Palestinian Conflict." *Middle East Report*, September 2010. http://www.merip.org/mero/interventions/another-war-zone.

Kurzweil, Baruch. *Ben chazon le-ven ha-absurdi*. [*Between Prophecy and the Absurd*.] Jerusalem: Schocken, 1973. [Hebrew]

Lacan, Jacques. "Touché and Automaton." *The Four Fundamental Concepts of Psychoanalysis*, ed. Jacques-Alain Miller, 53–66. Trans. Alan Sheridan. New York: W. W. Norton, 1988.

Landsman, Ohad, and Roy Bendor. "Animated Recollection and Spectatorial Experience in *Waltz with Bashir*." *Animation: An Interdisciplinary Journal* 6, no. 3 (2011): 353–70.

Laor, Yitzhak. "Dor shalem doresh tashlum." ["A Whole Generation Demands Compensation."] *Ha'aretz*, February 29, 2009. http://www.haaretz.co.il/hasite/pages/ShArt.jhtml?itemNo=1067189. [Hebrew]

Lebanon. [*Levanon*.] Dir. Samuel Maoz. Israel, 2009. DVD. [Hebrew]

Levine, Laura. "The Performative Force of Photography." *Photography and Culture* 2, no. 3 (2009): 327–36.

Levy, Gideon. "Nothing but a Charade." *Ha'aretz*, February 21, 2009. http://www.haaretz.com/gideon-levy-antiwar-film-waltz-with-bashir-is-nothing-but-charade-1.270528.

Lewis, Bernard. *The Crisis of Islam: Holy War and Unholy Terror*. New York: Random House, 2003.

———. *What Went Wrong? The Clash between Islam and Modernity in the Middle East*. New York: Harper Perennial, 2003.

Lindsey, Ursula. "Shooting Film and Crying." *Middle East Report Online*, March 2009. http://www.merip.org/mero/interventions/shooting-film-crying.

Linfield, Susie. *The Cruel Radiance: Photography and Political Violence*. Chicago: University of Chicago Press, 2010.

Linor, Irit. "Anti-Semitism Now." *Ynet*, July 2, 2006. http://www.ynetnews.com/articles /0,7340,L-3212503,00.html.

Lloyd, David. "Ruination: Allan deSouza's Irish Photography." *Third Text* 18, no. 3 (2004): 263–72.

———. "Settler Colonialism and the State of Exception: The Example of Israel/Palestine." *Past Is Present: Settler Colonialism in Palestine.* Spec. issue of *Settler Colonial Studies* 2, no. 1 (2012): 59–80.

Lopate, Phillip. "In Search of the Centaur: The Essay-Film." *Beyond Document: Essays on Nonfiction Film*, ed. Charles Warren, 243–70. Middletown: Wesleyan University Press, 1998.

Lott, Eric. "A Strange and Bitter Spectacle: On 'Without Sanctuary.'" *First of the Month: A Website of the Radical Imagination.* http://www.firstofthemonth.org/culture/culture _lott_sanctuary.html.

Makdisi, Saree. "The Architecture of Erasure." *Critical Inquiry* 36, no. 3 (2010): 519–59.

———. *Palestine Inside Out: An Everyday Occupation.* New York: W. W. Norton, 2008.

Mansbach, Daniela. "Normalizing Violence: From Military Checkpoint to 'Terminals' in the Occupied Territories." *Journal of Political Power* 2, no. 2 (2009): 255–73.

Mansfield, Natasha Jane. "Loss and Mourning: Cinema's 'Language' of Trauma in *Waltz with Bashir.*" *Wide Screen* 2, no. 1 (2010): 1.

Manzo, K. "Imaging Humanitarianism: NGO Identity and the Iconography of Childhood." *Antipode* 40, no. 4 (2008): 632–57.

Maoz, Ayelet. "The Privatization of the Checkpoints and the Late Occupation," n.d. hagada .org.il/2008/10/10/הפרטת-מחסומים-והכיבוש-המאוחר/. [Hebrew]

Marks, Laura. "Invisible Media." *Digitextuality: Theses on Convergence Media and Digital Reproduction*, ed. Anna Everett and John T. Caldwell. Routledge: New York: 2002.

Massad, Joseph. "Conceiving the Masculine: Gender and Palestinian Nationalism." *Middle East Journal* 49, no. 3 (1995): 467–83.

———. "The Weapon of Culture: Cinema in the Palestinian Liberation Struggle." *Dreams of a Nation: On Palestinian Cinema*, ed. Hamid Dabashi. New York: Verso, 2006.

Mayer, Tamar. "From Zero to Hero: Nationalism and Masculinity in Jewish Israel." *Gender Ironies of Nationalism: Sexing the Nation*, 283–308. London: Routledge, 2000.

McClintock, Anne. *Imperial Leather: Race, Gender and Sexuality in the Colonial Conquest.* London: Routledge, 1995.

———. "Slow Violence and the BP Coverups." *Counterpunch* 23 (August 2010). http:// www.counterpunch.org/2010/08/23/slow-violence-and-the-bp-coverups/print.

Menick, John. "The Occupied Imagination of Elia Suleiman." *John Menick blog*, June 2003. http://www.johnmenick.com/writing/the-occupied-imagination-of-elia-suleiman.

Merleau-Ponty, Maurice. *The Visible and the Invisible.* Trans. Alphonso Lingis. Chicago: Northwestern University Press, 1969.

Merom, Gil. "Israel's National Security and the Myth of Exceptionalism." *Political Science Quarterly* 114, no. 3 (1999): 409–43.

Meyer, Morris, ed. *The Politics and Poetics of Camp.* New York: Routledge, 1994.

Minh-Ha, Trinh T. "The Totalizing Quest of Meaning." *Theorizing Documentary*, ed. Michael Renov, 90–107. New York: Routledge, 1993.

Miron, Dan. "S. Yizhar: Some General Observations." *Midnight Convoy and Other Stories.* S. Yizhar, 257–73. Jerusalem: Israeli University Press, 1969.

———. "Ghostwriting: Working Out Visual Culture." *Journal of Visual Culture* 1, no. 2 (2002): 239–54.

Mirzoeff, Nicholas. "Invisible Empire: Visual Culture, Embodied Spectacle, and Abu Ghraib." *Radical History Review* 95 (2006): 21–44.

Mitchell, W. J. T. "Christo's Gates and Gilo's Wall." *Critical Inquiry* 32, no. 4 (2006): 587–601.

———. "Holy Landscape: Israel, Palestine and the American Wilderness." *Critical Inquiry* 26, no. 2 (2000): 193–223.

Moeller, Susan D. *Compassion Fatigue: How the Media Sell Disease, Famine, War and Death.* New York: Routledge, 1999.

Mondzain, Marie-Jose. *Image, Icon, Economy: The Byzantine Origins of the Contemporary Imaginary.* Trans. Rico Franses. Stanford, CA: Stanford University Press, 2004.

Monterescu, Daniel. "Stranger Masculinities: Gender and Politics in a Palestinian-Israeli 'Third Space.'" *Islamic Masculinities*, ed. Lahoucine Ouzgane, 123–42. London: Zed Books, 2006.

Moon, Michael. "Memorial Rags." *Professions of Desire: Lesbian and Gay Studies in Literature*, ed. George E. Haggerty and Bonnie Zimmerman, 233–40. New York: Modern Language Association, 1995.

Morag, Raya. "Chronic Trauma." *Framework* 49, no. 1 (2008): 121–33.

Mosse, George L. *The Image of Man: Creating Modern Masculinity.* Oxford: Oxford University Press, 1996.

Muir, Diana. "'A Land without a People for a People without a Land.'" *Middle East Quarterly* 25, no. 2 (2008): 55–62. http://www.meforum.org/1877/a-land-without-a-people-for-a-people-without.

Muller, Nat. "Shifting Roles (A Conversation with Azza El Hassan)." *Mute: Culture and Politics after the Net.* October 23, 2002, 1–5. http://www.metamute.org/editorial/articles/shifting-roles-conversation-azza-el-hassan.

Muñoz, José E. "Photographies of Mourning: Melancholia and Ambivalence in Van Der Zee, Mapplethorpe, and Looking for Langston." *Race and the Subject of Masculinities*, ed. Harry Stecopoulos and Michael Uebel, 337–58. Durham, NC: Duke University Press, 1997.

Naaman, Dorit. "The Silenced Outcry: A Feminist Point of View from the Israeli Checkpoints in Palestine." *National Women Studies Association Journal* 18, no. 3 (2006): 168–80.

Nagel, Joan. "Masculinity and Nationalism: Gender and Sexuality in the Making of Nations." *Nations and Nationalism: A Reader*, ed. Philip Spencer and Howard Wollman, 110–31. New Brunswick, NJ: Rutgers University Press, 2005.

Nathansohn, Regev. "Metsalmim kibutsh: Sotsiologiya shel yetsug chazuti." ["Shooting Occupation: Sociology of Visual Representation."] *Theory and Criticism* 31 (winter 2007): 127–54. [Hebrew]

Nayar, Pramod K. "Scar Cultures: Media, Spectacle, Suffering." *Journal of Creative Communications* 4, no. 3 (2009): 147–62.

Neale, Steve. "War Films." *Hollywood and War: The Film Reader*, ed. J. David Slocum, 23–30. London: Routledge, 2006.

Nervus Rerum. Dir. Otolith Group. *Homeworks 4: A Forum on Cultural Practices.* 2008. DVD.

Nevo, Eshkol. *Arba'a batim ve-ga'agu'a.* [Homesick.] Tel Aviv: Zemora bitan, 2004. [Hebrew]

———. *Homesick.* Trans. Sondra Silverston. Champaign: Dalkey Archive Press, 2010.

Newsinger, John. "Do You Walk the Walk? Aspects of Masculinity in Some Vietnam War Films." *You Tarzan: Masculinity, Movies and Men,* ed. Pat Kirkham and Janet Thumim. London: Palgrave Macmillan, 1993.

News Time. [*Zaman al-akhbar.*] Dir. Azza El-Hassan. Palestine, 2001. DVD. [*Arabic*]

Notre Musique. Dir. Jean-Luc Godard. Wellspring Media, 2004. DVD.

"October 2000 Killings." *Adalah: The Legal Center for Arab Minority Rights in Israel,* n.d. Accessed September 18, 2012. http://adalah.org/eng/Articles/1773/October-2000 -Killings.

Ofrat, Gidon. "Ruins, Remains, Ruination." *Me-chorbotaikh avnekh: Dimuyi ha-churva be-yisrael 1803–2003,* 7–77. [From Your Ruins I Shall Build You: The Image of Ruins in Israel 1803–2003.] Tel Aviv: Zman le-omanut, 2003. [Hebrew]

Oliver, Kelly. *Witnessing beyond Recognition.* Minneapolis: University of Minneapolis Press, 2001.

Ophir Adi, "A Time of Occupation." *The Other Israel: Voices of Refusal and Dissent,* ed. Roane Carey and Jonathan Shainin, 51–66. New York: New Press, 2004.

Ophir, Adi, Michal Givoni, and Sari Hanafi, eds. *Power of Inclusive Exclusion: Anatomy of the Israeli Rule in the Occupied Palestinian Territories.* London: Zone, 2009.

Oppenheimer, Yohai. *Ha-zekhut ha-gdola lomar lo: Shira politit be-yisrael.* [The Great Right to Say No: Political Poetry in Israel.] Jerusalem: Magnes, 2004. [Hebrew]

Oz, Amos. "Chofrim." ["Digging."] *Temunot me-chayie kfar,* 51–102. [Scenes from a Village Life.] Tel Aviv: Keter, 2005. [Hebrew]

———. "Digging." *Scenes from a Village Life.* Trans. Nicholas de Lange, 39–82. New York: Houghton Mifflin Harcourt, 2011.

———. *A Perfect Peace.* Trans. Hillel Halkin. Orlando: Harcourt Brace, 1985.

Ozguc, Umut. "Beyond the Panopticon: The Separation Wall and Paradoxical Nature of Israeli Security Imagination." Annual APSA (Australian Political Science Association) Conference, University of Melbourne, Melbourne, Australia, September 27–29, 2010. Conference paper.

"Palestinian Celebration of Murder Dooms Hope for Peace." *NY Daily News,* March 8, 2008. http://www.nydailynews.com/opinion/palestinian-celebration-murder-dooms -hope-peace-article-1.287580.

Paradise Now (Al-jannah al-an). Dir. Hanny Abu-Assad. Palestine/Israel, 2005. DVD [Arabic].

Pealsee, Robert Moses. " 'It's Fine as Long as You Draw, but Don't Film': *Waltz with Bashir* and the Postmodern Function of Animated Documentary." *Visual Communication Quarterly* 18, no. 4 (2011): 223–35.

Peteet, Julie. "Male Gender and Rituals of Resistance in the Palestinian 'Intifada': A Cultural Politics of Violence." *American Ethnologist* 21 (1994): 31–49.

Peterson, V. Spike. "Sexing Political Identities: Nationalism as Heterosexism." *International Feminist Journal of Politics* 1, no. 1 (1999): 33–65.

Pile, Steve. *Real Cities: Modernity, Space and the Phantasmagoria of City Life.* London: Sage, 2005.

Pisters, Patricia. "Violence and Laughter: Paradoxes of Nomadic Thought in Postcolonial Cinema." *Deleuze and the Postcolonial*, ed. Simone Bignall and Paul Patton, 201–19. Edinburgh: Edinburgh University Press, 2010.

Piterberg, Gabriel. *The Returns of Zionism: Myths, Politics and Scholarship in Israel*. New York: Verso, 2008.

Porton, Richard. "Notes from the Palestinian Diaspora: An Interview with Elia Suleiman." *Cineaste* 28, no. 3 (2003): 24–27.

Puar, Jasbir K. *Terrorist Assemblages: Homonationalism in Queer Times*. Durham, NC: Duke University Press, 2007.

Pullan, Wendy. "A One-Sided Wall." *Index on Censorship* 33, no. 3 (2004): 78–82.

Quinn, Anthony. "Review of *Waltz with Bashir*." *Independent*, November 21, 2008. http://www.independent.co.uk/arts-entertainment/films/reviews/waltz-with-bashir-18-1027847.html.

Rana's Wedding ('Urs Rana). Dir. Hany Abu-Assad. Palestine/Israel, 2002. DVD. [Arabic/Hebrew]

Rancière, Jacques. *Disagreement: Politics and Philosophy*. Trans. Julie Rose. Minneapolis, MN: University of Minnesota Press, 2004.

———. *Dissensus: On Politics and Aesthetics*. Trans. Steven Corcoran. London: Continuum, 2010.

———. *The Emancipated Spectator*. Trans. Gregory Elliott. London: Verso, 2009.

———. *The Future of the Image*. Trans. Gregory Elliott. New York, Verso, 2007.

Rancière, Jacques, Fulvia Carnevale, and John Kelsey. "Art of the Possible: Fulvia Carnevale and John Kelsey in Conversation with Jacques Rancière." *Artforum*, March 2007. http://www.egs.edu/faculty/jacques-ranciere/articles/art-of-the-possible/.

Rappaport, Meron. "Cellcom ve-chomat ha-ha-frada: Kakha malbinim matspun." ["Cellcom and the Separation Wall: The Way to Clear One's Conscience."] *Ha'okets*, November 11, 2009. www.haokets.org/2009/11/11/מצפון-מלבינים-ככה-ההפרדה-וחומת-סלקום/. [Hebrew]

———. "Ha-sefer tsioni, ha-seret lo." ["The Book Is Zionist, the Film Is Not."] *Ha'aretz*, March 23, 2005. http://www.haaretz.co.il/misc/1.1513268. [Hebrew]

Rascaroli, Laura. "The Essay Film: Problems, Definitions, Textual Commitments." *Framework: The Journal of Cinema and Media* 49, no. 2 (2008): 24–47.

Rekhess, Elie. "The Arabs of Israel after Oslo: Localization of the National Struggle." *Israel Studies* 7, no. 3 (2002): 1–44.

Renov, Michael. *The Subject of the Documentary*. Minneapolis: University of Minnesota Press, 2004.

Robbins, Bruce. "Sad Stories in the International Public Sphere: Richard Rorty on Culture and Human Rights." *Public Culture* 9, no. 2 (1997): 209–32.

Rose, Jacqueline. *Proust among the Nations: From Dreyfus to the Middle East*. Chicago: University of Chicago Press, 2011.

Rosenthal, John. "*Waltz with Bashir*, Nazi Germany, and Israel." *Pajamas Media*, February 18, 2008. http://pajamasmedia.com/blog/waltz-with-bashir-nazi-germany-and-israel/2/.

Ross, Reuben. "*Waltz with Bashir* and *Persepolis*: Culturally Specific Universal Animations." *Film Matters* 1, no. 3 (2010): 26–30.

Rotbard, Sharon. "Wall and Tower: The Mold of Israeli Architecture." *A Civilian Occupation: The Politics of Israeli Architecture*, ed. Rafi Segal and Eyal Weizman, 39–56. New York: Verso, 2002.

———. "Wall and Tower: The Mold of Israeli Adrikhalut." *Babel Architectures*, December 17, 2008. http://babelarchitectures.blogspot.com/2008/12/wall-and-tower-mold -of-israeli.html.

Rothschild, Nathalie. "*Waltz with Bashir*: Post-Zionist Stress Disorder." *Spiked*, November 19, 2008. http://www.spiked-online.com/index.php/site/article/5944/.

Sa'ar, Amalia, and Targhreed Yahia-Younis. "Masculinity in Crisis: The Case of Palestinians in Israel." *British Journal of Middle Eastern Studies* 35, no. 3 (2008): 305–23.

Sabouraud, Frédéric, and Serge Toubiana. "La Force du faible: 'Noce en Galilée,' entretien avec Michel Khleifi." *Cahiers du cinéma* 401 (1987): 111.

Said, Edward. Afterword. "The Consequences of 1948." *The War for Palestine: Rewriting the History of 1948*, ed. Eugene L. Rogan and Avi Shlaim. Cambridge: Cambridge University Press, 2001.

———. "Permission to Narrate." *London Review of Books* 6, no. 3 (1984): 13–19.

———. "Preface." *Dreams of a Nation: On Palestinian Cinema*, ed. Hamid Dabashi. New York: Verso, 2006.

———. "Propaganda and War." *Al Ahram Weekly On-line* 550 (2001). http://weekly.ahram .org.eg/2001/550/op2.htm.

Salti, Rasha. "From Resistance and Bearing Witness to the Power of the Fantastical: Icons and Symbols in Palestinian Poetry and Cinema." *Third Text* 24, no. 1 (2010): 39–52.

Saxton, Libby. "Fragile Faces: Levinas and Lanzmann." *The Occluded Relation: Levinas and Cinema*. Spec. issue of *Film-Philosophy* 11, no. 2 (2007): 1–14.

Schechia, Joseph. "The Invisible People Come to Light: Israel's 'Internally Displaced and the Unrecognized Villages.'" *Journal of Palestine Studies* 31, no. 1 (autumn 2001): 20–31.

Schlunke, Katrina. "Animated Documentary and the Scene of Death: Experiencing *Waltz with Bashir*." *South Atlantic Quarterly* 110, no. 4 (2011): 949–62.

Schulze, Kirsten E. "Israeli Crisis Decision-Making in the Lebanon War: Group Madness or Individual Ambition?" *Israel Studies* 3, no. 2 (1998): 215–37.

Schwab, Gabriele. *Haunting Legacies: Violent Histories and Transgenerational Trauma*. New York: Columbia University Press, 2010.

Schwartz, David. "Al chorvot: Dimuee ha-chorva ha-falestinit ba-kolno'a ha-yisraeli besof shnut ha-shiv'im." ["On Ruins: On the Image of the Palestinian Ruin in Israeli Films from the Late 1970s."] Published talk delivered during the conference "The Palestinian Nakba in Israeli Cinema and Literature," organized by Zochrot, May 28–29, 2012. http://zochrot.org/sites/default/files/qvbts_hrtsvt.pdf. [Hebrew]

Segal, Chagai. "Hora im Folman." ["Hora with Folman."] *Ma'ariv: De'ot*, February 21, 2009. http://www.nrg.co.il/online/1/ART1/856/177.html?hp=0&loc=302&tmp=20 22%E2%80%8F. [Hebrew]

Seikaly, Sherene. "All That Is Chic: Geography and Desire." *Chic Point: Fashion for Israeli Checkpoints*, 160–64. Exhibition Catalog. Tel Aviv: Andalus, 2007.

Sekula, Allan. *Photography against the Grain: Essays and Photo Works, 1973–1983*. Halifax: Press of the Nova Scotia College of Art and Design, 1984.

Shabi, Rachel. "*Ajami* and *Lebanon*: Two Filmic Faces of Israel." *Guardian*, May 6, 2010. http://www.theguardian.com/film/2010/may/06/ajami-lebanon-israel-filmmaking.

———. "Anger over Ex-Israeli Soldier's Facebook Photos of Palestinian Prisoners." *Guardian*, August 16, 2010. http://www.theguardian.com/world/2010/aug/16/israeli-soldier-photos-palestinian-prisoners.

Shaked, Gershon. "Eretz Yisrael ha-yafa shel ha-milim." [Israel of the Words."] *Sifrut az, kan ve-akhshav*, 181–203. [Literature Then and Now.] Tel Aviv: Zmora bitan, 1993. [Hebrew]

———. *Gal chadash ba-sifrut ha-ivrit: Masot al siporet yisra'elit ts'ira.* [A New Wave in Hebrew Literature: Essays on Young Israeli Prose.] Tel Aviv: Sifriyat ha-po'alim, 1974. [Hebrew]

Shalev, Mordechai. "Ha-aravim ke-pitaron sifruti." ["The Arabs as a Literary Solution."] *Mabatim mitstalvim: E'yunim be-ye'tsirat AB Yehoshua.* [Intersecting Sights: New Critical Essays on A. B. Yehoshua.] Ed. Amir Banbaji and Nitza Ben-Dov. Tel Aviv: Ha-kibuts ha-me'uchad, 2010. [Hebrew]

Shalhoub-Kevorkian, Nadera. "Palestinian Women and the Politics of Invisibility: Towards a Feminist Methodology." *Peace Prints: South Asian Journal of Peacebuilding* 3, no. 1 (2010): 1–21.

Shapira, Anita. "Hirbet Hizah: Between Remembrance and Forgetting." *Jewish Social Studies* 7, no. 1 (2000): 1–62.

Shapira, Avraham. *The Seventh Day: Soldiers Talk about the Six-Day War.* New York: Simon and Schuster, 1971.

Sharon, Moshe. "Tarbut shel chayim mul tarbut shel mavet." ["A Culture of Life versus a Culture of Death."] MIDA, November 23, 2012. http://mida.org.il/?p=3412. [Hebrew]

Sharoni, Simona. "Gendering Conflict and Peace in Israel/Palestine and the North of Ireland." *Millenium: Journal of International Studies* 27, no. 4 (1997): 1061–89.

Shaviro, Steven. *The Cinematic Body.* Minneapolis: University of Minnesota Press, 1993.

Shavit, Ari. "Ben Tsion Netanyahu in an Interview in 1998: 'There Is No Such Thing as a Palestinian.'" *Ha'aretz*, April 30, 2012. http://www.haaretz.co.il/news/education/1.1694581.

Shenhav, Yehouda, *Beyond the Two State Solution: A Jewish Political Essay.* Trans. Dimi Reider. Cambridge: Polity Press, 2012.

Shklovsky, Viktor. "Art as Technique." *Russian Formalist Criticism: Four Essays*, ed. Lee T. Lemon and Marion J. Reiss, 3–24. Lincoln: University of Nebraska Press, 1965.

Shnitzer, Meir. "Waltz im Bashir: Chidush kolno'ee." ["Waltz with Bashir: A Cinematic Innovation."] *Ma'ariv tarbut*, June 12, 2008. http://www.nrg.co.il/online/47/ART1/745/668.html?hp=47&cat=308. [Hebrew]

Shohat, Ella. *Israeli Cinema: East/West and the Politics of Representation.* 1989. London: I. B. Tauris, 2010.

Shohat, Ella, and Robert Stam. *Unthinking Eurocentrism: Multiculturalism and the Media.* New York: Routledge, 1994.

The Shooter. [*Al-Takheekh.*] Dir. Ihab Jadallah. Palestine, 2007. DVD. [Arabic]

Siisiäinen, Lauri. "From the Empire of the Gaze to Noisy Bodies: Foucault, Audition and Medical Power." *Theory and Event* 11, no. 1 (2008). http://muse.jhu.edu/journals /theory_and_event/v011/11.1siisiainen.html.

Siksek, Ayman. "Ta'atu'ai ke'elu." ["As If Illusions."] *Ha'aretz*, May 8, 2008. http://www .haaretz.co.il/literature/1.1341183. [Hebrew]

Silverman, Kaja. *The Threshold of the Visible World.* New York: Routledge, 1996.

Sivan, Emmanuel. "The Lights of Netzarim." *Ha'aretz*, November 7, 2003. http://www .haaretz.com/print-edition/opinion/the-lights-of-netzarim-1.104944.

Slyomovics, Susan. *The Object of Memory: Arab and Jew Narrate the Palestinian Village.* Philadelphia: University of Pennsylvania Press, 1998.

Sofian, Sheila. "The Truth in Pictures." *FPS Magazine* 1 (2005): 7–12.

Solomon, Keith. "The Spectacle of War and the Specter of 'The Horror': *Apocalypse Now* and American Imperialism." *Journal of Popular Film and Television* 35 (2007): 25.

Solomon-Godeau, Abigail. *Photography at the Dock: Essays in Photographic History, Institutions, and Practices.* Minneapolis: University of Minnesota Press, 1991.

Sontag, Susan. "Notes on Camp." *Partisan Review* 31 (1964): 515–30.

———. *On Photography.* New York: Anchor, 1990.

———. *Regarding the Pain of Others.* New York: Farrar, Straus, Giroux, 2003.

Spivak, Gayatri Chakravorty. "Can the Subaltern Speak?" *Marxism and the Interpretation of Culture*, ed. Cary Nelson and Lawrence Grossberg, 271–313. Urbana-Champaign: University of Illinois Press, 1988.

Srouji, Samir. "Nazareth: Intersecting Narratives of Modern Architectural Histories." *Third Text* 20, nos. 3–4 (2006): 355–71.

Stein, Rebecca. "Explosive: Scenes from Israel's Gay Occupation." *GLQ: A Journal of Lesbian and Gay Studies* 16, no. 4 (2010): 517–36.

———. "Impossible Witness: Israeli Visuality, Palestinian Testimony and the Gaza War." *Journal for Cultural Research* 16, no. 2–3 (2012): 135–53.

———. *Itineraries in Conflict: Israelis, Palestinians, and the Political Lives of Tourism.* Durham, NC: Duke University Press, 2008.

Stein, Rebecca, and Ted Swedenburg, eds. *Palestine, Israel and the Politics of Popular Culture.* Durham, NC: Duke University Press, 2005.

Stein, Rebecca, and Ted Swedenburg. "Popular Culture, Relational History, and the Question of Power in Palestine and Israel." *Journal of Palestine Studies* 33, no. 4 (2004): 1–16.

Stewart, Garrett. "Screen Memory in *Waltz with Bashir*." *Film Quarterly* 63, no. 3 (2010): 58–62.

Studlar, Gaylyn. "Masochism and the Perverse Pleasures of the Cinema." *Movies and Methods.* Vol. 2. Ed. Bill Nichols, 267–82. Berkeley: University of California Press, 1985.

Sturken, Marita. *Tangled Memories: The Vietnam War, the AIDS Epidemic, and the Politics of Remembering.* Berkeley: University of California Press, 1997.

Suleiman, Elia. Interview with Anna Bourland. "A Cinema of Nowhere: An Interview with Elia Suleiman." *Journal of Palestine Studies* 29, no. 2 (2000): 95–101.

———. Interview with Linda Butler. "The Occupation (and Life) through an Absurdist Lens: An Interview with Elia Suleiman." *Journal of Palestine Studies* 32, no. 2 (2003): 63–73.

———. Interview with Steve Erickson. "A Breakdown of Communication: Elia Suleiman Talks about *Divine Intervention*." The European Graduate School, January 15, 2003. http://www.egs.edu/faculty/elia-suleiman/articles/a-breakdown-in-communication/.

———. "The Other Face of Silence: Nathalie Handal Interviews Elia Suleiman." *Guernica: A Magazine of Art and Politics*, May 1, 2011. http://www.guernicamag.com/interview/2628/suleiman_5_1_11.

Tal, Kali. *Worlds of Hurt: Reading the Literatures of Trauma*. Cambridge: Cambridge University Press, 1995.

Tamir, Tali. "Against the Grain: The Paintings of Ruth Schloss," n.d. http://talitamir.com/catalog/album/191.

———. "Tsuba: Hafshata veʻevaron." ["Tsuba: Abstraction and Blindness."] *Larry Abramson Tsooba*. Exhibition Catalog. Tel Aviv: Kibbutz Art Gallery, 1995. [Hebrew]

Tartoussieh, Karim. "Chic Point and the Spectacle of the Body." *ArteEast: The Global Platform for Middle East Arts*, April 1, 2007. http://www.arteeast.dreamhosters.com/pages/artenews/article/94/.

The Time That Remains (Al-zaman al-baqi). Dir. Elia Suleiman. Israel/Palestine, 2009. DVD. [Arabic, Hebrew]

Thompson, David. "Villains, Victims, and Veterans: Buchheim's *Das Boot* and the Problem of the Hybrid Novel-Memoir as History." *Twentieth Century Literature* 39, no. 1 (1993): 59–78.

Tiglao, Sarah. "Israeli Strip Searches: A Partial List." *If Americans Knew*, August 1, 2008. http://www.ifamericansknew.org/cur_sit/strip-searches.html.

To See If I Am Smiling (leerot im ani mechayechet). Dir. Tamar Yaron, Israel, 2007. DVD.

Trigg, Dylan. "The Place of Trauma: Memory, Haunting and the Temporality of Ruins." *Memory Studies* 2, no. 1 (2009): 87–101.

Veracini, Lorenzo. "Historylessness: Australia as a Settler Colonial Collective." *Postcolonial Studies* 10, no. 3 (2007): 271–85.

———. *Israel and Settler Society*. London: Pluto, 2006.

Virilio, Paul. *Open Sky*. Trans. Julie Rose. New York: Verso, 1997.

———. *War and Cinema: The Logistics of Perception*. Trans. Patrick Camiller. New York: Verso, 1989.

Waltz with Bashir. [*Vals im bashir*.] Dir. Ari Folman. Israel, 2008. DVD. [Hebrew]

Warner, Michael. *The Trouble with Normal: Sex, Politics, and the Ethics of Queer Life*. New York: Free Press, 1999.

———, ed. *Fear of a Queer Planet*. Minneapolis: University of Minnesota Press, 1993.

We Began by Measuring Distance. Dir. Basma Al Sharif. Sharjah Art Foundation, 2009. DVD. [Arabic]

Weir, Alison. "Letting AP in on the Secret: Israeli Strip Searches." *Counterpunch*, July 29, 2008. http://www.counterpunch.org/2008/07/29/israeli-strip-searches.

Weizman, Eyal. *Hollow Land: Israel's Architecture of Occupation*. London: Verso, 2007.

———. "The Politics of Verticality" *Open Democracy*, April 23, 2002. http://www.opendemocracy.net/ecology-politicsverticality/article_801.jsp.

Westwell, Guy. *War Cinema: Hollywood on the Front Lines*. London: Wallflower Press, 2006.

White, Ben. "Behind Brand Israel: Israel's recent Propaganda Efforts," *The Electronic Inti-*

fada, February 23, 2010. http://electronicintifada.net/content/behind-brand-israel
-israels-recent-propaganda-efforts/8694.

Williams, Patricia J. "Diary of a Mad Law Professor: Without Sanctuary." *Nation* 270,
no. 6 (February 14, 2000): 9.

Wolf, Patrick. "Settler Colonialism and the Elimination of the Native." *Journal of Genocide
Research* 8, no. 4 (2006): 387–409.

———. "Structure and Event: Settler Colonialism, Time, and the Question of Genocide." *Empire, Colony, Genocide: Conquest, Occupation and Subaltern Resistance in World History*, ed. Dirk Moses, 102–32. Oxford: Berghahn Books, 2008.

Wright Andrew. "More Than Ink: Comic Realism in Film." *Pop Damage*, April 1, 2009.
http://pop-damage.com/?p=1213.

Yaqub, Nadia. "Azza El-Hassan and Impossible Filmmaking in Israel/Palestine." *Resistance in Contemporary Middle Eastern Cultures: Literature, Cinema, and Music*, ed. Karima
Laachir and Saeed Talajooy, 153–66. New York: Routledge, 2012.

———. "The Palestinian Cinematic Wedding." *Journal of Middle East Women's Studies* 3,
no. 2 (2007): 56–85.

Yehoshua, A. B. "Facing the Forests." *Three Days and a Child*. Trans. Miriam Arad, 131–74.
London: Peter Owen, 1971.

———. *Mul Ha-ye'arot*. [Facing the Forests.] *Kol ha-sipurim*. [All the Stories.] 1993. Tel
Aviv: Ha-kibuts ha-me'uchad, 2005. 99–127. [Hebrew]

Yizhar, S. *Khirbet Khizeh*. Trans. Nicholas de Lange and Yacob Dweck. Jerusalem: Ibis
Editions, 2008.

———. *Sipur khirbat hiz'ah ve-od shlosha siporai milchama*. [Khirbet Khizeh and Three Other
Stories.] Tel Aviv: Zmora Betan, 2006. [Hebrew]

Yosef, Raz. "Homoland: Interracial Sex and the Israeli-Palestinian Conflict in Israeli
Cinema." *GLQ: Gay and Lesbian Quarterly* 8, no. 4 (2002): 553–80.

———. "War Fantasies: Memory, Trauma and Ethics in Ari Folman's *Waltz with Bashir*."
Journal of Modern Jewish Studies 9, no. 3 (2010): 311–26.

Yossef Hassan, Budour. "The Second Intifada Puts Holes in Israel's Wall of Fear." *Electronic
Intifada*, October 4, 2013. http://electronicintifada.net/content/second-intifada-put
-holes-israels-wall-fear/12826.

Young, Marilyn. *The Vietnam Wars 1945–1990*. New York: HarperCollins, 1991.

Yuval-Davis, Nira. *Gender and Nation*. London: Sage, 1997.

Z32. Dir. Avi Mograbi. Israel, 2008. DVD. [Hebrew]

Zerubavel, Yael. "The Forest as a National Icon: Literature, Politics, and the Archeology
of Memory." *Israel Studies* 1, no. 1 (1996): 60–99.

———. *Recovered Roots: Collective Memory and the Making of Israeli National Memory*. Chicago:
University of Chicago Press, 1995.

Žižek, Slavoj. "Enjoy Your Nation as Yourself!" *Tarrying with the Negative: Kant, Hegel, and
the Critique of Ideology*, 200–238. Durham, NC: Duke University Press, 2003.

———. "A Soft Focus on War." *In These Times*, April 21, 2010. http://www.inthesetimes
.com/article/5864/a_soft_focus_on_war/.

Zureik, Elia. *Surveillance and Control in Israel/Palestine: Population, Territory and Power*. Oxford:
Taylor and Francis, 2011.

Index

homosexuality, 86–87, 92–95, 178n6, 178nn8–9. *See also* camp; homoeroticism; queer; terrorist: sexualization of
human rights organizations, 30–31, 115, 119–20
hypervisibility, 17, 24, 27, 119; poetics of, 59, 75; of Palestinian terrorist, 68–69, 75

IDF. *See* Israeli Defense Force
Intimacy (Rula Halawani, 2004), 97–106
invisibility, 7; of Israeli occupation, 63–64; political and poetic potential associated with, 65, 75, 120, 163; vs. visibility, 75, 166. *See also* ghost; haunting; invisibility; specter; visibility
invisibility, of Palestinians, 17, 75, 97, 163; in Israel, 61–66; in fashion commercial, 23. *See also* ghost, figural: in Elia Suleiman's films; ruins, of Palestinian villages
Israeli-Arab. *See* Palestinians, citizens of Israel
Israeli-Palestinian conflict: dominant representations of, 6, 60, 69; history of, 3–5
Israeli Defense Force, 11, 101, 145, 167n2, 182n12; and Aberjil photograph scandal, 14; film representation of, 64–69, 185n7. *See also* Lebanon War; occupation, Israeli; Operation Cast Lead; soldiers, Israeli

Jadallah, Ihab: *The Shooter* (2007), 117
Jarrar, Khaled: *At the Checkpoint* (2007), 97–98, 106–12
Jerusalem: on film, 63–69
Jewish National Fund, forestation, 46, 173nn17–19
JNF (Jewish National Fund), forestation, 46, 173nn17–19

Khirbet Khizeh (S. Yizhar, 1949), 44–46

Lebanon (Samuel Maoz, 2009), 32, 139, 142, 144, 155–62, 186nn16–17
Lebanon War, 139, 142–66, 184n4. See

also *Lebanon* (2009); Second Lebanon War; *Waltz with Bashir* (2008)
Levanon (Samuel Maoz, 2009), 32, 139, 142, 144, 155–62, 186nn16–17
literature, Israeli, 39, 42–51, 173n20

Machsom Watch, 31, 37, 177n2, 180n13. *See also* human rights organizations
Maoz, Samuel: *Lebanon* (2009), 32, 139, 142, 144, 155–62, 186nn16–17
masculinity: "crisis of," 86–87, 93–94; and nationalism, 86–87, 93–94, 153, 177–78nn5–7
Massad, Joseph, 86, 177–78n5, 178n7
media: global/international, 6, 8–10, 13, 17, 30–31, 115–20, 137, 163, 168nn7–8, 182n16; and images of violence, 9–10, 13–15, 69, 72, 168–69n11; visual regimes of, 119; Western, 9–10, 72, 124. *See also* documentary; documentary conventions; human rights organizations; news footage; spectator; testimonial; visual evidence; witnessing
memory, 46, 147–49, 152–53, 156–57, 173n18, 185nn12–13
militarization, of Israeli society, 10–12
military, Israeli: *See* Israeli Defense Force; soldiers, Israeli
Mirzoeff, Nicholas, 3, 98. *See also* visual rights, uneven distribution of
Mitchell, W. J. T., 52
Mul Ha- ye'arot (A. B. Yehoshua, 1971), 41, 46–48

Nakba, 4, 24, 44; as haunting presence, 37–42, 49, 55. *See also* 1948 War; ruins, of Palestinian villages
al-naksa, 3–5, 49, 132
Nazareth, on film, 63–64, 67–69, 175n7
Nervus Rerum (Otolith Group, 2008), 31, 115, 117–29, 136, 181n5, 182–83nn16–17. *See also* essay film
news footage, 130–33
nongovernmental organization (NGO), human rights, 30–31, 115, 119–20
Notre Musique (Jean-Luc Godard, 2004), 116. *See also* essay film

occupation, Israeli, 3–8, 16, 27, 30, 33, 59, 70, 164, 167n5, 175n5, 177n2, 179n5, 181n12; in/visibility of, 10–11, 14, 63–66, 74; representation of, 15, 63–66, 102–4, 116–19, 168n7, 184n7. *See also* body: at Israeli checkpoint; checkpoint, Israeli; fashion: for Israeli checkpoints; invisibility: of Israeli checkpoint; Jarrar, Khaled: *At the Checkpoint* (2007); Occupied Palestinian Territories; settlements, Jewish-Israeli; settler-colonialism, Zionist-Israeli

Occupied Palestinian Territories (OPT), 17, 21, 24, 33

Operation Cast Lead (2008), 4, 118, 128–29

Oslo Accords period (1993–2000), 4, 33, 59–62, 67–68, 115, 175n5. *See also* Second Palestinian Intifada

Otolith Group, 31, 115, 117–29, 136, 181n5, 182–83nn16–17

Oz, Amos: *A Perfect Peace* (1985), 39–41

painting, Israeli: abstract/modernist tradition (1950s–1960s), 39, 42, 52, 54

Palestinian cinema, 58–59, 73, 74, 118–23, 176n13; *Chronicle of a Disappearance* (1996), 60–67; *Divine Intervention* (2002), 67–74, 177nn16–17; Suleiman, Elia, 17, 24, 57–75, 157–58, 175–77nn7–9, 177nn14–17; *The Time That Remains* (2009), 57–58, 174n2

Palestinians: representation as victims, 116–19, 130; subgroups according to Israeli state, 4

Palestinians, citizens of Israel: in/visibility of, 61–62, 67–68; representation of, 57–59. *See also* Palestinians; Palestinians, occupied noncitizens

Palestinians, occupied noncitizens: public invisibility of, 97

Palestinian Territories, 17, 21, 24, 33

Paradise Now (2005), 73, 146

parody: in Elia Suleiman films, 67–69, 71–73, 176n14

Perfect Peace, A (Amos Oz, 1985), 39–41

perpetrator: humanization of, 144–47, 155, 162; trauma of, 30, 32, 139, 146–47, 155, 185n9

Pessoa, Fernando, 124, 127, 182n17

photographs, 29; by Rula Halawani, 97–106; of Israeli checkpoints, 82, 85–86, 91–93; by Khaled Jarrar, 97–98, 106–12; political potential of, 103–6, 111–12; and scandals of prisoner abuse, 14–16; in Sharif Waked's *Chic Point: Fashion for Israeli Checkpoints* (2003), 80–95; spectator of, 97, 99, 102–12

poetics: of invisibility, 59–60, 120; of opacity, 125–29, 182n15; of "traumatic realism," 119–20

"present absentees," 17, 38, 174nn2–3

queer, 92, 178n6; aesthetics of, 86–87; camp, 88, 90; and checkpoint exchange between Israeli and Palestinian men, 82–95; terrorist as, 93. *See also* masculinity: "crisis of"; homoeroticism; homosexuality

queer reading, 61; of *Chic Point: Fashion for Israeli Checkpoints* (2003), 82–95

Rachel's Tomb: paintings on wall near, 20–21

Rascaroli, Laura, 117. *See also* essay film

refugee camp, 181n8, 182n12; of Jenin, 118–27, 182nn16–17; of Sabra and Shatila, 143, 148, 154, 157

resistance, Palestinian, 10, 24, 41, 55, 66, 75, 176n13, 182n14; "poetics of opacity" as, 8, 125–26, 182n15; spectacle of, 66, 69, 71

ruins, of Palestinian villages: as haunting presence for Israelis, 40–51, 55; images of, 37–38, 52; literary and poetic image of, 40–51; in/visibility in Israeli landscape, 38–39, 46, 52–55; in Israeli abstract landscape paintings, 39; in painting, 52–53

Sabra and Shatila refugee camp: massacre at, 142–43, 148, 154, 157, 185–86n15. *See also Waltz with Bashir* (2008)

violence, 139–41; in cinema vs. actual, 71; film and media representation of, 69, 71, 127, 133; of gaze, 91; international media images of, 13–14; in/visibility of at checkpoint, 81–82; of Israeli military, 4, 14, 32, 118, 128–29; Palestinian images of, 9; spectacle of, 14, 69–73; "spectacular" vs. "suspended," 13, 15–16; of state, 84. See also occupation, Israeli; war

Virilio, Paul, 151, 156, 159–60, 185n14

visibility, 24; conditions of, 3–4; Palestinian struggle for, 17; political power of, 126. See also invisibility; visible invisibility; vision

visible invisibility: of Palestinians in Israel, 38; of Nakba, 38–41; of ruins, 51–52. See also ghost; haunting; invisibility; specter; visibility

vision, compromised, 159–62; in literary example, 47–48

visual field, 97–98, 102, 109, 155–56, 161, 164–65; at checkpoint, 79, 81, 90; dominant Israeli, 38, 51–52, 57, 79, 81, 111–12, 168n10

visual icons: Palestinian, 127; of victimhood, 119, 130

visual proof, 8–9, 30–31, 116–24, 137, 163–65. See also documentary; documentary conventions; news footage; testimonial

visual rights, uneven distribution of, 3–5, 29, 97–98, 104–6

visuality, 51, 164, 168n6; denaturalization of, 5; Israeli and Palestinian politics of, 3–6, 24, 34, 98; predetermined field of, 6; proof, 31; re-/distribution of, 5–7; regimes of, 7. See also visual field; visual proof; visual rights, uneven distribution of

Waked, Sharif: Chic Point: Fashion for Israeli Checkpoints (2003), 80–95

Waltz with Bashir (Ari Folman, 2008), 139–58, 161–62, 185nn8–13

war: cinematic experience of, 151, 157; images of, 154, 185n15; victims of, 145–46; memories of, 151. See also antiwar films; war films; violence

war films, 140–41, 144, 147, 156–57, 184n1, 185n7; inherent violence of, 141. See also antiwar films; Lebanon (Samuel Maoz, 2009); violence; Waltz with Bashir (Ari Folman, 2008); war

We Began by Measuring Distance (Basma Al Sharif, 2009), 117, 127–37. See also essay film

West Bank, 17, 21, 24, 33

witnessing, 8 , 29–32, 109, 115, 118, 130–37, 139–42, 149, 155–56, 161–62; crisis of, 129; ethics of, 127; failed, 139, 142, 149, 155, 162; of violence, 142. See also evidence, visual; testimonial

Yehoshua, A. B.: Mul Ha-ye'arot (Facing the Forests), 41, 46–48

Yizhar, S. [Smilansky]: Khirbet Khizeh (1949), 44–46

Yom Kippur War, 49

Zionism, 3–5, 17, 38, 43, 46, 52, 58, 61, 167n3, 172n12; blindness of, 43, 52; and forestation, 46, 173nn17–19; and gender, 178n6; resignification of Palestinian ruins within, 39–41, 54. See also Jewish National Fund; occupation, Israeli; settlements, Jewish-Israeli; settler-colonialism, Zionist-Israeli

Žižek, Slavoj, 144–45

Zritsky, Yosef: Tsuba paintings, 52. See also Tsóob'ä (Larry Abramson, 1993–94)